*Anthropologists and
Their Traditions across
National Borders*

Histories of Anthropology Annual

Anthropologists and Their Traditions across National Borders

Histories of Anthropology Annual, Volume 8

EDITED BY REGNA DARNELL
& FREDERIC W. GLEACH

University of Nebraska Press | *Lincoln and London*

© 2014 by the Board of Regents of
the University of Nebraska

All rights reserved
Manufactured in the United States of America
♾

Anthropologists and their traditions across national
borders / edited by Regna Darnell, Frederic W. Gleach.
pages   cm.—(Histories of anthropology annual)
Includes bibliographical references.
ISBN 978-0-8032-5336-0 (paperback)
ISBN 978-0-8032-5688-0 (epub)
ISBN 978-0-8032-5689-7 (mobi)
ISBN 978-0-8032-5687-3 (pdf)
1. Anthropology—Methodology. 2. Anthropology—
Fieldwork. 3. Anthropologists—History.
4. Anthropologists—Biography. I. Darnell, Regna. II.
Gleach, Frederic W. (Frederic Wright), 1960-
GN33.A4455 2014
301.01—dc23
2014023474

Set in Arno Pro by Renni Johnson.
Designed by A. Shahan.

CONTENTS

ILLUSTRATIONS

EDITORS' INTRODUCTION

We begin by apologizing to our readers for the recent hiatus in publication of our ostensibly annual publication. *Histories of Anthropology Annual* began in the University of Nebraska book division and moved to the journals category after it had established reasonable visibility among anthropologists and historians. We discovered, however, that our readers are more inclined to buy single volumes than to subscribe. Thus we are returning to the book division. This has required rethinking and rescheduling, especially to accommodate the peer review process now in place through the Press in addition to the editors' review. We are confidant that this will improve the quality of each issue and that the regular annual appearance of *HoAA* is sustainable into the foreseeable future.

Another important change is that each volume will now appear with a subtitle indicating something about the nature of its contents. Hence *Volume 8: Anthropologists and Their Traditions across National Borders.* We emphasize that this does not mean we are moving to thematic volumes. *HoAA* was established to provide a publication outlet across subject matters and approaches to history for specialists and for scholars whose primary interests lie elsewhere but who on occasion delve into historical questions of wider interest to the discipline. Volume 8 integrates fairly easily around how anthropologists' careers have intersected across different professional generations and allowed them to navigate national boundaries and national traditions. The essays are partly biographical, moving from the iconic heroes of the discipline to their little known contemporaries. Authors often deal with the foundational relationship of anthropologists to the people(s) they study. In each previous volume, while consciously encouraging the greatest possible diversity, we have in practice been startled by recurrent patterns as we juxtapose the scholarship of diverse contributors. Henceforth, we will make this explicit at the point of assembling a volume, rather than seeking out integrated themes in advance.

Likewise we have sought variation in genres of historical writing. Lindy-Lou Flynn's meticulous documentation of the teaching styles of two quite different undergraduate mentors offers an informal and deeply personal commentary about professional socialization. Simultaneously, the paper provides a fascinating glimpse of how a British-trained social anthropologist and a First Nations cultural anthropologist coexisted as departmental colleagues and were perhaps not as far apart as a more abstract treatment might suggest. We continue to be open to reflexive memoir and oral history materials from or about anthropologists as well as to more conventional research articles.

National traditions dominate volume 8, but these traditions refuse to stay in their separate boxes. Anthropologists working in the Americanist tradition will be aware of Boas's Jesup expedition foray into Asian ethnography, whereas Laurel Kendall explores Berthold Laufer's Chinese work and its abortive anthropological context at the American Museum of Natural History, which has been largely forgotten. Several papers trace the British national tradition through its far-flung geographical distribution: Charles Laughlin reexamines the comparative ethnographic approach of A. M. Hocart, which was eclipsed in its own time by the reputations of Radcliffe-Brown and Malinowski. Mark Lamont places Malinowski squarely within British colonialism and attributes the success of his functionalism to its administrative utility in dealing with the "native question." Another guise of functionalism, Radcliffe-Brown's "applied anthropology," was tested at the far ends of empire during his appointments at Sydney, Australia, and Cape Town, South Africa; Ian Campbell demonstrates that British social anthropology was not a position confined to or developed solely within the British Isles. Geoffrey Gray and Doug Munro continue their institutional documentation of anthropology in Australia and New Zealand as they skip ahead in time to 1957 and the politics of filling S. R. Nadel's chair at Australian National University after his sudden death the previous year.

Three short papers, best read as a set, assess the legacy of structuralism not long after the death of Claude Lévi-Strauss, its founder and most distinguished anthropological proponent. Regna Darnell emphasizes the interplay between culture-specific pattern and cognitive universals in the widespread empirical exemplars of kinship, myth, and language. Abraham Rosman and Paula Rubel focus on the application of Lévi-Strauss's structuralist method to the classificatory systems of the North Pacific Coast, where Boas established an ethnographic database that has become iconic for the discipline. Michael Asch assesses Lévi-Strauss's claim to have accessed universal mental structures in his renditions of history, tying the French anthropologist to the European philosophical traditions usually outside the sphere of attention of practicing anthropologists. The death of the major figure in a theoretical school of thought offers the disciplinary historian a unique opportunity to stand back and take stock. These papers begin to define the ongoing legacy.

Lars Rodseth contextualizes the complex career of Marshall Sahlins, albeit further surprises may yet come from this contemporary maverick across national traditions and theoretical debates. Sahlins's career has wended its way from renewed neo-evolution to Lévi-Straussian structuralism to an ambitious philosophical reworking of history in which cultural encounter figures as miscommunication at mythic epistemological levels whether in ancient Greece or the near-contemporary South Pacific.

Stay tuned for new twists on these and other issues in volume 9.

REGNA DARNELL

FREDERIC W. GLEACH

*Anthropologists and
Their Traditions across
National Borders*

LAUREL KENDALL

1

"China to the Anthropologist"

Franz Boas, Berthold Laufer, and a Road Not Taken in Early American Anthropology

"I shall place the ethnography and archaeology of this country on an entirely new and solid basis, that I shall conquer China to the anthropologist. China no longer the exclusive domain of travelers and sinologues, both narrow-minded and one-sided in their standpoints and researches, China to all who have anthropological interests" (Laufer to Boas, 12 August 1903, 1903-13, DAA, AMNH). Thus did Berthold Laufer address his mentor, Franz Boas, the founding father of American anthropology, with a euphoric vision of future anthropological researches in China. A century later, Laufer has been eulogized as the premier Sinologist of his generation, best known for his studies on Han period ceramics (1909), jade (1912a), and ancient bronzes (1922) and a list of wide-ranging, original, erudite, and sometimes eccentric publications from Nestorian inscriptions (1911a) to singing crickets (1928), Chinese theater (1923) to Chinese hermaphrodites (1920), with historical reconstructions of the introduction of vaccinations (1911b), corn (1907) and tobacco (1924) into East Asia.[1] His association with American anthropology, indeed the very existence of an early anthropological project in China, is largely forgotten. As an anthropology graduate student, I found Laufer's name on a course syllabus, an article on the origin of the word "shaman" (Laufer 1917), but did not recognize him as one of our own, much less a protégé of Franz Boas, whose students included nearly all the luminaries of early twentieth-century American anthropology (Handler 1990). Maurice Freedman's summation of the history of China anthropology makes no mention of Laufer, describing China anthropologists as relative latecomers to the discipline (Freedman 1979).

Boas biographies give, at best, passing mention to the Jacob H. Schiff expedition that sent Laufer to China.[2] Douglas Cole notes that the "Chinese enterprise" was part of a major project that loomed large in Boas's AMNH years (1999:207–208, 287). George W. Stocking Jr. observes that Boas "worked rather hard" to raise funds from the business community and "capitalize on public interest in the Far East," suggesting that this was something of a temporary fall from grace (Stocking 1974:285). Stanley A. Freed's recent history of anthropology at the American Museum of Natural History devotes less than two pages to Laufer and the Schiff expedition in contrast with two full chapters devoted to the Jesup North Pacific expedition, which preceded it (Freed 2012:310–311). John Baick (1998: 24–83) describes Boas's efforts in the business community as part of a social history of New York elites around 1900 and their brief infatuation with Asia.[3] John Haddad (2006) and Roberta Stalberg (1983) give descriptive accounts of Laufer's activities in China and Boas's support of it; Steven Conn (1998:80–81) makes passing reference to the global reach of Boas's ambitions.[4] Regna Darnell (1998:160) notes Boas's attempts to broaden the geographic scope of anthropology at Columbia by conscripting Laufer to teach there. But no one has yet considered this project as part of a larger Boasian vision of what American anthropology might be or become, an anthropology that from the moment of its professionalization would have been cognizant of "peoples with history" (cf. Wolf 1982). The full import of the Boas-Laufer collaboration is lost in a disciplinary might-have-been, an anthropology that might just possibly have sidestepped its now very dated (but in popular culture tenacious) association with the study of "simple societies" and "primitive peoples."

Boas envisaged a major Asian Studies enterprise with New York City as its hub, collaboration between the American Museum of Natural History, the Metropolitan Museum of Art, and Columbia University with Berthold Laufer as the premier anthropologist in the mix. The story of this failed enterprise and its subsequent consignment to the dustbin of disciplinary history is worth revisiting because it cuts against the grain of what we think we know about early American anthropology, a history that, with few exceptions (e.g., Oppenheim 2005), has not considered East Asia as part of the story.

Critiques of early anthropology and of anthropological collecting as its salient enterprise have assumed, following Stocking's assertion, that "anthropology through most of its history has been primarily a discourse of the culturally or racially despised" (1985:112) and Clifford's description of the western museum as a colonial contact zone "usually involving conditions of coercion, radical inequality, and intractable conflict" (1997:192). Yes, in 1900, Chinese residents of the United States were counted among the "racially despised," and Boas was supremely cognizant of this, but he worked "rather hard" in another direction. Boas described the work of collecting and exhibiting as a means of impressing upon the general public "the fact that our people are not the only carriers of civilization, but that the human mind has been creative everywhere" (quoted in Jacknis 1985:107). Boasian humanism was very far from an Orientalist act of collecting and representing as an assertion of "European superiority over Oriental backwardness" (Said 1978:7), imperialism's "imagined ecumene" (Clunas 1997:414–415; Breckenridge 1989:196), or, as was the case with most other foundational anthropological collections, a hierarchical demonstration of cultural achievement with western civilization at the apex (Conn 1998:90). China in 1900 had been humiliated by a series of western incursions, acquiescing to a system of treaty ports to abet foreign commerce. When Laufer arrived in Beijing in December 1901, the foreign troops that had occupied the capital city in the aftermath of the Boxer Rebellion had only recently departed. But in contrast with prior anthropological subjects, the "China" of Boas's and Laufer's conversations was a still sovereign imperial power and a sophisticated "civilization" in the language of the day, a place that, in their thinking, the American public ought better to know and appreciate. "Respect" was a central concept in their project and conversations.

The Jacob C. Schiff expedition to China was a consequence of the meeting of two unique individuals, a soon-to-be-archaic style of anthropological fieldwork, and a particular historical moment. It rested on a wobbly triangulation of interest between Boas's humanistic regard for nonwestern cultures, his perception of the pragmatic interests of his potential backers, and Laufer, the brilliant but mercurial researcher in the field whose results were intended to seduce future support but who also had his own research agendas. This is the story of an ambitious and ultimately failed project, what they set out to do, how Laufer tried to carry it out, and how it ended, with some speculations on the consequences of this failure for the discipline of anthropology.

THE PLAN

By 1901, when he dispatched Laufer to China, Boas was already developing the nascent anthropology program at Columbia. Along the way, he was also rethinking American anthropology as an intellectual commitment to cultural relativism, with the premise that all peoples have "cultures" of equal value independent of any social evolutionary ranking (Sanjek 1996). A visionary with a research agenda, Boas had already successfully convinced AMNH president Morris K. Jesup to fund the ambitious Jesup North Pacific expedition (1897–1902), five years of research by multiple teams of international scholars. With the official objective of proving that the Americas had been peopled via the Bering Strait, the expedition effectively garnered a huge resource base of object collections, physical and linguistic data, and published ethnographies, although its contribution to the Bering Strait question was negligible (Freed, Freed, and Williamson 1988; Krupnik and Vakhtin 2003). That Boas delayed in producing a synthesis of the expedition research with a definitive answer to the question of the peopling of the Americas would be a source of growing tension between him and Jesup, his primary backer. Jesup's mounting impatience would cast a shadow over Boas's efforts during and immediately after the Schiff expedition (Freed 2012:446–448).

As with the Jesup expedition, Boas's plans for an anthropological enterprise in Asia were strategic and wide-ranging. With the conclusion of the Spanish American War in 1898, the United States gained possession of the Philippines, adding colonial interests in Asia to its already well-established commercial interests in China and Japan. Baick describes a critical moment when "a number of New York institutions made China and Japan a priority" (1998:2) and sought institutional support for cultural and scholarly projects—from museum collections to Chinese language instruction. This task required "convincing a broad cross-section of the city's cultural leadership that 'knowing' East Asia was a crucial step in the elevation of the city from a commercial center to a cosmopolitan capital" (Baick 1998:4). In this period, Boas articulated an urgent interest in creating both practical knowledge and cultural understanding of the subjects of the United States' enlivened Pacific interests (East Asiatic Committee, 1894–1907 Correspondence Files, DAA, AMNH). Like many a future academic seeking private or government funding to innovate, expand, or sustain an Asian studies program, Boas made his appeal on the grounds that professional knowledge of Asia was a necessary component of commerce and diplomacy. He observed that "special schools of Oriental culture, museums, and universities that include these subjects in the scope of their work" were already established in Paris, Berlin, and St. Petersburg, and he devoted a summer of European travel to visiting several of them and assessing their facilities with a practical eye toward creating a similar institution in New York (Boas to Schurz, 6 November 1901, East Asiatic Committee, 1894–1907 Correspondence Files, DAA, AMNH).

In developing a language to justify this project, Boas tacked between the broad humanistic perspective of his own scholarship—the cultural relativism for which he is best-remembered today—and pragmatic appeals to the business interests of potential donors, as if the connections were seamless. In a report prepared for the Asiatic Committee, he stated that Laufer would make "collections which illustrate the popular customs and beliefs of the Chinese, their industries, and their mode of life" on the assumption that these collections "bring out the complexity of Chinese culture, the high degree of technical development achieved by the people, the love of art, which pervades their whole life, and the strong social ties that bind the people together. . . . These will demonstrate the *commercial and social possibilities* of more extended intercourse. We also wish to imbue the public with greater *respect* for the achievements of Chinese civilization" (Boas to Jesup, 27 December 1902, East Asiatic Committee, 1894–1907 Correspondence Files, DAA, AMNH, my emphasis). This language appealed to Jacob Schiff (1847–1920), a New York banker and philanthropist with business interests in China who responded favorably to Boas's appeal for funds to send Laufer to China: "Personally, I am much taken with your idea, for even without being a territorial expansionist, one can readily see that if we wish to expand our commercial and industrial activities, we should know more than we do now of the customs . . . of the people with whom we desire to trade and come into closer contact" (Schiff to Boas, 24 December 1900, East Asiatic Committee, 1894–1907 Correspondence Files, DAA, AMNH).[5] Schiff provided $18,000 for a three-year expedition.[6] Boas considered the Schiff expedition the cornerstone of an ambitious edifice of East Asian scholarship. There would be a program of instruction at Columbia University emphasizing language, history, literature, cultural life, and commerce, a research library at Columbia, and museum collections for teaching, research, and public education at the American Museum of Natural History and the Metropolitan Museum of Art. AMNH would sponsor broad anthropological studies in Asia and use the resulting collections to introduce Asian cultures to an American popular audience.

In an age before the professionalization of institutional fund-raising, and with limited support from his own trustees for research, it was up to Boas to secure patronage for this and other projects (Jacknis 1985:83–84). With Jesup's blessing, he engineered the creation of the East Asiatic Committee, a group of prominent businessmen and cultural figures with interests in Asia who would meet periodically at the American Museum of Natural History from 1900 to 1905. Jesup chaired the committee, and Boas himself was secretary and prime mover (East Asiatic Committee, 1894–1907 Correspondence Files, DAA, AMNH; Baick 1998:24–83).[7] Prospective members received this invitation:

> Owing to the ever-increasing importance of the relations between America and the countries and peoples of eastern Asia, it is highly desirable that we should have a better knowledge of them. At the present time there is no place in the United States, in fact on the whole of this continent, where it would be possible to pursue studies in relation to eastern Asia. The experience of foreign countries, more particularly of Russia, France, and Germany, shows that the only method of attaining this object is to introduce the study of east Asiatic countries and civilizations. . . . Owing to the importance of foreign trade with New York, there ought to be no city in the United States in which an interest in the development of a knowledge of for-

eign countries should be keener. (Villard invitation, 11 April 1900, East Asiatic Committee, 1894–1907 Correspondence Files, DAA, AMNH)

The appeal is practical, urgent, and with just a hint of a competitive edge in its evocation of "the experience of foreign countries," a well-crafted pitch.

The Committee would include financiers, bankers, railway magnates, the president of Columbia University, a trustee of the Metropolitan Museum of Art, and the leader of an association of patrician art aficionados. The agenda was clear: convince potentially sympathetic leaders of the business community that it was in their common interest to develop university and museum resources for both specialist and public knowledge of Asia. Reference to "the ever-increasing importance of our intercourse with eastern Asia," to the need for better knowledge of those who live there, and to New York's prominence in foreign trade appear with mantra-like frequency in Boas's solicitations (East Asiatic Committee, 1894–1907 Correspondence Files, DAA, AMNH).

Throughout the work of the Committee, Boas was emphatic that the China expedition was just the beginning of a larger Asian studies enterprise, more than "simply making an interesting museum collection . . . we are trying to work towards a more far-reaching plan. . . . [A] foundation must be laid particularly in India and in China" (Boas to Schiff, 31 January 1901, East Asiatic Committee, 1894–1907 Correspondence Files, DAA, AMNH). He had been incubating this idea for some years, exchanging Native American artifacts for material from the Dutch East Indies (Accession file 1898–50, DAA, AMNH), enlisting missionaries as museum collectors (Hasinoff 2010)—most successfully C. C. Vinton in Korea (Accession files 1901-78, 1908-32, DAA, AMNH)—and seizing upon opportunistic circumstance, as when Bashford Dean, on a zoological expedition to Japan, collected Ainu material in Hokkaido (Accession file 1901-77, DAA, AMNH). Laufer also collected Japanese material en route to and from his Siberian fieldwork for the Jesup expedition (Accession file 1898-36, DAA, AMNH). As an intended sequel to Laufer's project, Boas developed a research strategy for "pretty thorough work in the Malay Archipelago" (Boas to Jesup, 15 March 1901, East Asiatic Committee, 1894–1907 Correspondence Files,

DAA, AMNH), drafted a prospectus, located a potential scholar to carry out the work, and continued to beat the drum for the project in his correspondence with members of the Asiatic Committee throughout the Committee's existence (East Asiatic Committee, 1894–1907 Correspondence Files, DAA, AMNH). In China, Laufer was also cognizant of the larger enterprise, writing to Boas of his encounter with a Mr. Unger, based in Yokohama, who can commission "some Japanese" to make a collection on the Luchu (Ryukyu) Islands (Laufer to Boas, 7 March 1902, 1902-4, DAA, AMNH). He reports a meeting with Dr. Reid, a missionary based in Seoul, who spoke "about a curious kind of very ancient crude pottery recently excavated around Seoul" and "asked him to secure some of such pieces for the museum" (Laufer to Boas, 19 September 1901, 1901-69, DAA, AMNH).

AMNH's leadership in this project might have ensured a prominent place for anthropology in the development of American thinking about East Asia and made East Asia visible in the imagination of an emergent anthropology, but it was an anthropology that would soon become something else. In the early years of the twentieth century, anthropology was still a material as much as an ethnographic enterprise and fieldwork took the natural science expedition as its model, what James Clifford has called "a sensorium moving through extended space" (1997:69). Never anywhere for very long, anthropological expeditionists would make observations of social life, take physical type measurements, photographs, and head casts, record songs and stories on wax cylinders, and make what were described as "comprehensive" collections of the material culture of those whom they encountered, measured, photographed, and recorded. Early professional anthropology, in kinship with the natural sciences, was an enterprise grounded in material evidence (Edwards 1992; Jacknis 1985, 1996), "specimens," "artifacts," texts, vocabulary lists, and physical measurements that could be worked up at leisure once the expedition was completed, a "thingishness" congenial to museum environments even as nineteenth-century social evolutionists worked comfortably inside natural history museums (Gosden and Larson 2007) and as physical anthropologists and archeologists still do. Ethnographic collecting loomed large in Boas's appeals to the Asiatic Committee. He saw the China collection financed by Schiff, "although complete in itself," as "only the first step toward a much larger under-taking" (Boas to Jesup, 7 January 1901, East Asiatic Committee, 1894–1907 Correspondence Files, DAA, AMNH). The materials that Laufer sent back from China would have to convince the Committee of the practical value of scholarly research, collecting, and documentation. These were the stakes.

THE EXPEDITIONIST

Berthold Laufer (1874–1934) was an unlikely anthropologist. He had been a student of Oriental languages at the University of Berlin, earned a doctorate in philology from the University of Leipzig by the age of twenty-three, and had already studied Persian, Sanskrit, Pali, Malay, Chinese, Japanese, Manchu, Mongolian, Dravidian, and Tibetan from some of the greatest scholars of the day (Latourette 1936:49). Owing to Laufer's extraordinary linguistic skills, Boas commissioned him in 1897 for fieldwork among the peoples of Sakhalin and the Amur River in the Russian Far East (eastern Siberia) as part of the Jesup expedi-tion. In retrospect, it is surprising that Boas would have sent to Siberia a budding European savant whose explorations into Asian cultures had theretofore been conducted in the rarefied air of a German university. Laufer's background was not unlike Boas's own, an assimilated German Jewish intellectual who had come to anthropology via a circuitous path. Boas had initially trained in physics, but had turned to geography and a stint of fieldwork with the Inuit on Baffin Island which turned him to ethnography (Baick 1998:32–33; Cole 1983; Sanjek 1996: 72). Still, one misses the logic of Boas's assertion that "Dr. Laufer had devoted himself to the study of the Tibetan language and of the history of Asi-atic cultures, and was well prepared to take up the problems offered by the Amur tribes" (Boas 1903:93–94). Even so, Laufer flourished in the field, working among the Ainu and Gilyak (Nivkh) of Sakhalin and the Gold (Nanai) of the Amur River region. He zealously collected objects and made wax cylinder recordings, but showed much less enthusiasm for photographic documentation or for taking the head and body mea-surements that were a component of turn-of-the-century anthropologi-cal practice. The plaster required for head casts seemed always to miss him at the last stop (Accession File 1900-12, DAA, AMNH; Kendall 1988).

In Siberia, Laufer had proven himself to be a comprehensive collector gifted with an aesthetic eye. As an ethnographer, however, his contribution to the Jesup expedition was thin: an aptly named publication of "Preliminary Notes" in *American Anthropologist* (1900) and a lavishly illustrated monograph on *The Decorative Art of the Amur Tribes* (1902) wherein he decoded textile patterns in the manner of arcane glyphs. The peripatetic expedition style, intended for a comprehensive survey of the vast culture area that spanned the Bering Strait, did not foster the extended, in-depth observation and deep linguistic competence that would be expected of subsequent generations of anthropologists.[8] In China, Laufer would meld his experience of expedition anthropology, acquired in the trenches of Siberian fieldwork, with the Sinological erudition he had acquired in Berlin, but he would continue to work in the expedition model. Significantly, and in contrast with most other ethnographic terrains circa 1900, China was also a place where Laufer, trained as a textual scholar, could purchase books that had been written, published, and read by some of his ethnographic subjects or their ancestors—significant collections of old and rare volumes that he was charged to purchase for the American Museum of Natural History and Columbia University (Edgren 1984, 1991).

Laufer's prior training in philology colored his approach to fieldwork. Commenting on the proofs of Laufer's Amur River textile monograph, Boas had chided him for relying overmuch on his own interpretations and for failing to distinguish them from local knowledge recorded in the field (Boas to Laufer, 25 October 1901, 1901-69, DAA, AMNH). In reply, Laufer maintained that "all explanations obtained by natives are merely fragmentary and must be put together into a whole by us like the pieces of a broken jar" (Laufer to Boas, 27 November 1901, 1902-4, DAA, AMNH). As an extension of his interest in ancient and exotic scripts, Laufer seemed sometimes to regard the material world as signs to be decoded and wide-ranging etymologies to be traced.[9] In China, he speculated that "shields of the Malayan tribes, including the so-called demon-shields of the Dayak of Borneo, derived from Chinese shields as still used in [the] 18th century" (Laufer to Boas, 11 January 1903, 1903-13, DAA, AMNH). In describing to Boas the "very curious representation of birds, fishes, insects, and other animals" on a collection of Chinese kites he had purchased during the lunar New Year, he suggested "a strange resemblance of this ornamentation to that of your friends in British Columbia, as set forth in your paper on the decorative art of the North Pacific Coast" (Laufer to Boas, 1 March 1902, 1902-4, DAA, AMNH). With an echo of his earlier contempt for the limitations of native knowledge, he wrote from Nanjing, explaining to Boas why he could not provide adequate documentation on the enormous puppet collection he had assembled, citing the limitations of his puppeteer informant and of informants more generally:

> The oral statements of the people are all superficial and unreliable, generally speaking, [and] as all their knowledge is derived from written sources, we have, of course, to look up literature to verify their statements. I do not think it wise, therefore, to give designations for these figures for labeling before I have gone through the subject in detail. I also hope you will understand … why I bought such a number of books. There is no oral tradition, and properly speaking, no folklore in China; everything is literature and art. The books which I bought ought to be considered as the text-books illuminating and explaining the collection and to form together with these an inseparable unit. (Laufer to Boas, 7 March 1903, 1903-13, DAA, AMNH)

For Laufer, texts contained the key to an antiquarian China, "up to the fatal year 1900 … the only country where the life of antiquity was really still alive" (Laufer 1912b:137). It was a romance, but its logic was not so far from the work of other turn-of-the-century ethnographers who privileged precontact native cultures over the contemporary conditions of those they studied. Boasian anthropology was in its own way "textual"; Boas and his students produced "endless recordings of texts" of folklore and linguistic data (Freed 2012:301, 454) but with human encounters mediating the recording ethnographer and the desired myth or tale. Recording in the informant's own words became a precept of Boasian anthropology where endangered native languages offered fragile windows on vanishing cultural knowledge (Darnell 1998:129, 186; 2001:11, 14). Laufer's privileging of printed textual knowledge, on the other hand, would have been reinforced through his encounters with educated Chinese who similarly valued erudition and the authority of classical texts: "received the visits of a number of scholars ... had talks about Confucianism and the antiquities and famous paintings of the place" (Laufer to Boas, 9 November 1901, 1901-69, DAA, AMNH). And Laufer was not a modest man. He observed how the antiquities deal- ers knew nothing about the material they sold and how highly liter- ate Chinese matched his own difficulty in decoding inscriptions and seals. In Beijing he reported with obvious pride, "I have found out that I know more about Buddhism, its history and literature, than any Chi- nese monk or even Lama." He bested the knowledge of his language tutor, a Lama who was instructor to the imperial family. "I could explain to him in his own language a number of terms which he never knew before, and tell him about books which he had never seen nor read" (Laufer to Boas, 14 March 1902, 1902-4, DAA, AMNH).

While Laufer's prior training led him in the direction of antiquar- ian research, Boas developed a plan for the China expedition in cogni- zance of the perceived interests of potential future backers on the Asi- atic Committee. He listed, as the expedition's first objective, a study of "the use of natural products by the people of eastern Asia, and manu- factures based on such products, methods of manufacture, embracing the whole range of industrial life of the people [and their] consumption of manufactured products, illustrating the extent to which the various natural products and manufactured objects enter into the daily life of the people" (Laufer Expedition to China, MSS.E973, Library Special Collections Archives, AMNH). As part of this same plan, the expedi- tion would document a cultural "China," attentive to how science, tech- nology, religion, and art were present in "the daily life of the people." Boas's outline for the work of the expedition reflected an apprecia- tion of the historic depth, complexity, technological sophistication, and sheer enormity of "China," but betrays naïve expectations of how much China could be caught within the net of a three-year expedition or embraced by the interest and energy of a single ethnographer, even one so gifted and versatile as Laufer.

Like the Jesup expedition (on the Siberia side), and in contrast with the shorter field "seasons" of anthropologists working with North American populations, the scope of the project was expeditionary, an extended period of fieldwork in a place not otherwise easily accessed,

Fig. 1. Laufer (rt.) in Hankou. Courtesy Field Museum, A98299.

a broad agenda, and a mobile engagement with the terrain. Boas was well aware of the difference between China and the small populations of hunters and gatherers, herders and horticulturalists who had theretofore been (and for much of the twentieth century would continue to be) regarded as anthropology's proper domain. But in accepting the idea of a historically and temporally unified China, he could com-

Fig. 2. AMNH 70/10577. Paper kite collected by Laufer, "a strange resemblance of this ornamentation to that of your friends in British Columbia."

mit the ethnographic sleight-of-hand of rendering the Qing Empire the lexical equivalent of the Kwakiutl [10] or the Koryak. In his "Plan of Operations" he argued, "Since the culture of China is, on the whole, uniform, owing to the centralization of government, the collections do not require elaborate subdivisions, except in so far as the historical influences which molded Chinese culture must be considered" (5 February 1901, East Asiatic Committee, 1894–1907 Correspondence Files, DAA, AMNH).[11] Boas, probably in consultation with Laufer, added the possibility that the research would include "the important culture of Tibet . . . and the life of the Miao-tse [Miao]" (5 February 1901, East Asiatic Committee, 1894–1907 Correspondence Files, DAA, AMNH). In China, Laufer soon realized that these geographic ambitions were overblown. His correspondence reveals a practical awareness of regional diversity within China and the difficulties of working through several local dialects, even in the Chinese heartland (e.g., 31 May 1903, 1903-13, DAA, AMNH). He reluctantly abandoned his own plans to extend his research into Central Asia, owing to lack of funds (Laufer to Boas, 1 March 1902, 1902-4, DAA, AMNH).

But if Boas described China as a place of extraordinary cultural unity over time and space, Laufer's China was far from homogenized (Laufer 1912b.). Intellectually omnivorous, he pursued diverse historical evidence, perusing stone inscriptions in Chinese, Manchu, Mongol, Tibetan, Sanskrit, Turkish, and Arabic, and acquiring old books and rubbings as opportunities arose throughout his travels (Laufer to Boas, 10 April 1902, 1902-4, DAA, AMNH). He collected Tibetan tangka paintings and masks for tantric liturgical dramas and supplemented his growing library with texts on borderland peoples.[12] China's ethnically complex past continued to tantalize him, as when he suggested that a future trip might involve research in the homeland of the eleventh- and twelfth-century Xi Xia (Tangut) Kingdom in the far northwest of China (Laufer to Boas, 18 May 1902, 1902-4, DAA, AMNH).

Despite the limitations of time, space, and money, Laufer's sense of ethnographic mission was encyclopedic, straddling contemporary observations and antiquarian research. At the end of his fieldwork, he would propose twenty-one topics of future scholarly studies, "ample material for which is already collected." These proposed projects ranged from the Chinese Neolithic to bronzes to ancient and modern pottery to the influence of religious dances in the development of Chinese theater to Chinese representations of "foreign tribes" (Laufer to Boas, 8 July 1904, 1904-2, DAA, AMNH). Because Laufer's primary task was to acquire and document collections that would be written up after his return to New York, he conducted his researches with great dispatch during his three years in China: Shanghai, an extended tour of Jiangsu and Zhejiang provinces including Suzhou, Hangzhou, Ningbo, Putuoshan (in the East China Sea) and Haimen (in Jiangsu), then on to Beijing with trips to the Great Wall, the Ming Tombs, the imperial kilns, and Chengde (Jehol) in the Manchu homeland. He returned to Shanghai as a jumping off point for a journey to Nanjing and Hankou and eventually Xian, then back to Beijing, on to Shandong, and from Qingdao back to Shanghai before sailing from China in April 1904.

The frenetic pace of his work and the astonishing breadth of his interests are well witnessed in his letters to Boas. In Hangzhou, he fought the onset of a sudden and violent intestinal complaint by accelerated activity, ten hours on horseback during which he saw "all [the] remarkable places of interest . . . collected a large number of rubbings made from old temples inscriptions . . . obtained also historical materials regarding these interesting places of worship and recorded some traditions and legends told by the priests." He adds, "The ride was, of course, very painful to me, as that disease is accompanied by a constant pricking heat and boiling in the bowels" (Laufer to Boas, 9 November 1901, 1901-69, DAA, AMNH).

Laufer did the wide-ranging work of an early twentieth-century anthropological expedition, generating material (including textual) and aural data for future research and future museum exhibitions. From Shanghai, he reported that he had made sixty-one recordings including two complete dramas with all songs and dialogues. "I engaged a band of female actors and took the plays on the stage of their theatre. I used two machines which were working at the same time, one for the orchestral music, the other one for the vocal music, so that the two cylinders are corresponding to each other" (Laufer to Boas, 27 September 1901, 1901-69, DAA, AMNH). The next month, in Suzhou, he commissioned the woodworkers at a Jesuit school to make models of a village,

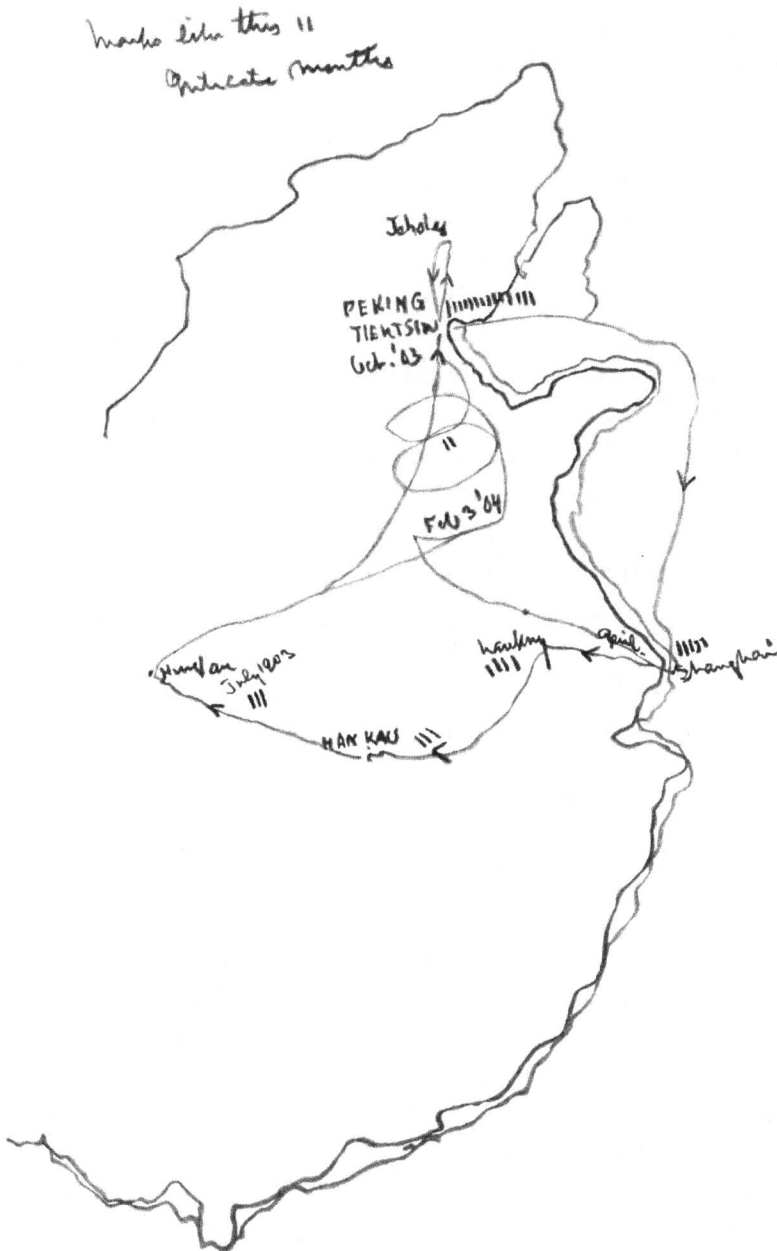

Fig. 3. Laufer's hand-drawn map of his travels during the final segment of the Schiff expedition, American Museum of Natural History, Expedition to China Correspondence, 1900–1904, MSS.E973, AMNH Library Special Collections Archives.

a pagoda, and a temple. "They have worked up similar models for the Paris Exhibition, and what I have seen of their work is very satisfying" (Laufer to Boas, 12 October 1901, 1901-69, DAA, AMNH). In November 1901, back in Shanghai, he reported arrangements for photographing actors and musicians, locating an Italian who could make plaster casts, and commissioning a street scene carved out of wood according to his own detailed plan and reports.[13] In addition, he wrote, "I am entering into negotiations with Chinese officials to obtain heads of executed criminals" (Laufer to Boas, 9 November 1901, 1901-69, DAA, AMNH). This would not have been the last time that Chinese officials trafficked in criminal body parts or that anthropologists brought skulls home from the field, but there is no record of either the projected criminal heads or the plaster casts having ever reached the Museum. The file does contain the following note: "Enclosed I beg to send you an X-ray photo taken from the crippled feet of a Chinese woman, which I hope may interest you to some degree. Yours very truly, B. Laufer" (Laufer to Boas, 28 February 1902, 1902-4, DAA, AMNH).

Correspondence between Boas and Laufer reveals a shared and passionate sense of purpose in elevating western perceptions of China. Boas's first report to the Asiatic Committee on Laufer's progress would claim that "the material sent by Dr. Laufer is very valuable and attractive, and gives a fair insight into the great achievements that the Chinese have accomplished" (1 May 1901, East Asiatic Committee, 1894–1907 Correspondence Files, DAA, AMNH). To Laufer himself he wrote, "You know perfectly well what we are driving at. It is to bring home to the public the fact that the Chinese have a civilization of their own, and to inculcate respect for the Chinese" (Boas to Laufer, 21 April 1902, 1902-4, DAA, AMNH). A year later, this conviction verged on self-righteousness when Laufer tried to dissuade Boas from accepting, on Columbia's behalf, the gift of a Kangxi encyclopedia from the Foreign Department of the Qing government. Laufer saw this as another instance of exploitation such as China had experienced in the aftermath of the recent Boxer Rebellion. Boas responded: "It is the ideal aim of our work to change . . . public opinion towards the Chinese, and anything that we may be able to contribute in this direction is a service rendered to China. From this point of view we have the right to utilize all the influence that we can possibly get in China in order to further our ends" (Boas to Laufer, 23 April 1903, DAA, AMNH). Back in New York, Boas was struggling, unsuccessfully, to persuade the Eastern Asiatic Committee to include in its membership "one or two wealthy and influential Chinese who live in this city" (Boas to Ford, 7 March 1903, East Asiatic Committee, 1894–1907 Correspondence Files, DAA, AMNH). The archive contains no response; the appeal seems to have fallen on deaf ears.

For his part, Laufer derided the "silly prejudices" of the "white residents of this place [Shanghai]. . . . The deeper the narrow mindedness of foreign residents, the higher is the intelligence of the Chinese who show a much better understanding for the character of my work" (Laufer to Boas, 30 August 1901, 1901-69, DAA, AMNH). Toward the end of his time in China he wrote, "The Chinese culture is in my opinion just as good as ours and in many things far better, especially in practical ethics. [If] I regret something it is not having been born a Chinese" (Laufer to Boas, 3 June 1903, 1903-13, DAA, AMNH).

VICISSITUDES OF COLLECTING

While Boas was secure in Laufer's sense of common purpose, they did not always see eye to eye regarding other aspects of the fieldwork, and their correspondence during the Schiff expedition sometimes erupts in mutual expressions of frustration. These altercations have been interpreted as a conflict between Boas's ethnographic agenda and Laufer's interests in art and antiquarian pursuits (Freed 2012:310; Haddad 2006; Stalberg 1983:38). This, however, misses the full charge of Laufer's mission and Boas's stake in it. Boas did sometimes find it necessary to curb Laufer's raptures over antique paintings and ancient bronze drums, reminding him to not "give undue prominence to Chinese art" and to always keep in mind that from the perspective of the Anthropology Department and the Museum, "the most important point is always the significance of an object in the cultural life of the people, and the use to which a work of art is put or the ideas which it represents" (Boas to Laufer, 3 February 1902, 1902-4, DAA, AMNH). A close reading of the correspondence suggests not that Laufer shorted his ethnographic project—work in which he engaged from nearly the moment of his arrival in China—but that he was not fulfilling a more specific and challenging mission to document Chinese handicraft industries and acquire the tools of production.

Collecting technology was high on the agenda of early field anthropology, initially as evidence for different stages of cultural evolution (Gosden and Larson 2007). While Boas is credited with turning the course of American anthropology away from cultural evolutionist models and pursuits, Jacknis describes how, consistent with his characteristic relativism, Boas felt that "manufactures would be improved by the exposure of craftsmen to the accumulated heritage of the world's cultures" (Jacknis 1985:87). It seems also to have been standard practice at AMNH to ask collectors for full sets of tools and materials in order to illustrate the production of characteristic crafts, "a piece of the cloth partly woven on the loom; also specimens of the grass itself" (Putnam to James, 20 March 1898, 1898-17, DAA, AMNH). However, in the case of China and in contrast with virtually everywhere else that AMNH had theretofore collected, handicrafts were produced at a high level of sophistication; they had long been consumed as decorative art in American and European homes and exhibited in world's fairs and other venues (Clunas 1997; Conn 2000; Rydell 1987). Detailed information on Chinese manufactures was the piece of the project most likely to entice potential backers on the East Asiatic Committee.

After receiving Laufer's first shipment of objects, Boas expressed his disappointment: "In collecting the material illustrating industries, please do not forget to obtain everything that is required in making the various objects; for instance, all the implements used in making the matting that you sent us, embroidery-frames and needles, carving-knives for wood-work, etc.... You must lay just as much stress on the technical side as on the artistic, social, and religious sides" (Boas to Laufer, 21 January 1902, 1902-4, DAA, AMNH). This theme would be struck, with varying degrees of emphasis, specificity, and conciliation throughout Boas's correspondence with Laufer in the field. One month after the previous directive he prodded Laufer again: "So far, your collections contain very little showing, for instance, the whole industrial side of weaving, embroidery, basketry, wood-carving,—all classes of objects represented in your collection. We ought to have samples of the various kinds of fabrics, thread, embroidery-silks, dyes, spinning apparatus, loom[s], etc.; and not only for this industry, but for others as well,—agriculture, wood work, metal-work, leather-work, lacquer-work, etc." (Boas to Laufer, 3 February 1902, 1902-4, DAA, AMNH). By April 1903, at the start of Laufer's last year in China, Boas's impatience was acute:

> You ought, for instance, to obtain for us the agricultural implements used in the cultivation of rice, the agricultural implements used in raising cotton and other products. You ought to make a collection of the ordinary every-day bamboo things,—a subject which you yourself referred to in one of your letters. You ought to illustrate the manufacture of paper, the preparing of skins, stone-cutting, the manufacture of glass, spinning, and a selection of some of the thousands of industries that are important in the daily life of China. . . . You will readily see that all the series which you have sent us are very special; and with the collections that you have made so far, we are not able to illustrate adequately the ordinary industries of China. (Boas to Laufer, 13 April 1903, 1903-13, DAA, AMNH)

A few days later, responding to pressure at AMNH, Boas waxed even more emphatic, implying that Laufer's future prospects in New York and Boas's own larger Asian project depended upon the documentation of local industries:

> [T]he whole development of your vast Asiatic work depends upon your strictest compliance with this request. Every time the matter of the East Asiatic work comes up, it is again and again brought forward that what the committee wants to do is to exhibit the products and consumption of the Chinese people. We want the agricultural implements. You ought to collect as much as you can bearing upon the silk industry, beginning with raising the silkworms to the manufacture of the silk. You ought to get specimens illustrating the carpentry-work, building, manufacture of porcelain, etc. . . . What you have done up to this time is altogether too special and too fragmentary. (Boas to Laufer, 24 April 1903, 1903-13, DAA, AMNH)

In October 1903, well into Laufer's final year in China, Boas offered one last prod to the recalcitrant Laufer, noting that having unpacked most of the material that Laufer sent and placed it in cases, he was struck "more forcefully than ever before" by the paucity of industrial material.

On the home front, Boas was under pressure to show results, both with respect to the promised synthesizing monograph on the Jesup expedition and for Laufer's continuing researches. By 1902, Jesup had even suggested that Laufer receive no further support, owing to the disappointing nature of his collections (Freed 2012:448). Boas was operating in a less congenial climate than had theretofore blessed his projects. His aging patron, Morris Jesup, began to defer administrative matters to the far less sympathetic director, Hermon Bumpus, and was no longer providing financial support for ambitious research and publication projects, a situation that would ultimately result in Boas's resignation from AMNH in 1905 (Cole 1999:235, 241, 244–248; Haddad 2006; Freed 2012:446–456). For his part, Laufer alternated between enthusiastic reports of the progress of his collecting and frustrated attempts to explain to Boas why it was so difficult to document handicraft industries in China.

When he went to China, Laufer's primary interests were textual and historical. His correspondence recounts work with a succession of tutors, visits to temples and historic sites, and his relentless acquisition of rubbings of historical inscriptions. In Beijing, in order to work uninterrupted with his tutor, he turned over the task of documenting a significant puppet collection to an unreliable assistant who allegedly made off with some of the puppets (Laufer to Goodnow, 12 August 1903, 1903-13, DAA, AMNH). In June 1902, making another promise to Boas to "stick to the plan as developed by you," he confessed to confusion about how to proceed and admitted "that the work of collecting does not always coincide with my scientific aims, and there is necessarily a dilemma between these two agents, which sometimes exclude one another entirely. Now, after a long fight, I have arrived at last at a compromise between those two hostile powers" (Laufer to Boas, 20 June 1902, 1902-4, DAA, AMNH).

But Laufer also struggled to impress upon Boas the particular difficulty of documenting the highly developed and often jealously protected techniques of Chinese handicraft production, underscoring the differences between collecting such material in China and the museum anthropologist's common practice of obtaining tools and materials from the local weavers, potters, or woodcarvers encountered in other fieldwork. Far from simply "going shopping," it required special ordering, which demanded "a good deal of nerves, the self-control of a god, and an angel's patience" over many cups of tea and gaining trust "before starting into real business. . . . All conditions of life and work are entirely different here from those in Japan, Siberia, or America" (Laufer to Boas, 28 February 1902, 1902–4, DAA, AMNH). He elaborates in subsequent correspondence:

> The man who sells the embroideries is not the same as the maker, and the maker is not the same as the man who makes the needles, thread, or frames or other instruments, and so with all objects. (Laufer to Boas, 10 March 1902, 1902-4, DAA, AMNH)

> You will hardly believe how many hours and days and even weeks one has to run about to hunt up such and such a thing, and at last, even if you have ordered it to be made, you will be disappointed at ever getting it. (Laufer to Boas, 18 May 1902, 1902-4, DAA, AMNH)

Laufer soon realized that among the producers of skilled and elegant handicraft, "the Chinese manufacturers have their own secrets like our own people and are not willing to betray them" (Laufer to Boas, 10 March 1902, 1902-4, DAA, AMNH). Owners of local industries "are suspicious of foreigners. . . . People really fear we might imitate their work at home, and it requires an Iliad of speeches in each and every case to convince them of the contrary" (Laufer to Boas, 20 June 1902, 1902-4, DAA, AMNH).

If industrial spying was a hidden agenda of the Asiatic Committee, Laufer was not cut out to be an industrial spy. In the spring of 1902, writing from Beijing, he had confessed his own limitations: "Subjects like weaving silk and cotton industry, agriculture and a number of other technicalities are entirely foreign to me and there is hardly anybody . . . [who can] master them all. . . . I cannot buy or order things which I do not understand" (Laufer to Boas, 10 March 1902, 1902-4, DAA, AMNH). After a heated exchange in the spring of 1902 and renewed promises to do his best, he reported in August a successful visit to an imperial brick kiln where he was permitted to observe the entire process of manufacture and was presented with several specimens (Laufer to Boas, 2 August 1902, 1902-4, DAA, AMNH). In May 1903, during a stint in Hankou, he reported that he had "particularly enjoyed the work of the ironsmiths." He was also finding ways to combine his textual interests with the collecting project. Having studied "the whole domain of agriculture according to the illustrated works of Chinese literature," he said, "I shall surely make a collection as complete as possible in this line" (Laufer to Boas, 31 May 1903, 1903-13, DAA, AMNH). In June 1903, however, collecting in Hankou, he again felt called upon to offer yet another explanation for both the complexity and confidentiality surrounding major Chinese manufactures:

> Take silk, for example. It would be necessary to live in a silk district for at least one year so as to observe all the stages of mulberry trees, the caterpillars, etc. The working of the silk industry takes place somewhere else. If of value, such collections can only be pursued by a silk expert. . . . I made inquiries about the porcelain manufacture to illustrate [that] it is out of the question. At present the only factory is imperial property located in King-te-chen [Jingdezhen] on the Yangtse [Yangtze]. The production is a carefully guarded secret, and a European can hardly expect to gain admittance. Repeatedly foreigners have been driven away from there. You remember that I was refused any industrial artifacts from the imperial brick factory in Peking, and the same thing is likely to happen at the porcelain factory if not worse. Travelling in these regions is complicated and tedious and I don't feel like . . . [going there and being] taken for a fool. (Laufer to Boas, 3 June 1903, 1903-13, DAA, AMNH)

In his remaining months in China, perhaps effectively shaken by the urgent tone of Boas's correspondence and aware that the clock was ticking, Laufer did make a significant effort to document handicraft industries. On his return to Beijing in September 1903, he immediately decamped for a six-day residence in a village at the foot of Beijing's eastern hills, interviewing farmers and blacksmiths and managing to make observations and collections at a nearby tile kiln (23 October 1903, 1903-13, DAA, AMNH). Back in the city he "made a special study of modern pottery and all metal industries, iron, copper, brass, tin, pewter, silver, and various others" (4 March 1904, 1904-2, DAA, AMNH). Boas had secured another behest enabling Laufer to make collections and studies of the ceramics industry near Beijing, from Po-shan in Shandong, and in Yixing on the Yangtze. But even during his self-described "winter campaign" in Shandong, where ceramics and glass production loomed large in his intentions, he managed to simultaneously pursue his own research interests. "I found more than twenty-five new stone sculptures in relief of the Han Dynasty which were heretofore unknown to Chinese epigraphists as well as to foreign scholars. I have paper rubbings of them. Still more important is the discovery of Mongolian inscriptions in these different places where nobody would search for them nor anybody ever found them" (Laufer to Boas, 10 February 1904, 1904-2, DAA, AMNH).

Early in 1904, perhaps encouraged by Laufer's progress, Boas expressed optimism about the future of the East Asian project and remained steadfast in his commitment to Laufer's continuing role in it: "My dear Laufer . . . I do not need to tell you how much I desire and wish to keep you here in New York and how ardently I hope for your assistance in developing the study of Oriental subjects in this country. Your point of view and my own coincide so happily, that I am certain that each in his proper field can do much towards bringing about a just appreciation of the achievements of a foreign race" (Boas to Laufer, 11 January 1904, 1904-2, DAA, AMNH). On February 10, Boas was able to inform Laufer of his likely appointment as assistant ethnologist whose duties would include cataloguing the Schiff expedition collection, arranging a public exhibition, and teaching the ethnology of China at Columbia University, an appointment confirmed a month later in a letter from AMNH director Hermon Bumpus (4 March 1904, 1904-2, DAA, AMNH).

CHINA FOR THE SINOLOGIST?

Laufer, the ultimate polymath, had balked at the broad expectations of Boas's agenda when they ran counter to his interests, temperament, and most important, his recognition of the incompatibility between the agendas of early expedition anthropology and the reality of docu-

Fig. 4. Carpenters in Beijing. Laufer Scrapbook, AMNH Library Special Collections Archives, neg. # 33610.

menting jealously protected handicraft industries in imperial China, a society with complex craft and art specializations. Recent and careful research on Chinese handicrafts has confirmed Laufer's instincts; these are domains of complex embodied knowledge and subtle interactions between the artisan, the user, the natural and social world, and a complex and historically contingent regime of production and distribution (Bray 1997; Eyferth 2009). The flying surveys of expeditionary anthropology were ill-suited to more than a passing acquaintance with sophisticated handicraft production. Even so, and despite all the misgivings that he had expressed to Boas, Laufer would observe, "If the manufacturers of this country [the United States] had taken the trouble to study the native industries of the Chinese and their products in museum collections with a view to adapting our manufactures to their peculiar needs, American business with China would have assumed much larger dimensions" (Laufer 1912b:138).

His unpublished guide to the exhibit he mounted at the AMNH after his return reveals a fidelity to the objectives of the exhibition, to document industries and patterns of consumption and to inculcate respect

Fig. 5. AMNH 70/2490. Cloisonné vase collected by Laufer in Beijing where he was able to document the entire casting and enameling process.

for his Chinese subject. The guide includes brief notes on such object-related topics as ceramic and glass making processes, plant fibers used in textile production, varieties of silk, cloisonné production, and blacksmithing. Visitors would see examples of the glazed Chinese wares that Boettger of Dresden had studied and eventually successfully reproduced. They would learn that after the fall of the Roman Empire, the most spectacular textiles came from the East and that familiar European patterns of dragons, griffons, and birds were influenced by Persian fabrics that copied Chinese motifs. Tin and silver ornaments were produced with creativity in endless variety to entice potential customers, an example to counter the common belief that Chinese artisans merely copy "things of the past." An exhibit of embroidery would include steel needles as a markedly rare example of a western commodity that had successfully supplanted a Chinese tool (Laufer n.d.). Laufer's celebratory presentation of Chinese handicraft past and present was far from the evolutionary displays of most contemporary museums and—in its referencing then-contemporary Chinese tastes and practices—far also from the strictly antiquarian exhibits that would dominate most museum presentations of China.

Had Laufer remained in Europe, he would undoubtedly have distinguished himself as a textual scholar. Had he gone to China by other means, he would probably also have enjoyed the conversations with Chinese scholars and antiquarians that he relates in his correspondence. But it is far less likely that he would have spent time in a rural village, at a pottery kiln, or in a cloisonné workshop. Boasian anthropology and his own polyglot curiosity had drawn him into a social and material encounter with late Qing China that was pulling his scholarship in multiple new directions. His report to Boas, after an ecstatic encounter with a living Buddhist tradition at Putuo Shan, suggests that even in the early months of fieldwork, he had begun to imagine contemporary observations and textual analysis as an integrated enterprise. He proposed a return to Putuo Shan after thoroughly studying ("in my few hours of leisure") the epigraphic and historical materials obtained on this first trip to compare the results of literary investigation with reality "to obtain a perfectly reliable fact." The resulting work would include a topographical description of the island, Chinese maps, his own observations, a chapter on the goddess Kwan Yin and the historical background of her worship, "the drama in which the story of her arrival . . . is performed together with a translation, musical notation of the songs, and descriptions of masks used in it," the modern traditions of the place, the lives of the monks, pilgrimages, and recent developments (Laufer to Boas, 9 November 1901, 1901-69, DAA, AMNH). Many of us might regret that such a monograph was never completed, although Laufer did succeed in re-creating the ritual drama under exhibition glass at the Field Museum in Chicago. The scholarship through which Laufer would eventually gain renown also bears the mark of his early fieldwork in descriptions of how jade is mined, distributed, and worked (Laufer 1912a) or the similarities between Han ceramics and some early twentieth-century wares (Laufer 1909). His writing on Chinese theater draws upon his own familiarity with performance as well as text (Laufer 1923). When he returned from his first trip to China, he had begun to master a style of China scholarship uniquely his own and for which he would eventually be eulogized as an "ethnologist" for want of any better term (Latourette 1936).

But anthropology would soon take another turn.

OBLIVION, OR NEARLY SO

At the end of 1905, the East Asiatic Committee had run out of steam and voted to dissolve. Apart from Schiff's generosity, Committee members' contributions to Boas's projects had been minimal, small subsidies for the collection of ceramics and smoking equipment. What is now arguably the most extensive ethnographic collection from pre-revolutionary China in North America had failed to impress them. The endeavor ended when Boas himself left the museum to teach full time at Columbia University. The precipitating cause was his nemesis, Director Bumpus, who had opposed a permanent appointment for Laufer and the kind of research-oriented fieldwork that had characterized both the Jesup and Schiff expeditions (17 May 1905, DAA, AMNH; Baick 1998:76–80; Cole 1999:243–248; Darnell 1998:142–147; Haddad 2006; Freed 2012). Boas's prescient vision of an Asian studies that combined fieldworking anthropologists with textual scholars and sometimes imagined them in the same person would not be realized for many more decades. Until the 1920s, North American anthropologists would work primarily in North America (Darnell 1998:160). Boas's successor at the Museum, Clark Wissler, defined the Anthropology Department as an "American department" with no space for continuing researches on China (Wissler to Lucas, 27 May 1912, East Asiatic Committee, 1894–1907 Correspondence Files, DAA, AMNH). When Schiff attempted to revive plans to publish Laufer's guide to the China collection, already in edited proofs, Museum president Henry Fairfield Osborn took the decidedly pre-Boasian view that "the whole subject lies somewhat beyond the true field of the Museum of Natural History, which concerns itself only with the prehistoric cultures and races", an image that the discipline has long since tried to live down (Osborne to Schiff, 5 May 1911, East Asiatic Committee, 1894–1907 Correspondence Files, DAA, AMNH). There was even correspondence with the Metropolitan Museum of Art with the aim of selling the China collection (Osborn to de Forest, 17 May 1911, Central Archives, 975, Special Collections Archives, AMNH).

After teaching Chinese at Columbia and holding an "assistant" position at AMNH, Laufer would join the staff of the Field Museum in 1908 and spend the rest of his career leading two more expeditions to China (Latourette 1936:44–45; Bronson 2006). Between 1908 and 1910 he would spend time in the Tibetan-speaking borderlands of western China, but he would fail in several attempts to reach Tibet itself (Bronson 2006). With the irony that history makes of youthful enthusiasms, Laufer in his disillusionment with Republican China would become the very model of an antiquarian, albeit a more wide-ranging and creative antiquarian than he might have been without his early anthropological adventure.

CONCLUSION

The history of American anthropology marks Boas's departure from AMNH as a critical disciplinary turning from the museum to the university and from museum collections to more abstract notions of "culture" (Conn 1998:102; Darnell 1998:149; Cole 1999:253–254; Jacknis 1985, 1996:205; Hegeman 1998), but East Asia and the study of complex state societies was also left behind in a neglected corner of the museum.

Fig. 6. AMNH 70/12870. Model of a potter's kiln, collected by Laufer.

Sixty years after the Schiff expedition, Maurice Freedman would critique the brief history of China anthropology, a story that, in his telling, began with village studies in the 1920s and 1930s. The authors of these studies engaged in participant observation through extended residence in and in-depth knowledge of a circumscribed community following Malinowski's model, an approach that has been broadly recognized for much of the twentieth century as "doing anthropology" (Clifford 1997). While Freedman valued the quality of information that deep participant observation produced, he faulted these efforts as narrow and limited, incapable of reaching beyond the well-examined village to a broader vision of Chinese society. But Freedman's 1979 history of China anthropology contained no memory of Laufer, who, if anything, had erred in the opposite direction. In the manner of assigning "proper names" (de Certeau 1984), what Laufer did was no longer recognized as anthropology and consequently forgotten. Freedman's comments on the brief history of China anthropology echo Eric Wolf's 1982 critique of the entire discipline in his *Europe and the People without History*, with its recognition that in their exquisite examination of microcosms, anthropologists had generally ignored the integration of their subjects into larger social, political, and economic systems. It is worth resurrecting the story of Boas's failed East Asian project now that Freedman's own summation has become history. Freedman's call for a new anthropology of China assumed the sort of area studies training, including cultural and historical literacy, that most practicing anthropologists of East Asia receive today.[14] The "area studies" moment has itself passed, but not without leaving a broader and more historically proficient anthropology in its wake.

Many of the topics that Laufer pursued—the tension between text and social practice, the importance of non-Han peoples in the larger "Chinese" mix, and the global traffic in goods and ideas—are matters of no small interest today. Laufer's studies of the circulation of such things as tobacco, maize, and textile motifs can be read as harbingers of our contemporary cognizance of global systems. Material culture studies have returned in a new incarnation and "multi-sited" ethnographies are considered valuable ways of recording mobile subjects and the things they make and consume (just don't call these projects "expeditions"). One can read the eclipse of this small chapter in the history of early American anthropology as a mistaken overinvestment in a soon to be outdated research model, a loss of nerve on the part of the intellectual community, a nadir in institutional politics, or a consequence of the risky business of marketing an academic enterprise, something many of us find ourselves doing from time to time. One possible reading is a cautionary tale about the sometimes irreconcilable expectations that freight many visionary enterprises, inside museums and out. What would anthropology have been like had it been able to digest Laufer and China into the twentieth-century mix? Could we have gotten sooner to where we are now—wedding the powerful tool of fieldwork with the abiding challenge to rigorously contextualize these studies in time, space, political economy, and global flow—if complex societies bearing their own voluminous histories had stayed within the anthropological gaze? History does not allow space for speculation about what might have been, but it is possible to suggest that something was lost from the discipline at large—or at least significantly delayed—when China fell out of early twentieth-century anthropology's gaze so completely that the telling of this story becomes a spectral counterhistory (Derrida 1994).

ACKNOWLEDGMENTS

This project emerged from the Division of Anthropology Archive (DAA) at the American Museum of Natural History (AMNH). I am grateful to former archivist Belinda Kaye and current archivist Kristen Mable for pointing me in the right direction and to Renate Khambatta for her translations from German of Laufer's Jesup expedition correspondence. Kristen Olsen and Katherine Skaggs, curatorial assistants in the DAA, helped me to prepare several drafts of this essay. Elizabeth Berger and Laura Warren provided invaluable research assistance during their internships in the DAA. Stanley Freed, Erin Hasinoff, and Robert Oppenheim kindly advised me of materials related to Boas/Laufer from their own archival researches. Myron Cohen, Soren Edgren, and Ira Jacknis also gave me much appreciated critical readings as did two anonymous reviewers. I alone am responsible for the shortcomings of this effort.

NOTES

1. See Latourette (1936:57–68) for a complete bibliography of Laufer's work.

2. For example, Cole (1999:2, 287). Stocking's Boas reader includes a report on the work of the East Asiatic Committee, which Stocking describes as part of Boas's attempt to "expand the horizons of his anthropological activity" (Stocking 1974:283, 294–297), but there is no further reference to this project in any of Stocking's four edited anthologies on anthropology's early history (Stocking 1983, 1989, 1991, 1996). Marshall Hyatt describes Laufer as "a friend" of Boas but does not explain the connection (Hyatt 1990:31). Darnell mentions Laufer and East Asia in relation to Boas's anthropology program at Columbia (Darnell 1998:160). In their summations of Boas's life and work, Goldschmidt (1959), Handler (1990), Hegeman (1998), Pierpont (2004), and Sanjek (1996) make no mention of Boas's anthropological interest in Asia.

3. Boas and the Asiatic Committee also get a deserved mention in the history of the development of Asian studies at Columbia (deBary 2006:594).

4. Bennet Bronson (2006) also mentions the Schiff expedition as prelude to Laufer's work in China on behalf of the Field Museum.

5. Schiff was more than casually interested in the Far East. He had unsuccessfully sought to establish banking interests in China for his firm, Kuhn, Loeb and Company. The firm would decisively fund Japan in the Russo-

Japanese War (1904–1905), in part owing to Russia's anti-Semitic policies. For this support, Schiff would travel to Japan in 1906 and be decorated by the emperor with the Order of the Rising Sun (Cohen 1999:33–36).

6. Schiff initially offered to cover the expenses of the first year to encourage other donors. When funds were not forthcoming, Schiff agreed to subsidize the entire expedition. This was the most significant contribution made by any member of the Asiatic Committee. Columbia, meanwhile, received an important behest for Chinese studies, given in the name of "Dean Lung" but assumed to have been provided by General Horace Walpole Carpentier, a trustee (Baick 1998:84–152; deBary 2006:594). Despite effort on Boas's part, Carpentier could not be persuaded to join the Committee (East Asiatic Committee, 1894–1907 Correspondence Files, DAA, AMNH).

7. The Committee included Edward D. Adams, a financier and trustee of the Metropolitan Museum of Art; Nicholas Murray Butler, president of Columbia University; Clarence Cary and C. C. Cuyler, bankers; John Foord, secretary of the American Asiatic Association, a business interest group; E. H. Harriman and James J. Hill, railway magnates; Clarence H. Mackay, president of Commercial Pacific Cable Company; Howard Mansfield, a lawyer and president of the art aficionados' Groiler Club; James R. Morse, president of a trading company who would invest in Korean gold mines; William Barclay Parsons, president of the American China Development Company and a trustee of Columbia University; George A. Plimpton, a trustee of Barnard College; and Jacob H. Schiff, banker. AMNH representation included Morris K. Jesup, president of the Asiatic Committee; Hermon C. Bumpus, director; John H. Winser, treasurer of the Asiatic Committee; and Franz Boas, curator and secretary of the Asiatic Committee.

8. His fellow Siberia expeditionists, Waldemar Bogoras and Waldemar Jochelson, although equally peripatetic, drew upon years of prior ethnographic observation, painfully acquired as political exiles in Siberia, in preparing their detailed monographs on the Chukchi, Koryak, Yukaghir, and Yakut (Sakha) (Freed, Freed, and Williamson 1988; Krupnik and Vakhtin 2003).

9. Indeed, he even suggested to Boas that the museum establish "an epigraphical department to show the development of writing in Asia and Europe and picture writing in Australia and the Americas" (Laufer to Boas, 18 May 1902, 1902-4, DAA, AMNH).

10. Now called Kwakwaka'wakw.

11. When asked if the Asiatic Committee should not prioritize Philippines research over the planned China expedition, "owing to the present political importance of the Philippine problems," Boas argued forcefully for China on the grounds that "Philippines (that is Malay) culture is an outgrowth of aboriginal Indian, West Asiatic, and East Asiatic cultures; consequently if we confine ourselves to work in Malay countries, we are building without a foundation, which must be laid particularly in India and in China" (Boas to Schiff, 31 January 1901, East Asiatic Committee, 1894–1907 Correspondence Files, DAA, AMNH). Although a dominant scholarly view at the time, this is an unexpected assertion from a man whose life's work affirmed the worth of "cultures" constructed by hunters, gatherers, and horticulturalists, but in January of 1901, having carefully primed Laufer for fieldwork, and aware of interests in developing Chinese studies at Columbia, he was likely loath to see this unique opportunity slip away.

12. Laufer's rubbings now reside in the Field Museum, where he ended his career.

13. There is no evidence that these commissions were ever fulfilled or that the street scene or the models ever reached New York.

14. Area studies, and most particularly the growth of East Asian studies in North America, is commonly regarded as a child of the Cold War, with an intensification of government and other institutional support for China studies prompted by the so-called loss of China to revolution in 1949. With the end of the Cold War, strategic and economic interests would remain prominent. The arguments that Boas had made in the name of national interest are very much alive in this corner of the academy.

REFERENCES

Baick, John. 1998. Reorienting Culture: New York Elites and the Turn toward East Asia. PhD diss., New York University.

Bray, Francesca. 1997. Technology and Gender: Fabrics and Power in Late Imperial China. Berkeley: University of California Press.

Breckenridge, Carol. 1989. The Aesthetics and Politics of Colonial Collecting: India at World Fairs. Society for Comparative Study of Society and History 31(2):195–216.

Boas, Franz. 1903. The Jesup North Pacific Expedition. American Museum Journal 3:69–107.

Bronson, Bennet. 2006. Berthold Laufer. In Fieldiana: Curators, Collections, and Contexts: Anthropology at the Field Museum, 1893–2002. Anthropology n.s. 36:117–126.

Clifford, James. 1997. Routes: Travel and Translation in the Late Twentieth Century. Cambridge MA: Harvard University Press.

Clunas, Craig. 1997. Oriental Antiquities/Far Eastern Art. *In* Formations of Colonial Modernity in East Asia. T. E. Barlow, ed. Pp. 416–417. Durham NC: Duke University Press.

Cohen, Naomi Wiener. 1999. Jacob H. Schiff: A Study in American Jewish Leadership. Hanover NH: Brandeis University Press.

Cole, Douglas. 1983. The Value of a Person Lies in his Herzensbildung: Franz Boas' Baffin Island Letter-Diary, 1883–1884. *In* Observers Observed: Essays on Ethnographic Fieldwork. George W. Stocking Jr., ed. Pp. 13–52. Madison: University of Wisconsin Press.

———. 1999. Franz Boas: The Early Years, 1858–1906. Seattle: University of Washington Press.

Conn, Steven. 1998. Museums and American Intellectual Life, 1876–1926. Chicago: University of Chicago Press.

———. 2000. Where Is the East? Asian Objects in American Museums, from Nathan Dunn to Charles Freer. Winterthur Portfolio 35(2–3):157–188.

Darnell, Regna. 1998. And Along Came Boas: Continuity and Revolution in Americanist Anthropology. Philadelphia: John Benjamins.

———. 2001. Invisible Genealogies: A History of Americanist Anthropology. Lincoln: University of Nebraska Press.

de Certeau, Michel. 1984. The Practice of Everyday Life. S. Rendall, trans. Berkeley: University of California Press.

de Bary, Wm. Theodore. 2006. East Asian Studies at Columbia: The Early Years. *In* Living Legacies at Columbia. Wm. Theodore de Bary, ed. Pp. 594–604. New York: Columbia University Press.

Derrida, Jacques. 1994. Specters of Marx. New York: Routledge.

Edgren, Soren. 1984. Chinese Rare Books in American Collections. New York: China House Gallery, China Institute in America.

———. 1991. The Laufer Library in New York. Committee on East Asian Libraries Bulletin 93 (June): 2–7.

Edwards, Elizabeth. 1992. Introduction. *In* Anthropology and Photography, 1860–1920. Elizabeth Edwards, ed. Pp. 3–17. New Haven: Yale University Press.

Eyferth, Jacob. 2009. Eating Rice from Bamboo Roots: The Social History of a Community of Handicraft Papermakers in Rural Sichuan, 1920–2000. Cambridge: Harvard University Asia Center.

Freed, Stanley. 2012. Anthropology Unmasked: Museums, Science, and Politics in New York City. Wilmington OH: Orange Frazer.

Freed, Stanley, Ruth Freed, and Laila Williamson. 1988. Capitalist Philanthropy and Russian Revolutionaries: The Jesup North Pacific Expedition (1897–1902). American Anthropologist 90(1):7–24.

Freedman, Maurice. 1979 [1963]. A Chinese Phase in Social Anthropology. In The Study of Chinese Society. G. W. Skinner, ed. Pp. 380–397. Stanford CA: Stanford University Press.

Goldschmidt, Walter, ed. 1959. The Anthropology of Franz Boas: Essays on the Centennial of His Birth. Menasha WI: American Anthropological Association.

Gosden, Chris, and Frances Larson. 2007. Knowing Things: Exploring the Collections at the Pitt-Rivers Museum. Oxford: Oxford University Press.

Haddad, John. 2006. "To Inculcate Respect for the Chinese": Berthold Laufer, Franz Boas, and the Chinese Exhibits at the American Museum of Natural History, 1899–1912. Anthropos 101:123–144.

Handler, Richard. 1990. Boasian Anthropology and the Critique of American Culture. American Quarterly 42(2):252–273.

Hasinoff, Erin. 2010. The Missionary Exhibit: A Frustration and a Promise for Franz Boas and the American Museum of Natural History. Museum History Journal 3(1): 81–101.

Hegeman, Susan. 1998. Franz Boas and Professional Anthropology: On Mapping the Borders of the "Modern." Victorian Studies 41(3):455–483.

Hyatt, Marshall. 1990. Franz Boas, Social Activist: The Dynamics of Ethnicity. New York: Greenwood Press.

Jacknis, Ira. 1985. Franz Boas and Exhibits: On the Limitations of the Museum Method of Anthropology. In Objects and Others: Essays on Museums and Material Culture. George W. Stocking Jr, ed. Pp. 75–111. Madison: University of Wisconsin Press.

———. 1996. The Ethnographic Object and the Object of Ethnology in the Early Career of Franz Boas. In Volksgeist as Method and Ethic: Essays on Boasian Ethnography and the German Anthropological Tradition. George W. Stocking Jr., ed. Pp. 185–214. Madison: University of Wisconsin Press.

Kendall, Laurel. 1988. Young Laufer on the Amur. In Crossroads of Continents: Cultures of Siberia and Alaska. W. W. Fitzhugh and A. Crowell, eds. Washington DC: Smithsonian Institution.

Krupnik, Igor, and Nikolai Vakhtin. 2003. "The Aim of the Expedition . . . Has in the Main Been Accomplished": Words, Deeds, and the Legacies of the Jesup North Pacific Expedition. In Constructing Cultures Then and Now: Celebrating Franz Boas and the Jesup North Pacific Expedition. Laurel Kendall and Igor Krupnik, eds. Washington DC: Arctic Studies Center, National Museum of Natural History, Smithsonian Institution.

Latourette, K. 1936. Berthold Laufer, 1874–1934. National Academy of Sciences of the United States of America, Biographical Memoir 18:43–68.

Laufer, Berthold. n.d. Guide to the Southwest Gallery (Chinese Hall). Unpublished ms. Anthropology Division Archive, AMNH.

———. 1900. Preliminary Notes on Explorations among the Amoor Tribes. American Anthropologist 2:297–338.

———. 1902. The Decorative Art of the Amur Tribes. Memoirs of the American Museum of Natural History VII. New York: American Museum of Natural History.

———. 1907. The Introduction of Maize into Eastern Asia. Pp. 223–257. Quebec: Congrès international des américanistes.

———. 1908. Chinese Pigeon Whistles. Scientific American (May):394.

———. 1909. Chinese Pottery of the Han Dynasty. Leiden: E. J. Brill.

———. 1911a. King Tsing, the Author of the Nestorian Inscription. Open Court (August):449–454.

———. 1911b. The Introduction of Vaccination into the Far East. Open Court (September):525–531.

———. 1912a. Jade: A Study in Chinese Archeology and Religion. Field Museum of Natural History Publication 154 (Anthropological Series 10):1–28.

———. 1912b. Modern Chinese Collections in Historical Light. American Museum Journal 12:135–138.

———. 1916. The Beginnings of Porcelain in China. Field Museum Anthropological Series 15.

———. 1917. Origin of the Word Shaman. American Anthropologist 29:361–371.

———. 1920. Sex Transformation and Hermaphrodites in China. American Journal of Physical Anthropology 3(2):259–262.

———. 1922. Archaic Chinese Bronzes of the Shang, Chou, and Han Periods. New York: Parish-Watson.

———. 1923. Oriental Theatricals. Chicago: Field Museum of Natural History.

———. 1924. Tobacco and Its Use in Asia. Chicago: Field Museum of Natural History.

———. 1927. Insect-Musicians and Cricket Champions of China. Field Museum Anthropological Leaflet 22.

———. 1928. Cricket Champions of China. Scientific American (January):30–34.

———. 1931a. The Domestication of the Cormorant in China and Japan. Field Museum Anthropological Series 18(3):205–262.

———. 1931b. Paper and Printing in Ancient China. Chicago: Caxton Club.

Oppenheim, Robert. 2005. "The West" and the Anthropology of Other People's Colonialism: Frederick Starr in Korea, 1911–1930. Journal of Asian Studies 64(3):677–703.

Pierpont, Claudia Roth. 2004. The Measure of America: How a Rebel Anthropologist Waged War on Racism. New Yorker (March 8, 2004): 48–63.

Rydell, Robert. 1987. All the World's a Fair: Visions of Empire at American International Expositions, 1876–1916. Chicago: University of Chicago Press.

Said, Edward. 1978. Orientalism. New York: Pantheon.

Sanjek, Roger. 1996. Boas, Franz. In Encyclopedia of Social and Cultural Anthropology. A. Barnard and J. Spencer, eds. Pp. 71–74. London: Routledge.

Stalberg, Roberta. 1983. Berthold Laufer's China Campaign. Natural History (2):34–39.

Stocking, George W., Jr., ed. 1974. The Shaping of American Anthropology 1883–1911: A Franz Boas Reader. New York: Basic Books.

———. 1985. Objects and Others: Essays on Museums and Material Culture. Madison: University of Wisconsin Press.

———. 1989. Romantic Motives: Essays on Anthropological Sensibility. Madison: University of Wisconsin Press.

———. 1991. Colonial Situations: Essays on the Contextualization of Ethnographic Knowledge. Madison: University of Wisconsin Press.

———. 1996. Volksgeist as Method and Ethic: Essays on Boasian Ethnography and the German Anthropological Tradition. Madison: University of Wisconsin Press.

Wolf, Eric. 1982. Europe and the People without History. Berkeley: University of California Press.

2

A. M. Hocart

Reflections on a Master Ethnologist and His Work

Why do we gather customs all the world over? Because science is comparative; it has to be, for the reason that one case is never sufficient to serve as a basis for theory; no more is a large number of cases all identical. It is only in the variations that we can observe under what conditions certain phenomena appear, and under what conditions they do not appear. Thus it is only through them we arrive at causes.

A. M. HOCART, "Spirits of Power" (1936)

Arthur Maurice Hocart (1883–1939), better known as A. M. Hocart, was a British sociocultural anthropologist living and working in the same era as A. R. Radcliffe-Brown and Bronislaw Malinowski. Yet despite his extensive ethnographic fieldwork, scientific sophistication, and prolific writings, his legacy is far less known than his more famous contemporaries. Indeed, Thomas O. Beidelman (1972) referred to Hocart as a "neglected master," and Meyer Fortes (1967) spoke of him as a "neglected pioneer." An accomplished master he was, being far more scholarly, experienced, and methodologically and theoretically astute in his explanations than the functionalist accounts of either Malinowski or Radcliffe-Brown. The works of A. M. Hocart should be better known by both American and British anthropologists. It is my hope that this essay will serve to keep Hocart's thinking in the forefront of our historical, methodological, and theoretical reflections, especially for those who are interested in the history of theoretical orientations in ethnology.

HOCART, THE MAN

A. M. Hocart was born on April 26, 1883, in Etterbeck, Belgium. He was educated in Brussels and at Elizabeth College for boys on Guernsey in the Channel Islands, where some of his kinsmen lived (Needham 1967, 1970:xvii; Gaillard 2004:47–48). He was classically trained and spoke a number of European languages, including French and German. He attended Exeter College, Oxford, 1902–1906, where he studied history, Greek, and Latin. He later learned Sanskrit, Pali, Tamil, and Sinhalese.

After he graduated from Oxford, he undertook training in psychology and philosophy at Berlin University (Evans-Pritchard 1939, 1970), where he carried out research on auditory perception with the great British physician and social psychologist William McDougall (1871–1938). McDougall supported the notion that human beings are driven by a finite set of instincts, a view that may well have influenced Hocart's notion of "the quest for life" (see below). McDougall was a graduate medical student under the great British ethnologist, neurologist, and psychiatrist W. H. R. Rivers (1864–1922). Both Rivers and McDougall accompanied Alfred Cort Haddon on the Second Torres Straits Expedition in 1898. Hocart himself later accompanied Rivers on the Percy Sladen Trust Expedition to the Solomon Islands in 1908 and became Rivers's close friend. It is not known whether Rivers introduced Hocart to McDougall during Hocart's Berlin days, although Rivers did supervise the latter's research on perception.

Keeping in mind that Germany was the world's leader in scientific anthropology at the time and that Hocart was exposed to the ideas of ethnographers of such stature as Adolph Bastian (1826–1905) and Friedrich Ratzel (1844–1904), it is small wonder that the directions he took in his work were far more complex, scholarly, scientific, and empirically enduring than those of many of his peers in England. From 1908 until the First World War, he traveled extensively and carried out ethnographic fieldwork in the Pacific (the Solomon Islands, Fiji, and other societies of the western South Pacific), and while there he did work with Rivers. He and Rivers returned to England in 1914 and served as captains during World War I, Hocart with army intelligence in France, and Rivers as a physician and psychiatrist.[1] After the Great War, Hocart became the consummate English "ex-pat" and took a variety of positions in the colonies. He became the archaeological commissioner of Ceylon (1920–1925), where he supervised numerous archaeological surveys and excavations. He returned to England to recuperate from a serious illness, and then, after repeatedly failing to obtain a faculty position at Cambridge, returned to Ceylon where he again suffered ill health. He retired with a pension in 1929 and in 1934 moved to Cairo to become a professor of sociology at the Egyptian University (the only faculty position he ever held). Unfortunately for us, he remained in ill health and died in Cairo in March 1939 (Evans-Pritchard 1939; Paranavitana 1939; Marett 1939). During the last decade of his life, he penned some of the most interesting studies in the history of ethnology and social anthropology, including *Kingship* (1927), *The Progress of Man* (1933), *Kings and Councillors* (1936; a continuation of his thoughts in *Kingship*; see Raglan 1941), *Caste* (1950), and *Social Origins* (1954), some of which were published posthumously. His essays have been published in a number of volumes including *The Life-Giving Myth and Other Essays* (1952a) and *Imagination and Proof* (1987).

HOCART'S PLACE IN THE HISTORY OF ANTHROPOLOGY

It is obvious that had it not been for the efforts of Lord Raglan and Rodney Needham (1923–2006), much of his oeuvre would still be languishing in manuscript form (Needham 1970:xxi).[2] There are several reasons why Hocart failed to receive the accolades and attention he certainly earned during his life, and why the histories of the discipline have usually neglected his work.

Hocart was effectively alienated from academic life in England, in part because his theoretical work stood outside and counter to mainstream British thought: "For most of his life he held no post in academic social anthropology which would have provided an institutional base for the propagation of his ideas, and his historical and comparative preoccupations were unfashionable in the heyday of functionalism" (Needham 1967:9). Hocart's project was influenced by and similar to that of Adolph Bastian (Koepping 1983, 2007; Lowie 1937:chapter 4; Laughlin 2011:38–43; Throop and Laughlin 2007). As the epigraph above implies, the whole purpose of doing ethnography and ethnology in Hocart's opinion was to collect a wide variety of comparative data from societies all over the globe upon which to ground nomothetic theories of psycho-social causation. In other worlds, Hocart was a structuralist— but with a difference. Unlike Lévi-Strauss, for whom cultural variance was mere noise, Hocart recognized the importance of diffusion in the history of cultures (Hocart 1954). His was not diffusion in the grand, global sense of British scholars William James Perry (1887–1949) and Grafton Elliot Smith (1871–1937), or the German *kulturkreis* (culture circle) ethnologists Fritz Graebner (1877–1934) and Wilhelm Schmidt (1868–1954), but rather more like the historical anthropology of Franz Boas (1858–1942):

> For with the advent of Franz Boas a major break was made with the past, resulting not so much from his program for cultural anthropology as in its selective implementation. Boas in "The Limitations of the Comparative Method" (Boas 1940 [1896]) outlined a program which included two major tasks. The first task involved detailed studies of individual tribes in their cultural and regional context as a means to the reconstruction of the histories of tribal cultures and regions. A second task concerned the comparisons of these tribal histories, with the ultimate objective of formulating general laws of cultural growth, which were psychological in character (1940[1896]:278–279). This second task, which Boas thought of as the more important of the two, was never to be fully implemented by his students. (Eggan 1954:748)

The similarity between the thinking of Boas and Hocart was not a coincidence by any means. In a very real sense, they were on the same page, having both been influenced by Bastian during their formative years. Once again, it is important to remember that during this period, Germany was the center of scientific ethnology, and Bastian was the leading figure in that milieu (Needham 1970:lxxii). Bastian's project was to study precolonial societies as rapidly as possible and before they had been influenced by western culture. He held that every human mind inherits a complement of species-specific "elementary ideas" (*Elementargedanken*), and hence the minds of all people, regardless of their race or culture, operate in the same structural way—there is a "psychic unity of mankind" that underlies all cultures. It is the contingencies of geographic location and historical background that we have to thank for the different elaborations of these elementary ideas, the different sociocultural traditions, and the various levels of sociocultural complexity. According to Bastian, there also exists a lawful genetic principle by which societies develop over the course of their history from exhibiting simple sociocultural institutions to becoming increasingly complex in their organization—up to and including civilizations—a theme we shall see repeated in Hocart's thinking below.

These inherent, elementary psychological processes can be studied in a systematic, objective, and comparative way, Bastian taught, and the more one studies various peoples, the more one sees that the historical influences on the culture *are of secondary importance compared with the elementary psychological structures that mediate culture.* Through the accumulation of ethnographic data, we can study the psychological laws of mental development as they reveal themselves in diverse regions and under differing conditions. Although one is speaking with individual informants, Bastian held that the object of research is not the study of the individual per se but rather the "collective mind" of a people. In other words, the ethnographer is after the "folk ideas" (*Volkergedanken*) of a particular people. The individual is like the cell in an organism, a social animal whose mind is influenced by its social background. The "elementary ideas" (*Elementargedanken*) are the ground from which the folk ideas develop. From this perspective, the social group has a kind of group mind, a social soul (*Gesellschaftsseele*) if you will, in which the individual mind is embedded.

Bastian's influence on Franz Boas was telling. Boas, a German physicist and geographer, studied the Inuit of Baffin Island, thus developing a lifelong interest in North American native peoples. He returned to Germany to study under Bastian at the Royal Ethnographic Museum in Berlin during 1886–1887. Boas, however, was a Jew, and because of intense anti-Semitism in his home country and his growing curiosity about North American indigenous cultures, he immigrated to the United States, where he did much to develop professional ethnology from his position at Columbia University.

Bastian's work was even more telling on Hocart, who was fluent in German and spent some time at the University of Berlin, where he was exposed to the works of Bastian. However, Hocart carried Bastian's project much further than did Boas. While Boas spent much of his professional energies in America fighting against racism and guiding his students to expend their time doing basic ethnographic research, Hocart continued along a more obvious structuralist course, balancing fieldwork with theory building. Like Bastian before him, Hocart carried out far more ethnographic fieldwork than most ethnologists do, even by today's standards. Hocart was a world traveler, spending most of his life outside of the British Isles. He spent six years living in various island communities in the South Pacific, and he is still recognized as one of the finest ethnographers of Oceania. His monographs on the Lau Archipelago of Fiji, *Lau Islands, Fiji* (1929) and the posthumously published *Northern States of Fiji* (1952b; edited by Lord Raglan), as well as numerous articles on Fijian languages, kinship, religion, and historical relations (see Needham 1967 for references), remain standard sources to this day.

When he moved to Ceylon (now Sri Lanka) in 1920, Hocart continued to publish material on western Oceania, even while he carried out archaeological surveys of his new home, as well as articles about Vedic rituals, Buddhist iconography, and other issues of South Asian ethnology and archaeology. He continued these scholarly interests when he made his final move to Cairo in 1934.

In order to get a feeling for Hocart's idiosyncratic brand of ethnology, it is perhaps easiest to explore what he had to say on some of the more seminal and perennial issues in ethnology.

HOCART ON PSYCHOLOGY, EXPERIENCE, THOUGHT, INNOVATION, AND CULTURE

In doing ethnography, Hocart never lost track of the fact that he was studying people influenced in their individual experiences, mind states, and behaviors by historical, social, linguistic, and cultural processes (Hocart 1912, 1915). For instance, he quickly rejected the idea that the minds of "savages" (read traditional or tribal peoples) were any different than our own. With his characteristic no-nonsense and witty style, he wrote in 1916, "The mythopoeic man is not yet dead. He is still commonly resuscitated as a mode of explanation. It is necessary therefore to examine his claims to continued recognition. If he has none, the sooner we do away with him the better" (Hocart 1916:307). In that early paper and throughout his career he argued against the view that traditional peoples manifest anything like "primitive mentality" (contrasted with "civilized mentality") in the sense hypothesized by the early evolutionists and later espoused (and still later repudiated) by Lévy-Bruhl (1923, 1975; see Hocart 1933:27 on Lévy-Bruhl's ethnocentricity). He showed that the division of psychology into that of "savage" (or "mythopoeic") quasi-humans (prelogical, fanciful, childlike) and fully "civilized" humans (1) is a hypothesis that has never been proved, (2) is not required to account for the generation and use of myth by peoples, and (3) is unnecessary in order to explain ethnographic facts:

> The psychological explanation is bad psychology because it postulates a type of mind which no psychologist has ever observed. It involves the supposition that there was a mythopoeic age, when fancy reigned supreme, followed by a historic age, in which men were as they still are, handing on to their sons what they learnt from their fathers, with minor differences due to loss of memory or changes in taste. (Hocart 1954:5)

Hocart was particularly addressing the ethnocentric psychological theories of Edward Tylor (1920 [1871]) and James Frazer (1890), who proposed empirically unsupportable explanations for the origins of religion and generalized these explanations to the world.

For another instance, in addressing the functions of dual social organization, and in support of an alliance theory, he argues (again with caustic wit) against the view that dual organization exists to prevent incest.

> If you object that there was a much simpler way of [preventing incest] by proclaiming "Thou shalt not marry thy sister, nor thy mother, nor thy daughter," then the second method comes to the rescue with the reply, "Oh, but savages have undeveloped intelligences and could not keep in mind their relationships." ... I will not dwell further on these inconsistencies. I will merely remark that I have had some acquaintance with savages, and I never noticed that, like Lamb's Chinese, they burnt their houses down whenever they wanted to eat roast pig. (Hocart 1954:39)

After intense involvement with native peoples (usually referred to as "savages" according to the ethnographic custom of the era),[3] Hocart had concluded that the minds of all people everywhere operate along the same (today we might say structural or cognitive) lines and from the same properties.

> It is precisely because savages think in the same manner as we do that they think different things; for the same processes working on different inherited material must lead to different results. . . . The material upon which the savage mind works is inherited tradition and social organization. We imagine, indeed, that we proceed differently, that we white folks each individually derive our knowledge directly from objective reality and that we can see it, each for himself. We conclude that our knowledge is rational, objective, and obvious, and we are at a loss to account how the savage can be blind to facts and truths that are staring us in the face; we have to suppose that the eyes of his soul are closed and that he lives in a world of dreams and vague feelings. Men of all races and all generations are equally convinced that they individually draw their knowledge from reality. A savage will defend his beliefs by an appeal to experience, and his doubts as to the sanity of our own are ill-concealed, though he is too polite to express them. We think that we believe in atoms because they really exist; a Fujian thinks that he believes in ghosts because he has seen them with his own eyes, and after all if he does claim to have seen a ghost what have we to oppose to the testimony of his eyes by a skepticism which has no reasons but that ghosts do not fit in with European conceptions of the world and are to us an unnecessary hypothesis? (Hocart 1954:41–42)

People everywhere operate upon the world with the same brain, yet confront different worlds of local contingencies. Each person supports their beliefs, as Hocart says, by recourse to experience. But it is more often the case that we all see the world the way we do because we have been conditioned by tradition to apperceive it so.

> Everyone agrees that savages do not believe in ghosts because they see them, but see them because they believe in them. But it occurs to few [westerners] to say that we do not believe in our principle of inertia because it is self-evident, but that it is self-evident because

we believe in it, or that economic law of supply and demand is to a great extent created by our belief in it, and not our belief created by the law. (Hocart 1954:42)

Anticipating Homer Barnett's brilliant 1953 analysis of the structure of innovation by more than a generation, Hocart showed that cultural innovation rarely if ever occurs outside the context of history. Yes, individuals may invent things that have not previously existed, but these things are generally neither social nor institutional. Changes in customs and social organization, on the other hand, are essentially social and institutional processes and derive their structures and elements by way of cultural continuity (Hocart 1915). Hocart contrasts the modern novel, which is the product of a single individual's creativity and is neither social nor institutional, with myth and folktales that may be altered in the telling, but which retain the powerful stamp of history. "You can write a history of *Beauty and the Beast*," writes Hocart, "but not of *Pickwick Papers*" (1954:36).

He applied this perspective to a critique of the very common presumption during his day that because savage mentality is qualitatively different than civilized mentality, the languages of savages must therefore be different and more primitive than civilized languages:

This view may seem quite impregnable to the thinker at home, and, as it once seemed so to me, I cannot blame those whose faith has never been exposed to that powerful dissolvent, experience of savage life. A few linguistic facts picked from various treatises and isolated from their vast context, which is no less than the whole life of the people, are just what tends to breed a false confidence of truth secured once and for all. (Hocart 1912:267)

Hocart went on to show that reasoning from a language backward to the nature of the mind that created the language is impossible. There is no application of the comparative method that can reconstruct the origins of language, but only the historical developments of kindred languages. People speak the language that their elders speak—thus it is a matter of enculturation, not of psychology. The notion that some languages are somehow more advanced than other languages is preposterous, for some languages may make more detailed distinctions in certain domains and fewer distinctions in other domains of communication than do other languages, but this fact cannot be construed as evidence of superior intellect. It is rather an interesting fact that may lead to insights into the various cultural values of a people. Hocart once again anticipated the debate over whether there exists such a thing as a "primitive" language, an issue that is still being addressed in sociolinguistics (Hymes 1961; Swadesh 2006).

HOCART ON MYTH

> The truth may be very different from what we all expected, and that is only to be attained by a systematic study of the whole culture to which the myth belongs, together with neighboring cultures. Then the facts will force the conclusion on us, not we on the facts. (Hocart 1916:318)

In keeping with his view that there exists no real difference between the mental attributes of traditional people and people living in modern technocracies, he shows that an understanding of myth requires that (1) we understand that all cultures on the planet have their myths (Hocart 1922a), (2) we understand that the mental processes that produce myth are universal and influence explanatory theories in all societies (Hocart 1916:311), and (3) anthropologists must set aside their own ethnocentric cultural categories and come to appreciate that myth involves virtually all aspects of life for traditional peoples (Hocart 1954:2–9):

> So long therefore as an anthropologist confines himself to one of these departments [religion, technology, magic, polity, etc.] his material will be a useless congerie of facts because the key to nine-tenths lies outside his own province. One half of a custom will lie within religion, the other within social organization; a myth will have some of its roots in technology, others in religion, others in something which we do not know how to classify. If we cast our net wide enough to embrace the whole culture, the clues required to explain a myth will find it hard to escape us. (Hocart 1916:310)

Mythical explanations are too often discounted because they run counter to our western view of things. We take into the field our own western "scientific" explanations, and because the native theory explaining things differs in form and content from our own, and moreover they are couched in a story narrative, we discount it as so much primitive "fancy" (Hocart 1954:2):

> In explaining things we are simply driven to certain conclusions by our preconceptions and the facts they work upon. Why should it be otherwise with Fijians? If they think like us what will they do when they begin to take an interest in the physical peculiarities of their island? They will approach the problem from the point of view of their own preconceptions which are different from ours and therefore the result will be different from ours. (Hocart 1916:311)

Always keen on sharpening ethnographic methodology, Hocart decries the tendency of mythologists to study myths by demythologizing (a modern term here, not Hocart's) their meaning. The only avenue to accurately understanding a myth is to evaluate it within the context of the whole culture from which it springs and is embedded—only then will the myth explain itself: "I have merely wished to show that if, instead of merely skimming through a myth, guessing its origin, and passing on to another, we make a systematic investigation of a region, leaving nothing untouched, despising no trifle, myths will explain themselves without any coaxing, and will spontaneously reduce themselves into common sense" (Hocart 1916:318).

Hocart makes the point that theories that purport to explain how myths come about are usually specious, for there were no examples at the time that he was writing (nor none I am aware of today aside from the rare experimental study) in the ethnographic literature of a myth coming into being. "You can do so much with a 'may,' that there ceases to be any fun in the game; it is far more amusing to trace what actually did happen" (Hocart 1922a:63). Furthermore, similar mythic elements and motifs can occur in many places on the planet (Hocart 1916:316). He gives the example of the mythic hero appearing to stop the sun, a motif that occurs in the Bible when Joshua asks God to stop the sun (Joshua 10:14) and occurs as well in a myth from the island of Lakemba in Fiji and ritual practices in Rhodesia. While it is just possible, Hocart playfully suggests, that this motif may have occurred all over the world because Joshua may have indeed stopped the sun, however improbable that may seem, there are two other possibilities; this concurrence of motifs may be due to either historical diffusion or spontaneous creativity by the same brain operating in the same way on similar problems. The point is, he argues, there is no way to know unless we have the requisite evidence to discriminate between explanations. "It is as vain to look to Homer for the primitive significance of the myth as it would be to seek it in Malory" (Hocart 1952a:1).

Unlike the primitive origins of myths, examples of the loss of meaning and distortion of the form of myths is commonplace.

> We can readily see why, for customs are continually decaying, and with each one that passes away the meaning of some old tradition is lost; for a narrative always assumes that certain customs, or beliefs, or events are known to the audience; the speaker cannot stop at every turn to expound them; he takes them for granted; but it sometimes happens that this knowledge which he presupposes is wanting, because he is speaking to a generation or a people that does not possess his experience. (Hocart 1952a:63–64)

If we fail to bring the experiences and total range of knowledge had by historical people into the process of interpretation, the myth can be misconstrued and eventually changed. Hocart gives an example of a myth he had been told about a Fijian Flying Chief who was killed by an enemy, and as his people carried him to his burial, he "spoke" to his people about the proper site for his burial mound. Hocart notes that had he not been privy to the cultural context of this story, he would have jumped to the conclusion that this was an example of a corpse coming alive and speaking to the living. The actual meaning of that part of the myth was that people used divinatory methods to communicate with the dead chief's spirit (Hocart 1922a:64–65).

HOCART ON RITUAL

> Thus the myth is part of the ritual, and the ritual part of the myth. The myth describes the ritual, and the ritual enacts the myth. (Hocart 1952a:22)

Myth is the body of knowledge upon which action in the world may be grounded. "In other words, the myth is the precedent. It is not a tale told to while away the idle moment, nor is it a deep and purely inquisitive speculation about the phenomena of nature" (Hocart 1952a:15). Precedent for what? For ritual, both being requisite to accomplishing the good life by controlling the natural contingencies around us. "The myth is necessary because it gives the ritual its intention" (16). The myth embodies the knowledge presumed in performing the ritual process, the latter often being an intricate interweaving of behaviors and symbols that must be reiterated in precisely the correct way to gain effect. "One or two recitals are not enough; it had to be committed to memory, and its meaning and its reasons had to be expounded in lesson after lesson" (12).

> Let us stick to the real myth, the myth which has some relation to the serious business of life. It is a precedent, but it is more than that. Knowledge is essential for the success of the ritual. "He who knows this," ends our first myth, "conquers all the quarters." That is the conclusion which winds up myth after myth. The myth itself confers, or helps to confer, the object of men's desire—life. (Hocart 1952a:16)

People everywhere integrate the information provided by myth into their daily lives. Their life is the life that their ancestors lived and taught. People continue to live this life because it is life-affirming—it promises longevity, prosperity, vitality, and peace. The myths communicate the ceremonies upon which life itself depends. Reflecting upon Australian Aboriginal ritual:

> These ceremonies take up a great part of his time. We wonder how he can spare so much from the struggle for existence to spend on mere ceremonies, but he does so precisely because existence is so uncertain; the ritual aims at abolishing that uncertainty. There are years when kangaroos, snakes, grubs, yams are scarce, when pools dry up. The ritual is designed to ensure a supply. For every species of food there is a ceremony which causes its increase. That ceremony's performance by an ancestor is recorded in the myth. (Hocart 1952a:22)

The era in which our ancestors merely lived and experienced is long past. Humans not only live, but they conceive of life and living, and in thinking about life, they seek to ritually control it.

> Out of all the phenomena contributing to life he formed a concept of life, fertility, prosperity, vitality. He realized that there was something which distinguished the animate from the inanimate, and this something he called life. . . . If life comes and goes it must come from somewhere and go somewhere. . . . [People] think they know in what objects life resides and into what objects it passes. Man has gone further: he has come to think he can control that coming and going. He has worked out a technique to the end of controlling it. (Hocart 1970[1936]:32)

Only more advanced societies can afford to detach their myth/ritual complex from the everyday struggle for existence. When myth is so detached, as happens in societies that have developed a priesthood, the "life-giving" aspect of myth is very likely doomed to the status of quaint antiquity.

> The ritual myth is not the result of perversion by that bugbear of scholars, an all-aspiring priesthood. It flourishes most where there is no professional priesthood, because there it remains in contact with reality. The myth detached from reality can continue to exist only in a society which is itself divorced from reality, one which has such a reserve of wealth that it can afford to maintain an intelligentsia exempt to intellectual play, to poetry, and to romance. . . . When a myth has reached that stage it is doomed. Myths, like limbs, atrophy and perish when they no longer work. (Hocart 1952a:25)

HOCART ON METHODOLOGY

Hocart never wrote an introductory textbook, nor a field guide for carrying out ethnographic research, more is the pity.[4] But there are methodological lessons, strictures, and cautions to be found throughout his oeuvre. Quite simply put, Hocart was an intuitive empiricist and a thorough historicist and linguist. Over and over again he urges us to stick with the facts obtained through observation and documented history and to keep our speculations at bay. "The great superiority of the historical method is that it assumes nothing which we do not know actually occurred. We have complete records of parent languages and their descendants, such as Latin and its derivatives, and can study in detail how new languages arise from old ones" (Hocart 1954:4). As Needham (1970:vi) notes, Hocart was skeptical of the grand generalizations of the sort that floated about in anthropology during the later nineteenth and early twentieth centuries. For instance, reflecting upon the considerable variety of tattooing traditions in the south Pacific, Hocart suggests:

> There are critics who will not be satisfied because they cannot *see* the initiatory use of tattooing being gradually narrowed down to specific ends. Such critics will never be satisfied, because if they could sit waiting till doomsday they would never see development. They think that they can see [cultural] evolution because they have been brought up to believe in it, but all that they really see is a great variety of [cultural] forms the existence of which can be satisfactorily explained only on the supposition that they have all developed out of the same originals. That is all that we have the right to expect in the development of human institutions: a theory that will explain all the variations in the simplest possible way without invoking any processes that have not been observed. (Hocart 1952a:170)

The sensible road to such a theory for Hocart is to study the whole culture as well as those around or historically related to the target culture. The ethnographer should record what the indigenous people have to tell in their own language and in their own way (Hocart 1952b:vii–x; note the influence of Bastian here, also reflected in Boas's methodology).

> Working through interpreters is certainly not ideal, and it is to be hoped that field-workers will in the future undergo a linguistic training and seek to work in the vernacular; but this is not given to all, and it is a great mistake to imagine that because interpretive work is not the best, it therefore is not good. (Hocart 1922c:72)

The ethnographic project is one of detailed and unbiased observation followed by comparative analysis: "One village can teach us nothing. It is only when we have the variations that we can begin to theorize.

The next step then was to go from one [Fijian] state to another noting the agreements and the differences" (Hocart 1952b:viii). In a more general vein:

> Why do we gather customs all the world over? Because science is comparative; it has to be, for the reason that one case is never sufficient to serve as a basis for theory; no more is a large number of cases all identical. It is only in the variations that we can observe under what conditions certain phenomena appear, and under what conditions they do not appear. Thus it is only through them we arrive at causes. (Hocart 1936:580)

So when an analyst takes up a particular custom—such as the ability of divine kings to fly through the air, snobbery, the king's image on money, caste structure, and so forth—he can lodge his understanding in the minutia of other related yet varying customs. If one asks how people can believe that divine kings fly through the air, one can relate the claim to the actual practice of carting the divine personage around from place to place on the shoulders of his subjects so that his feet never touch the ground (Hocart 1952a:28–32). When one then finds such a custom all over the world, it raises the question of diffusion or some other causal factor—e.g., psychology—operating in history. It is instructive to compare Hocart's methodology with that of A. L. Kroeber and others of the California school of historical anthropology who advocated precisely this kind of comparative trait analysis.[5]

HOCART ON SOCIAL ORIGINS AND KINGSHIP

Hocart's preeminent work was in the area of social organization and in particular the evolution of governance. In step with his denial of any fundamental distinction between savage and civilized mental functions, Hocart took exception to the view—quite common in his day—that human social organizations across the planet could be neatly assigned to one of two types, prehistoric, savage cultures and historical, civilized cultures (Hocart 1954). Savage cultures were supposed to be independent of historical relations, acculturative processes, and diffusion: "Every small group found its way to the place which was to be its home before it had acquired language or the knowledge of how to make fire or artifacts of any kind, and when it was still without the most elementary forms of social organization" (Raglan 1954:vii). Savage culture then fluoresced with cultural developments totally independent of outside influences. By comparison, civilizations were porous to acculturative influences from other societies and freely exchanged inventiveness, customs, institutions, and organizations among themselves. Savages really had no history (hence "prehistoric"), only myths and other folklore. Civilizations on the other hand have history—read this as *written stories*—about their past. As I say, Hocart rejected this view and instead argued from his usual stance that peoples are influenced most by their psychology (the same for people everywhere) and their history (oral and written), especially history manifesting as myth and ritual. By psychology Hocart included experience. Presaging the transpersonal anthropology of contemporary ethnologists like Edith Turner (1993), Hocart chose to believe his informants when they told them they had seen spirits and other supernatural beings:

> Men are inclined to question and ridicule customs they are not used to, and those who observe them retort by justifying them. A chief of Roviana in the Solomons, a staunch upholder of the customs of his land, once said to me, "The white men say there are no spirits. They are wrong. We know there are because we see their truth." That was the psychological approach: for him the belief in ghosts was based on observation: he saw the workings of spirits and accepted the evidence of his eyes. (Hocart 1954:1)

Because men believe their own senses, they organize themselves around the world they experience, which in this case is a world that admits of supernatural beings and relations.[6]

In what is now considered his magnum opus and a classic in social anthropology by any standard, *Kings and Councillors: An Essay in the Comparative Anatomy of Human Society*, he argued that all of the functions of government were present in society before government per se ever emerged: "We shall see all of the functions of government discharged among peoples without government" (1970[1936]:30). In a nutshell, Hocart makes the case that the social organization requisite to governance is present before the need for governance is felt. (I am reminded of Middleton and Tait's remarkable 1958 edited volume, *Tribes without Rulers,* which includes studies of African societies that carry out complex governance when necessary without the benefit of the enduring institution of chiefdomship.) Where is this organization to be found? In myth and ritual, in the life-giving and socially uniting activities of spiritual practices discussed above.

> Ritual is not in good odour with our intellectuals. It is associated in their minds with a clerical movement for which most of them nurse an antipathy. They are therefore unwilling to believe that institutions which they approve of, and which seem to them so eminently practical and sensible as modern administration, should have developed out of the hokus-pokus which they deem ritual to be. In their eyes only economic interests can create anything as solid as the state. Yet if they would only look about them they would everywhere see communities banded together by interest in a common ritual; they would even find that ritual enthusiasm builds more solidly than economic ambitions, because ritual involves a rule of life, whereas economics are a rule of gain, and so divide rather than unite. (1970[1936]:35)

In order for a society to carry out effective rituals, the society itself has to be organized such that the people can bring the rituals about. Relationship between social organization and ritual is evidenced clearly in the "big-man" systems of western Oceania. Really important giving is ritualized in these societies, and it is the personal power of the big-man that makes the rituals possible. An example is the effort that big-man Ongka had to go through to mount a great Moka ceremony among his Kawelka tribe of New Guinea (Strathern 1971, 1979). Ongka had spent much of his life helping others accumulate pigs, giving kinsmen pigs as an "investment" for the future (pigs being the major source of traditional wealth among the Kawelka and surrounding groups). The only ways in which one could obtain pigs were by stealing them from enemies, receiving them as gifts from kinsmen, and by natural accumulation. However, as pigs were rarely killed and eaten, and thus had to eat the same food as did people, there was a limit to how many pigs one family could support. Therefore, the major problem for Ongka in mounting his great Moka (meaning "giving" in Kawelka)—a ceremony that required giving away hundreds of pigs, plus other valuables—was by persuading others of his kin to donate their pigs and even their cash to the effort. Ongka could not just tell everyone in his group to cough up pigs and wealth the way, say, a feudal lord might have done. They had to willingly participate in making the great Moka happen. During the buildup to the main ceremony, the giving up of pigs (little Mokas) to Ongka was also a cause for minor ceremony and feasting. When all the requisite wealth was accumulated by Ongka and his family, the day for the Moka was set, and invitations were sent to the recipients of the wealth—that being another tribe who had themselves given a great Moka for the Kawelka many years earlier. Ongka was a big-man because, despite all the vicissitudes of everyday life, including political struggles between himself and other big-men, and despite the fact that he could not order the thing done, Ongka was able to muster his personal power and social networking skills to bring together the resources to make this rare event occur.

For Hocart, kingship and governance lie latent in the organization of such ritual enterprises—enterprises that have as their purpose the quest for the good life—the maintenance of vitality, equitable resource distribution, alliance among groups, and so forth. It only requires the social necessity to spark governance into existence. Hocart points to the institution of warfare among North American Indian tribes for an example. In these societies, leaders only have the authority of ruler when they are acting as war chiefs. At the cessation of hostilities, the authority enjoyed by the war chief disappears, and the society returns to its more acephalous peacetime structure.

Hocart centers his argument on "kingship" because in his estimation the first form of governance is monarchy, and the first form of organized religion is the divine king (i.e., the apperception of the monarch as a god; Hocart 1922b), while later forms of governance (republic, federation, etc.) arise in resistance to monarchy. Prior to monarchical governance, the organization for ritual "exists where there is no government and where none is needed. When however society increases [demographically] so much in complexity that a coordinating agency, a kind of nervous system, is required, that ritual organization will gradually take over the task" (Hocart 1970[1936]:35). As with the American Indian war chief, when the king ceases to fulfill his function, the structure of governance may vanish.

Hocart may have given us a clue to why the institution of the classic Maya divine kingship disappeared. The king (*ajau*) was a ritual specialist—actually a kind of shaman king—and the great cities were as much ritual centers as anything else (Coe 2002). Hocart argues in *Kings and Councillors* that the original motivation for the ancient city is to coalesce the population around a sacred ritual center, not for purposes of the market or administration. "Population first condenses round the centre of ritual, not round shops. In the West of England they talk of 'church towns,' not of 'shop towns,' although church towns are shopping towns, because the church is the primary fact" (1970[1936]:251). Early cities and their temples, like those of classic Maya, are essentially *cosmograms*—iconic representations of the cosmos within which rituals are performed.[7] Just as early humans built mounds as altars upon (or within) which to perform rituals, later Neolithic peoples flocked to their cities for the same purpose (1970[1936]: chapter 17). One explanation for the collapse of Maya civilization in the ninth century is that, due to deteriorating ecological conditions, the shaman king was gradually conceived by the people as ritually ineffectual and no longer able to intercede with the gods to ensure the good life through his mystical machinations. Hence they no longer flocked to the city temples, and they stopped adding to or renovating them or crafting inscriptions extolling the power of the shaman king. They all faded back into the forests where most of them had been living all along. It is interesting that many living Maya today still consider the cities as sacred.

Implicit in Hocart's account of the evolution of governance is a profound understanding of the nature of bureaucracy. The genius of the man emanates from his straightforward and simple insistence that the role of consciousness in human affairs is the biological, social, and cultural assurance of the good life (Hocart 1934). People living in simple societies are no different than people living in complex societies in that they all want the same fundamental thing—life. The furtherance of that universal desire may lead peoples in different directions depending upon how they construct a technical and social adaptation to local contingencies. But underlying it all is a common inexorable process of development:

Conscious purpose precedes the adaptation of behaviour, and the adaptation of behaviour is followed by adaptation of [institutional] structure. A community wants something; it shapes its actions so as to achieve that something, and the result of its action is to alter its organization. It is not indeed government that man wants, for how can he conceive of a government except by experience of it? It is life he wants, and in the effort to live he does one thing after another till he eventually finds himself governed, that is specialized into producers and into regulators of those producers. He does not want a priesthood or a civil service to control him; he wants to control nature for his own benefit; but in the pursuit of this aim he places some members of his community into new functions which in turn produce a new type of man, no longer the all-round handy man, but the man who lives largely by thinking. The conscious purpose is the impulse that sets the whole machinery in motion with results that are not foreseen. (Hocart 1970 [1936]:299)

In the pursuit of the good life, the organization of the acephalous tribal society gradually develops a hierarchy—it loses that horizontal organization typical of kin-based clan structure and takes on the form of officialdom. "Gradually the high rise higher, the low sink lower, until the state is rearranged in a vertical hierarchy such as ours" (Hocart 1970 [1936]):292). In ancient India this vertical structuring process resulted in a caste system (Hocart 1950). In each case of vertical structuration, the organization is grounded upon the society's mythology and organized ritual. The high castes perform the necessary ritual functions, while the king is associated with the sun or some other high god. The social structure mirrors the cosmology in both social roles and ritual activities. Within this social diversity arises the process of specialization of role. People are taken into the government and taught to do jobs that no longer are carried out in and for the old clan system. Specialization becomes more and more constraining upon the individual:

As there is little specialization in the South Seas [at the time of Hocart's fieldwork], there is little discrepancy between a man's work and his fitness for it. It is otherwise with us: a rivet-maker is far from being adapted to make nothing all day but rivets; still less is a cafeteria girl designed by nature to do nothing else but hand out knives and forks for hours on end. It follows that a very small part of their persons is exercised for one third of the day, and then it is exercised to excess. The great remainder is left hungering for activity till evening. It is the tragedy of our civilization: our men and women have not yet been narrowed down by nature to fit the narrowness of their tasks.... The pursuit of life is no longer a wide all-embracing exercise, but an alternation of limited reactions. (Hocart 1970 [1936]:297–298)

In pursuing the good life, people in our society are forced to adapt to roles that no longer fulfill that primal desire. Much of the pressure is driven by demographics. As the population grows, the competition for the means of attaining the good life becomes more and more difficult. Somewhere along the line, the "coordinating system" [bureaucratic state, corporations, etc.] absorbs more and more of the resources available to the society—it becomes as it were a society within the society and increasingly feeds its own needs, rather than the needs that gave rise to the institution in the first place. It ceases to carry out the functions of pursuit of the good life for all the people, but because it is now institutionalized, it thwarts the existence of alternative organizations that might answer that need more directly. In the end, society becomes so fragmented and specialized that the result is alienation of most of the people who find themselves blocked in their pursuit of life.

REFLECTIONS ON A MASTER ETHNOLOGIST

Man is a custom-making animal: that is one of his most prominent characteristics. Doubtless other animals hand on by example habits they have acquired by experience, but only to a very slight degree. Man has developed this power to such an extent that custom may actually override the most fundamental instincts—those concerned with food and sex. A man's conduct is determined not only by the structure of his nervous system but also by the teaching of his elders: it is the result of two factors—his nature and his upbringing. (Hocart 1954:1)

No brief summary of Hocart's work can do justice to the rich tapestry of insights he brings to his subjects. In many respects his work, grounded as it was on years of ethnographic experience, was way ahead of its time. The above quote pretty much sums up the core of Hocart's ethnology. Had he the access to a modern neuropsychology and neuroethology, he might well have been one of the first neuroanthropologists.[8] He was clearly a structuralist in the Bastian mold.[9] The products of a universal structure of mind-brain brought up in different environments and conditioned by a different process of enculturation will appear at the same time similar and varied. His intent was upon fostering the growth of anthropology into a science grounded in empirical research and hypothesis testing, especially ethnological research unencumbered by philosophical, ethnographically unsupportable speculation. "Explanations do not arise naturally, but are evoked by queries" (Hocart 1954:2)—queries raised by the data themselves in comparative perspective.

Over the course of my own career in anthropology, many authors, too numerous to mention, have influenced me with their insights and perspectives. But of all those anthropologists, most of whose works seem to fit into a school, an era, or a passing fad, only A. M. Hocart stands out as timeless to me, for I have returned again and again to his writings over the last forty-plus years to good effect. All I have to do is open anything he wrote (I have his whole oeuvre) at random and the fresh, rich, witty, caustic, and provocative mind of Hocart feeds me—makes me see old issues in a new way, yet keeps me grounded in the subject of my field—namely, people. As a demonstration, I just opened his *Progress of Man* at random to page 580, and here I read: "*The expression 'fear of the dead' is quite misleading, for it is not the corpse men are afraid of, but the spirit, and it is not even the spirit in its self, but its power to harm.*"[10] Brilliant insight—a "neglected master" indeed, for while the now (for me at least) simplistic theories of functionalists like Malinowski, Radcliffe-Brown, and Parsons read more as quaint stepping-stones on the path to modern anthropology, Hocart reads as a thinker for all ages. His understanding is a remarkable blend of common sense informed by years of ethnographic experience and tempered by heartfelt appreciation of and unquenchable curiosity about what it means to be a living, breathing, and experiencing person, of whatever cultural background.

1. Rivers carried out some of the first battlefield clinical work on what would later become known as posttraumatic stress disorder (Rivers 1923).
2. I refer here to FitzRoy Somerset, the 4th Baron Raglan (1885–1964), who was a notable anthropologist in his own right.
3. During Hocart's time, the English word "savage" had the same meaning as does the French word "*sauvage*" today—simply meaning "wild," or in the natural state. Still, it was as unapt a term then as it is today.
4. The closest Hocart came to writing a text in anthropology was when he set out to write *The Progress of Man*, but as he himself notes in the preface of that work, the field of anthropology at the time—and I would say the field as it remains to this day—was too fragmented to encompass within a single paradigmatic framework: "I soon found, however, that I was attempting a contradiction. Experts are not even agreed about fundamentals, without which it is impossible to proceed" (1933:vii).
5. Do not let the dates of publication of Hocart's ethnographic works lead to the mistaken idea that he was working in the field later than Kroeber and his students. Hocart carried out his Fijian research before the First World War.
6. I am particularly sensitive to this aspect of Hocart's methodology, for it mirrors my own work in transpersonal anthropology (see Laughlin 1989, 2011; Laughlin, McManus, and d'Aquili 1990). In this respect Hocart's transpersonal methodology was way before its time.
7. The term "cosmograms" was coined by George F. MacDonald (see MacDonald, Cove, Laughlin, and McManus 1988).
8. Hocart was in fact quite conversant with the physical anthropology of his day: "There are many functions of the brain which are left fluid at birth. They can be moulded during childhood and youth till they harden with old age" (Hocart 1933:3). "Man is not specialized to the same extent as some animals like the horse. He can live under a greater variety of conditions. His great brain makes it possible to adapt himself to almost any climate" (5).
9. Hocart was more an evolutionary structuralist, not a semiotic structuralist, of the Lévi-Straussian variety. See Laughlin, McManus, and d'Aquili 1979:3–4 for the distinction between evolutionary and semiotic structuralism.
10. He precisely describes the reality behind the oft remarked aversion of Navajo people, among whom I have lived, to dead bodies. They do not fear the body per se but rather the harm that may be done by the ghost of the dead person that keeps hanging around.

REFERENCES

Barnett, Homer G. 1953. Innovation: The Basis of Cultural Change. New York: McGraw-Hill.

Beidelman, Thomas O. 1972. Neglected Master: A. M. Hocart. Journal of Interdisciplinary History 2(3):311–316.

Boas, Franz. 1940 [1896]. The Limitations of the Comparative Method of Anthropology. In Race, Language, and Culture. Franz Boas, ed. Pp. 270–280. New York: Macmillan.

Coe, Michael D. 2002. The Maya. 6th ed. New York: Thames and Hudson.

Eggan, Fred. 1954. Social Anthropology and the Method of Controlled Comparison. American Anthropologist 56:743–763.

Evans-Pritchard, E. E. 1939. Arthur Maurice Hocart: 1884–March 1939. Man 39 (August):131.

————. 1970 Foreword. In Kings and Councillors: An Essay in the Comparative Anatomy of Human Society. A. M. Hocart. Rodney Needham, ed. Pp. ix–xi. Chicago: University of Chicago Press.

Fortes, Meyer. 1967. Of Installation Ceremonies. Proceedings of the Royal Anthropological Institute of Great Britain and Ireland 1967:5–20.

Frazer, James. 1890. The Golden Bough. London: Macmillan.

Gaillard, Gérald. 2004. The Routledge Dictionary of Anthropologists. London: Routledge.

Hocart, A. M. 1912. The Psychological Interpretation of Language. British Journal of Psychology 5(3):263–279.

————. 1915. Psychology and Ethnology. Folklore 26:115–137; reprinted in Imagination and Proof: Selected Essays of A. M. Hocart. Rodney Needham, ed. Pp. 35–50. Tucson: University of Arizona Press (1987).

————. 1916. The Common Sense of Myth. American Anthropologist 18(3):307–318.

————. 1922a. Myth in the Making. Folklore 33(1):57–71; reprinted in Imagination and Proof: Selected Essays of A. M. Hocart. Rodney Needham, ed. Pp. 51–60. Tucson: University of Arizona Press (1987).

————. 1922b. The Origin of Monotheism. Folklore 33(3): 282–293; reprinted in The Life-Giving Myth and Other Essays. Rodney Needham, ed. Pp. 66–77. London: Methuen.

————. 1922c. The Cult of the Dead in Eddystone of the Solomons (Part 1). Journal of the Royal Anthropological Institute of Great Britain and Ireland 52:71–112.

————. 1927. Kingship. London: Oxford University Press.

———. 1929. Lau Islands, Fiji (Bernice P. Bishop Museum, Bulletin 62). Honolulu: Bishop Museum.

———. 1933. The Progress of Man: A Short Survey of His Evolution, His Customs, and His Works. London: Methuen.

———. 1934. The Role of Consciousness in Evolution. Psyche Annual 14:160–164.

———. 1936. Spirits of Power. Anthropos 31(3/4):580–582.

———. 1941 [1927]. Kingship. Introduction by Lord Raglan. London: Watts.

———. 1950. Caste: A Comparative Study. New York: Russell and Russell.

———. 1952a. The Life-Giving Myth and Other Essays. Rodney Needham, ed. London: Methuen.

———. 1952b. The Northern States of Fiji (Occasional Publication No. 11). London: Royal Anthropological Institute of Great Britain and Ireland.

———. 1954. Social Origins. Completed by Lord Raglan. London: Watts.

———. 1970 [1936]. Kings and Councillors: An Essay in the Comparative Anatomy of Human Society. Rodney Needham, ed. Chicago: University of Chicago Press.

———. 1987. Imagination and Proof: Selected Essays of A. M. Hocart. Rodney Needham, ed. Tucson: University of Arizona Press.

Hocart, A. M., and William McDougall. 1908. Some Data for a Theory of the Auditory Perception of Direction. British Journal of Psychology 2(4):386–405.

Hymes, Dell H. 1961. Functions of Speech: An Evolutionary Approach. Indianapolis: Bobbs-Merrill.

Koepping, Klaus-Peter. 1983. Adolf Bastian and the Psychic Unity of Mankind: The Foundations of Anthropology in Nineteenth-Century Germany. St. Lucia: University of Queensland Press.

———. 2007. Bastian and Lévi-Strauss: From "Entelechy" to "Entropy" as "Scientific" Metaphors for Cultural Teleologies. In Adolf Bastian and His Universal Archive of Humanity: The Origins of German Anthropology. Manuela Fischer, Peter Bolz, Susan Kamel, and Emily Schalk, eds. Zurich: Georg Ohms.

Laughlin, Charles D. 1989. Transpersonal Anthropology: Some Methodological Issues. Western Canadian Anthropologist 5:29–60.

———. 2011. Communing with the Gods: Dream Cultures and the Dreaming Brain. Brisbane: Daily Grail.

Laughlin, Charles D., John McManus, and Eugene G. d'Aquili, eds. 1979. The Spectrum of Ritual: A Biogenetic Structural Analysis. New York: Columbia University Press.

————. 1990. Brain, Symbol, and Experience: Toward a Neurophenomenology of Human Consciousness. New York: Columbia University Press.

Lévy-Bruhl, Lucien. 1923. Primitive Mentality. 1966 ed. Boston: Beacon Press.

————. 1975. The Notebooks on Primitive Mentality. New York: Harper & Row.

Lowie, Robert H. 1937. The History of Ethnological Theory. New York: Rinehart.

MacDonald, George F., John Cove, Charles D. Laughlin, and John McManus. 1988. Mirrors, Portals, and Multiple Realities. Zygon 23(4):39–64.

Marett, R. R. 1939. A. M. Hocart. Stapleton Magazine 9:289.

Middleton, John, and David Tait, eds. 1958. Tribes without Rulers: Studies in African Segmentary Systems. New York: Routledge and Kegan Paul.

Needham, Rodney. 1967. Preface and Biographical Introduction. In A Bibliography of A. M. Hocart (1883–1939). Rodney Needham, ed. Pp. 13–16. Oxford: Blackwell.

————. 1970. Editor's Introduction. In Kings and Councillors: An Essay in the Comparative Anatomy of Human Society. A. M. Hocart. Pp. xiii–xcix. Chicago: University of Chicago Press.

Paranavitana, S. 1939. A. M. Hocart. Journal of the Ceylon Branch of the Royal Asiatic Society 34:264–268.

Raglan, Lord. 1941. Arthur Maurice Hocart (foreword). In Kingship. A. M. Hocart. London: Watts.

————. 1954. Foreword. In Social Origins. A. M. Hocart. Pp. vii–ix. London: Watts.

Rivers, W. H. R. 1923. Conflict and Dream. New York: Harcourt Brace.

Strathern, Andrew. 1971. The Rope of Moka: Big-Men and Ceremonial Exchange in Mount Hagen, New Guinea. Cambridge: Cambridge University Press.

————. 1979. Ongka: A Self-Account by a New Guinea Big-Man. London: Duckworth.

Swadesh, Morris. 2006. The Origin and Diversification of Language. Piscataway NJ: Aldine Transaction.

Throop, C. Jason, and Charles D. Laughlin. 2007. Anthropology of Consciousness. In Cambridge Handbook of Consciousness. P. D. Zelazo, M. Moscovitch, and E. Thompson, eds. Pp. 631–669. New York: Cambridge University Press.

Turner, Edith. 1993. The Reality of Spirits: A Tabooed or Permitted Field of Study? Anthropology of Consciousness 4(1):9–12.

Tylor, Edward B. 1920 [1871]. Primitive Culture. New York: J. P. Putnam's Sons.

MARK LAMONT

3

Malinowski and the "Native Question"

This anthropology would obviously be of the highest importance to the practical man in the colonies. Finally, since we are witnessing one of the greatest crises in human history, namely that of the gradual expansion of one form of civilization over the whole world, the recording of that event is an essential duty of those competent to do it. Now it is really the anthropologist, accustomed as he is to deal with the simple mind and to understand simple cultures, who ought to study the problem of the westernization of the world.

BRONISLAW MALINOWSKI (1929)

In Europe, social anthropology is a major social science that can now boast thousands of participants. This was not the case in the 1920s and 1930s, when the number of professional, university-trained anthropologists was limited to a few dozen individuals (Goody 1995; Kuper 1983). The subject is not taught in high schools, yet university recruitment remains robust, even in recent decades when government cutbacks threaten even some of the oldest, most established fields in the humanities and social sciences. It would seem, on the surface, that anthropology has something to offer. While the reasons individuals would choose to study anthropology are obviously very broad, one of the most common allures is that anthropology offers the possibility of opening up a sustained critique of western ideas about, or actions upon, the world. But how did this position come to be formed against anthropology's earlier deference to colonialism? And what were the preconditions that allowed this to happen?

This essay is intended as a polemic. Such a position risks ignoring, or otherwise pushing to the side, other perspectives on the subject. It will not read as a subtly researched, historically nuanced portrait of the discipline's early years. The full social history required of such a project awaits another occasion. At present, what is at stake is an argument, *pointe à ligne*. It is an argument-debate, struggle, fight for sorting out the politics of possibility that anthropology represents. It is as much about "really existing colonialism" in countries such as Canada, my home country, as it is about the crippled constitutions and denigrated economies that colonialism left behind worldwide. This is particularly acute in postcolonial African states where colonial policy fostered a devastating legal dualism between Africans and Europeans.

Anthropologists were active participants in debates about trusteeship, colonial jurisprudence, and institutional segregation. This essay argues for a sustained and critical examination of debates that anthropologists entered into after the First World War when, to use Lucy Mair's 1936 wording, "empire-consciousness" was the public recognition that trouble was brewing in the tropics. In seeking to synthesize an argument about anthropology's present relationship to its past, we level our questions at anthropologists' relationships to former debates. One of the debates being recalled in this essay is the "native question," an ultimately paternalistic and doomed debate that centered on how colonized peoples should be ruled.

This key debate of the interwar period, the native question, had far-reaching implications in the development of professional social anthropology in Britain and South Africa. To do justice to the ramifications issuing from this debate for anthropology, it is necessary to go beyond disciplinary history, written largely by anthropologists for anthropologists, toward a richly contextualized social history. What is required is a social history that seeks primarily to situate anthropologists within the broader politico-historical context of its earlier formative years, roughly from 1919 to 1939. My aim here is specific, to write the social history of anthropology's engagement with debates about what were called the "world race problem" and, latterly, the native question. To ground my research I have chosen to look at a key figure, Bronislaw Malinowski. I am primarily interested in synthesizing how he, and others he employed or supported, struck up institutionalized relationships with a variety of universities, philanthropic foundations, scholarly associations, and governments that were clearly committed to promoting problem-based social sciences in solving perceived threats to the colonial order.

Central to this development were funds acquired by the International Institute of African Languages and Cultures (IIALC) and the London School of Economics (LSE) from the Laura Spelman Rockefeller Memorial Fund, a subsidiary branch of the Rockefeller Foundation, one of the leading American philanthropic organizations that funded British universities at this time. In advocating problem-based social science, American philanthropy had its own political agendas, but this essay asks whether or not Malinowski's "functionalism" was an epistemological rupture, as disciplinary histories of anthropology have been at pains to ascertain, or whether the development of "functional anthropology" at the LSE was a branding effect aimed at promoting a pragmatic scientism and hence an ideology supportive of social engineering the "world race problem." To answer this question requires careful contextualization about the relationship of functionalist analysis and the doctrine of "indirect rule," which formed a significant policy debate in the native question as a whole. In order to contextualize the work of individual anthropologists working during his time, it will be necessary to examine, however cursorily, the work of several of Malinowski's first research students and fellows working mainly in rural settings in British colonial Africa.

These were foundational debates in the manufacture of anthropology as a discipline. Malinowski's penchant for being persuasive among leaders of the "Establishment," figures like J. H. Oldham, Lord Lugard, and Hans Vischer, gave the native question a scientific voice, one that they all exploited at some point or another as liberals. Malinowski's "functionalist" brand of anthropology was consciously promoted as instrumental, ideally developed for the solving of practical administrative problems, especially those identified as "problems" by colonial governments. Born out of the "colonial encounter," reared in metropolitan debates about the welfare of the changing native, contemporary anthropology's legacy to colonialism is well established. There is absolutely nothing novel to this claim.

Why then should this period of anthropology's history be reexamined? What is to be gained from studying the native question and the role anthropologists played in this formative debate? The answer lies in making analogies between earlier historical debates forming around problems of colonial administration and current concerns with indigenous peoples figuring around human rights, development, and identity. I argue that the native question that Malinowski and others addressed may be viewed as a generic form of governance that animates polemic within the discipline. Generic, in this sense, does not mean that there is some kind of cohering transhistorical ideology among anthropologists. By making the claim that the native question is at the heart of anthropology's deepest ideological premise, I aim to return to the foundational presence of colonial-era method and theory in contemporary anthropological practice. This ideology is the demand to make anthropology useful and relevant, to stress its suitability for solving perceived social problems. While this could be construed as a rather bold but naïve attack on the whole field of anthropology, making straw men out of the ancestors, I aim not to deliver a polemic for its own sake but to illustrate the specific form of governance that prevents anthropology from shedding its imperialist legacy.

EMPIRE-CONSCIOUSNESS AND THE ANTHROPOLOGIST

It has been more than forty years since Kathleen Gough asserted that anthropology is a "child of imperialism" (1968:403). This simple metaphor is now given as axiomatic in university lecture halls where anthropology is taught. As a preliminary attempt to historicize the discipline and demonstrate its political legacy, Gough's critique of anthropology and its liberal foundations stimulated further writings on the subject of anthropology and the "colonial encounter" (Asad 1973; Hymes 1974; Loizos 1977). These works have all contributed significantly to understandings of colonial subjectivities and historicizing anthropological careers.

At some point, however, the critique of anthropology's historical relationship to colonial administration was compelled to go further than axioms. Despite the emergence of what Peter Pels and Oscar Salemink have called "disciplinary histories," of which Adam Kuper's 1983 *Anthropology and Anthropologists* and Jack Goody's 1995 *The Expansive Moment* are exemplary, anthropologists themselves have made rather parochial assessments of the field with respect to its broader politico-historical context. This point was made by Regna Darnell when she argued that "a great deal of purported history of anthropology . . . is far from contextually accurate or historically sophisticated. Practitioners as quasi-historians frequently use history to argue for present theoretical concerns" (Darnell 1982:268, quoted in Pels and Salemink 1994). Yet today fewer social historians would continue arguing that the past can be known fully with self-evident conclusions and that all history is, in a sense, a public history for present concerns. Gough's argument, in 1968, must be put into its proper context before we can make use of this now axiomatic claim that anthropology was a "child of imperialism."

Gough was thinking primarily of the forty years that had preceded 1968. That year heralded new possibilities for anthropologists, the promise of a break with the world of empire that seemed to have dissipated in the violent ideological tensions of the Cold War. It brought events that were portent signs of possible revolution: student and worker revolt in Paris and Amsterdam; the beginning of the end for the American military in Vietnam; the ideological promises of the Prague Spring. There was a self-consciousness about rupture and change throughout 1968, mythologized as such by those who were young at the time.

In 1928, a differing critique of world events was being hatched by an older, but no less politicized generation of intellectuals, politicians, and administrators spread across the world. If for Gough, the ideologies of the Cold War merely masked the iniquities faced by nonwestern colonized peoples, bringing them into new ideological conflicts, for those entering into anthropological research in the interwar period, roughly 1919 to 1939, their debates were fired by deep, probing questions about the human dignity and legal status of nonwestern peoples subjected to colonial overrule. Today our axiomatic understandings of anthropologists as "reluctant imperialists" require historical fine-tuning (James 1973). To achieve this most effectively, some background to the growth of anthropology is needed.

Anthropology became a profession in the 1920s as British universities began to offer PhDs and new chairs. The University College London and the London School of Economics (LSE) established research programs that produced, respectively, twelve and twenty-four doctorate degrees by the end of the Second World War (Kuklick 1991:53–55).

In America, the newly appointed director of the Laura Spelman Rockefeller Memorial (LSM), Beardsley Ruml, worked on developing the social sciences in tandem with the rationalization of public administration. A relatively new ideology and faith that the social sciences could solve social problems led American philanthropic organizations, such as the Rockefeller Foundation, to invest heavily in foreign universities with the mandate to bring the social sciences into a "more equal relationship with the natural sciences" (Fisher 1980: 234). As will be detailed below, the LSE was a direct beneficiary of Laura Spelman Rockefeller Memorial funds, the provision being that social scientists turn to solving the world's many ills. One of these was often glibly referred to as the "world race problem."

A second development occurred some years before the influx of American philanthropic monies into British universities and scholarly institutions. With the growing recognition in the Colonial Office of increased conflict between governments, settlers, and subjected peoples in key British colonies, notably India and Malaya but also Kenya, the Rhodesias, and the Union of South Africa, rhetoric about the use of the "Science of Man" to solve problems of statecraft increasingly found an audience (see Myres 1929). The growing concern for conflict in the colonies on behalf of the Colonial Office was, in part, fueled by the controversies that raged among metropolitan public figures. It was into this climate of controversy that figures such as J. H. Oldham, author of *Christianity and the Race Problem* (1924), began to launch a liberal critique of white supremacy. Although not as radical as critics such as Norman Leys and W. M. Macmillan, whom the authorities dismissed because of their "savage attacks" on colonial land and labor policy, the liberal critique of racial segregation and excesses of empire was drawn to less overtly politicized questions like education. With increased emphasis on the utility of ethnology to questions of colonial policy and administration, the Colonial Office began to treat institutional bodies like the Royal Anthropological Institute and the World Council of Churches with serious if not guarded interest.

It is into this fold that Bronislaw Malinowski stepped in 1923 with his appointment at the LSE as reader of "social anthropology," a position that had been created alongside Charles Seligman's in the same institution. The two men's outlook on anthropology reflected markedly different points of view that would impact upon their relationship—and that of their respective students—quite dramatically. Malinowski viewed Seligman's anthropology as anachronistic, impractical for the place of the social sciences in the modern world and, in particular, to the world race problem and native question that Malinowski increasingly saw as relevant problems for his "functional" anthropology.

Anthropologists have long debated when the "revolution" occurred in anthropology, the theoretical shifting away from evolutionary and diffusionist concerns directed toward the study of origins, toward field-based empirical studies of contemporary human societies. For Europe, Ian Jarvie (1964) locates this roughly between 1919 and 1939, but we ought to question what justification there is for speaking of this shift as revolutionary. The interwar British "revolution" in anthropology is largely attributed to Malinowski's brand of functional anthropology, which he also tried to promote as applied or practical anthropology. While Malinowski was fond of mythmaking—part of how he succeeded in drawing such attention to social anthropology from diverse parties—I show how his relationships with diverse nonacademic actors and institutions in the United Kingdom, the United States, and the Union of South Africa led social anthropology, for quite an extensive period of time, to be widely recognized as the lead arbiter of the native question. Much of this development depended upon Malinowski's persuasive marketing of anthropology as well as the intensive training program that he set up at the LSE for a generation of research students. This is what anthropologists call Malinowski's "revolution." In the following section, I reconsider the notion of revolution within the context of Malinowski's functionalism, arguing that anthropologists need to look more intently at the circumstances of Malinowski's politics before such a claim of a rupture can be substantiated.

MALINOWSKI'S REVOLUTION?

Which parts of Malinowski's innovations in the 1920s were actual and which were mythic? This question is informed by skepticism raised over his purported innovations in theory, method, and pedagogy. Without a doubt, he was an able administrator and capable rhetor, but the mythmaking Malinowski has perhaps triumphed over the Malinowski of correspondence, memoranda, and grant proposals. Before questioning the Malinowskian revolution in social anthropology, we must assess the myths that anthropologists perpetuate about the man.

Indeed, one of the pitfalls in choosing Malinowski to center historical narrative about anthropologists' engagements with the native question is his mythic status among practicing anthropologists (see Firth 1988). The man himself was a mythmaker and became, possibly by his own intention, one of the anthropological "ancestors" that disciplinary histories focus so intently upon. His myths center mainly around a beach on Kiriwina, in the Trobriand Islands; his methodological borrowings from Seligman and Haddon that gave us an idea of how to do ethnographic research; his brand-name of anthropology theory, "functionalism"; the solid oak seminar table at the LSE and praise for his teaching style; his posthumously published "diary in the strict sense of the term"; and a tent.

The tent is perhaps the strongest example I can give to show how effective his mythmaking was. James Urry (1989) delivers one of the strangest Malinowski stories I've ever heard. After a call from one of Urry's former students in a Brisbane museum about some pieces of canvas that were wrapped around Papuan artifacts shipped from Port Moresby in October 1918, Urry carried out a heroic piece of archival sleuthing and unearthed irrevocable evidence that, indeed, the calico, earthy fragments of canvas were Malinowski's tent. These pieces of canvas were framed and auctioned off to bidding museums for a handy sum. We now have relics of Saint Malinowski!

The lasting debates about the native question that raged in the 1920s and 1930s fueled Malinowski's campaign to apply his functionalism to questions of administration. The result was a series of engaged studies of African societies by Malinowski's research students, marked by their cultural relativism, that questioned the impact of "native policy" in such domains of social life as diet and nutrition, wage and subsistence labor, migration, political organization, and "native law." Despite the empirical foci of much of this work, the preservation of African "culture" stood in contrast with the problem of the "westernization of the world" (Malinowski 1929). This lent anthropology the power to influence liberal conscience and deliberation on the development of racial segregation in countries like South Africa (Rich 1984: 54–76). Far-reaching in its consequences for developing "native policy," anthropology was viewed as a trained and disciplined watchdog for liberalism and its critique of colonial excesses. Why is it that this legacy is accorded less privilege than the figure of Saint Malinowski?

As Richard Fardon observed in the early 1990s, when anthropologists sought their own rupture with the past in the guise of postmodernism, Malinowski became a value, a precedent through which contemporary ethnographers could emplot their own departure from old orthodoxies (Fardon 1990: 571). "Malinowski" as value, of breaks and rupture, thereby voiced the possibility for revolution, and the more that anthropological discussion turned to changing their practice, the larger the scope for discussing history became. At least since Ian Jarvie's 1964 characterization of "functionalism" as a revolt against the evolutionists and the diffusionists, it has become a commonplace orthodoxy to conflate Malinowski with the "revolution in anthropology." Indeed, as critical an observer of Malinowski's thought and life as he was, Ernest Gellner emphasized the rupture that Malinowski stood for:

> The revolution over which Bronislaw Malinowski presided during the two inter-war decades from the London School of Economics, which then emerged for a time as the world capital of anthropology, really was a revolution, a total inversion, a literal over-turning of things. (Gellner 1986; quoted in Fardon 1990:572)

But what exactly did Malinowski turn over? In this narrative, Malinowski is represented as an agent unbarred and uninhibited by the vast social and ideological pressures that would have weighed in on a salaried academic in a field that was still seen to be the reserve of romantics and antiquarians. Even if his challenge to anthropology did harness the institutional and personal resources to transform anthropology, he certainly did not achieve this alone.

In order to substantiate a "revolution" in theory and method, historians of anthropology need to synthesize the conversation Malinowski had with others about indirect rule and "functionalism," on the one hand, and questions posed by anthropologists about cultural relativism, equality, colonial jurisprudence, on the other. The native question was, in many respects, much larger than Malinowski's project, encompassing the attention of the public's "empire consciousness" of both liberal and conservative strands of opinion. The "revolution" that is attributed to Malinowski, in this periodization, was the product of political work, mythologized as some form of Kuhnian rupture. Functionalism appealed to protagonists of indirect rule because it stressed the dangers of radical historical change and offered administrators the hope that the problems confronting colonial administrators could be overcome if they just let the "natives" respond to their own needs in their own time. Functional anthropology was a comforting narrative to liberals who saw British colonial interests threatened by rapid social change. To explore this in greater detail, the ideological agreement between functionalism and indirect rule ought to be more clearly drawn.

Malinowski's "Functional Anthropology" is an early example of academic branding. He was certainly conscious about how he promoted it, strategically choosing a rhetoric underlining its scientific method and pragmatic outlook. He took pains to ensure that his brand of anthropology stood apart from others as "Social Anthropology," insisting on capitalization and punctuation to call attention to his theoretical stance. There were various functional schools in other scholarly fields, such as Roscoe Pound's "Functional Jurisprudence" at the Brookings Institute in the United States.

Malinowski attacked what he identified as theoretical and methodological weaknesses in anthropological evolutionism and diffusionism. By the 1920s at least, these theoretical frameworks were coming under siege from a number of quarters, especially since more anthropologists were writing monographs about a specific society based on face-to-face interactions and exchange. A. R. Radcliffe-Brown's *The Andaman Islanders* and Malinowski's *Argonauts of the Western Pacific* were both published in 1922, establishing functionalism as an alternative to dominant theoretical persuasions. He accused evolutionist and diffusionist theorists of romantic longing for the *sauvage noblesse* and methodologically naïve antiquarianism, viewing the history of all societies as vestiges of contact with superior civilizations in some putative past. In both evolutionist and diffusionist thinking, he seems to have seen these theories as ideological props to imperialism, even if he frequently engaged with both polemically, aiming for political mileage. His "Functionalist Anthropology," in the proposals and essays he wrote, bore the mark of science, interested in both "civilized" and "primitive" peoples and capable of being applied to both. Seeing colonizer and colonized as part of the same world, each capable of being studied by the analytic methods of the functionalist anthropologist, Malinowski's brand of functionalism claimed the capacity to study both rapid and gradual change. Malinowski felt, however, that the possibilities for anthropology had been curtailed by the lack of detailed ethnographic studies of actually changing societies. The following was a proposal he wrote for promoting functionalist anthropology under the auspices of the African Institute:

> Anthropology even of the previous generation preferred to study man dead rather than alive—it was the science above all of skulls and skeletons, of Pleistocene or Neolithic man, of ages and forms known only from meagre survivals and reckless reconstructions. It chose as its pet subject, not the nearest human beings, but those most remote, the few native tribes surviving on the outskirts of civilization. And yet it called itself "science of man" unlimited and unqualified. Even the natives, however, were not studied in their full reality. They were made into "primitives" or "savages," into "pre-logical" beings, or into "representatives of prehistoric times." Thus it came about that we know a great deal about a little tribe in Central Australia, about some natives from Tierra del Fuego, about one or two atolls in the Pacific, about a few Veddhas huddled in inaccessible caves of the Ceylon jungle. While, all the time, we anthropologists almost completely ignored the very existence of such enormous portions of humanity as the masses of China, Malaya, and India. Anthropology also till recently regarded as outside its interest the study of hybrid races, of detribalised natives, of the processes of diffusion when these happen between European and native cultures. (Malinowski 1930: 406–407)

By the time Malinowski wrote this, initially in a 1926 proposal to the Rockefeller Foundation on behalf of the African Institute, he had a vision of anthropology as the study of the "changing native" and saw immediately the possibility for anthropology in the management of colonial affairs.

Functional Anthropology promised both methodological rigor and training in theory. Neither could be provided without money and other institutional supports. This he was most clear about, especially in his correspondence with J. H. Oldham once Oldham contacted him about developing an anthropological contribution to a grant being prepared for the Rockefeller Foundation's Laura Spelman Rockefeller Memorial fund. Initiated through Oldham, Lord Lugard, and Hans Vischer, the Rockefeller Foundation pledged to finance the International Institute of African Cultures and Languages on a five-year challenge grant. Oldham saw in Malinowski an academic who would bring international attention to the proposed institute, even when he had not conducted research in Africa. For Malinowski's part, he saw in Oldham, a senior public figure in the World Council of Churches, a diplomatic administrator who could indirectly further Malinowski's ambition to make anthropology into a practical and modern social science. Less clear are Malinowski's motivations to launch Functional Anthropology in such terms, but an examination of his visit to the United States, as a visiting scholar on Rockefeller Foundation stipends, hints that his functionalism was driven by far-reaching ideological concerns.

Connected to this, he was also clear on the purpose, or even moral duty, of the anthropologist. He would write that the anthropologist "ought to be able to make clear to traders, missionaries, and exploiters what the Natives really need and where they suffer most under the pressure of European interference" (Malinowski 1961:3). As Susan Sontag demurred, the anthropologist as hero! From numerous writings, it emerges that Malinowski was intensely aware of the injustices that the expansion of western interests had inflicted upon colonized peoples. Yet there was a profoundly contradictory character to Malinowski's critical liberalism, especially in his consistent calls to depoliticize the native question.

Part of the IIACL mandate was that it must remain nonpolitical: "By the constitution of the Institute all political issues are eliminated from its activities" (Malinowski 1929:23). Such a constitutional stance, interpreted from today's understandings of power and governance, can be interpreted in entirely ideological terms. Scientific method was in the service of "practical problems," immune to the idea that scientific endeavors were driven by political agendas. Malinowski's politics were subtle, and his political thinking shifted with the opportunities that came his way. That's human! Unfortunately, several commentators have accepted his rhetoric and mythmaking as evidence of his political neutrality. The author of a semiofficial history of the LSE, Ralf Dahrendorf, surprisingly states that "he was as near to an unpolitical being as was possible at LSE" (1995: 245). Yet Malinowski did have a politics of his own, and in the next section this will be represented in his first scholarly visit to the United States during 1929, when debates about the "world race problem" formed the crucible of think tank politics in the United States. This position, in turn, would shift even further with respect to his 1934 travels through southern and eastern Africa, a visit that was also funded through the LSM as part of the winding down of the system of grants and fellowships provided by the Rockefeller Foundation. In this later period, the world race problem lay entwined in Malinowski's answer to the native question. But first to Malinowski's 1929 tour of America and the politics of race.

WORLD RACE PROBLEM: MALINOWSKI IN AMERICA

What interests did American philanthropic organizations such as the Rockefeller and Carnegie Foundations have in funding research institutes and affiliated scholars outside the United States? This question has sparked answers among historians working on the subject of race relations, a term that originated in the United States and was then exported, notably to South Africa (MacMillan and Marks 1989: 73). Malinowski's growing emphasis on "culture contact" struck a resonant chord with Rockefeller interest in race relations (Fisher 1986:5). During the late 1920s when Malinowski traveled to the United States, race and culture were entangled in the popular imagination yet were subject to intensive academic and political debates about their similitude (Barkan 1993). The so-called world race problem was inescapable and broadcast particularly widely in Great Britain, the United States, and South Africa. Jack Goody (1995) suggests that the industrialization of the United States and the racialization of its workforce presented to the white American public the future menace of competition with blacks, giving form to a particular "Negro problem" not only in the southern United States but also in the northeast, where increased labor migration transformed the composition of the working class. Following John Cell's 1982 study of segregation in both South Africa and the southern United States, the directors of the Rockefeller Foundation may have sought a comparative understanding in countries that had their own race relations conflicts, in these cases British settler colonies.

Malinowski came to the United States in March 1929 to deliver a report to directors of the Laura Spelman Rockefeller Memorial about the activities of his grant and the scope of Functional Anthropology. Against general Rockefeller dissatisfaction with American anthropology, considered to be too eclectic and antiquarian for the foundation's interests in race relations and public administration, Malinowski's visiting scholarship would raise the issue of race politics and colonial administration inside the United States. Searching worldwide for new perspectives on race relations, Rockefeller funds also supported the Kaiser Wilhelm Institute in Nazi Germany, although this work was mainly directed toward physical anthropology and the scientific legitimation of biological race (see Schafft 2004). Malinowski's own correspondence and reports related to this visit reveal that the "world race problem," as it was sometimes referred to in his notes, formed a considerable focus for his itinerary.

A secondary, underlying conceit that he used in his reports to the Rockefeller Foundation and other institutes he visited was that American anthropology was mired in the outdated "historical school," an allusion to the American practice of reconstructing cultural history from the recollections of privileged informants, what we today call "salvage ethnography." This was a plug for functionalist anthropology. It was, however, an abrupt attack on what was the hallmark of Boasian historical particularism, a methodological position staunchly supported by prominent colleagues of Papa Franz. In front of Robert Lowie and Alfred Kroeber's students at the University of California, Berkeley, he delivered a functionalist critique of salvage ethnography, urging them to avoid the difficulties of conjectural history. The substance of this argument can be found repetitively, and perhaps pedantically, in almost all of Malinowski's writings about cultural change: "Because what exists nowadays is not a primitive culture in isolation but one in contact and process of change" (Malinowski 1961:6). The fact that Malinowski started to use the culture concept more frequently after his addresses to American anthropologists shows that he was not dismissive of ideas that challenged his own, despite his hostility to historicism. In a paper prepared during his tour of Berkeley, he employed the culture concept while admonishing historical particularism: "It is the essence of culture that all its aspects hang together and one cannot be understood without reference to another. The atomistic, one sided way of dealing with human culture is perhaps the most serious reproach that can be levelled at present day American field work."[1] Yet clearly Malinowski did not endear himself to many of his American counterparts. Kluckhohn called him a "pretentious Messiah of the credulous" (quoted in Kuper 1983:24).

Malinowski's visiting scholarship to the United States had enormous influence on his practical and theoretical work after 1930, yet it has scarcely been footnoted. It was significant, in the first place, because it raised the issue of race and culture in a way that went counter to that conventionally accepted in Boasian terms: that race and culture were independent of one another. With Malinowski, curiously, the inverse seems to hold; they were interdependent. The world race problem was hardly of frivolous interest to Malinowski, and what he had to say about race is suggestive of what he later had to say about cultures: that there were differences and that these differences mattered to public administration. His "functional" anthropology certainly could not be neutral in this respect.

His theoretical challenges to American anthropology aside, his notes from the 1929 visit to the United States demonstrate a vested interest in the political relations between the state and indigenous peoples, on the one hand, and black/white relations, on the other. Race and administration permeate his unpublished essays and correspondence at this conjuncture. At the risk of enforcing a stereotypic (and unfair) culturalist rendering of "Malinowski as Pole," it appears that the eminent anthropologist's acceptance of race was confusing "matters of fact, not of prejudice," to snatch Elazer Barkan's candid phrase (Barkan

1993:2). This came at a time when the scientific legitimacy of race as biological given between peoples came to be challenged by an ideologically reflective version of race as socially mediated inequality. Caught up in the context of wide-scale debates over the validity of race analysis, especially in Britain and the United States, Malinowski's position is characterized by a puzzling ambivalence. Did he believe race was a matter of fact? Or a matter of prejudice?

The distinction matters for anthropology. Undoubtedly, Malinowski's privileged relationship to the European offices and American directors of the Rockefeller Foundation shaped professional anthropology. We can only try to imagine what would have happened to anthropology if the bulk of Laura Spelman Rockefeller Memorial funds had gone to the University College London under the management of the diffusionist Grafton Elliot Smith. Malinowski's understanding of race cannot be interpreted as racist. Put into the context of the race debates that shaped 1920s intellectual life, it would be nothing short of a presentist bias to suggest he was racially political. Yet he failed to conceptualize race in the manner that he did for culture, function, and institution. He refused to be resolutely, steadfastly, and methodologically "scientific" about it. It remained the odd, taken for granted notion that people, in essence, were objectively different. Concealed within this, however, was a sense of urgency regarding this world of difference and of "culture contact." He seems to have seen the whole world undergoing significant structural changes, asserting in an almost prophetic manner: "I believe also that in the future the problems of racial contact and clash of cultures will become more and more urgent and important in the world's history." This was a position that he would reiterate more than once, with as much urgency; a position that, in the last analysis, equated "racial contact" with a "clash of cultures." Some eighty years later, the tenor of his argument sounds suspiciously familiar—as if Samuel Huntington had written it himself.

One possibility that presents itself about Malinowski's travels through the United States is that he was playing his part with his donors. This is not to suggest cynically that he was disingenuous in his pursuit of resources and support. Most of his students recalled his drive and conviction in what he believed to be the right course. Race in this context was simply a matter of fact that was of political importance to others; scientists, for their part, might inform policy, but they should refrain from making it. Scientists need only report back their findings and conjectures. Malinowski's public discussions of race were ideologically conservative, witnessed in this 1929 report to the Rockefeller Foundation:

> My opinion is also that racial prejudice is neither an illusion, nor that we can explain it away as the result of cultural or economic conflict. These factors very often enter and enhance, as well as distort the biological foundations of race prejudice, but I cannot help thinking that such biological foundations do exist. I am personally convinced that two independent divergent races are bound "to get on each other's nerves" and that there is a quota of irreducible hostility and division owing to the sole fact of racial difference. The relation between assimilated Jew and Gentile, between Latin and Teutonic people whenever they are brought into close contact, between Asiatics and Europeans in all colonies, show that even between such layers of society where there is no economic and cultural conflict, some antagonism remains. Mixed marriages and a systematic policy of ignoring the differences may, as in the Dutch Indies, offer a solution. But the problem is there, and the solution must be found. (LSE M 8/2)

The problem that he was alluding to was the problem of how to govern people whose adverse fate had been conquest. In suggesting the Dutch Indies as an example, he was warning against models of assimilation fostered by some protagonists of colonial policy. Briefly stated, Malinowski theoretically opposed assimilation because his functionalist analysis of social wholes saw change as gradual, based on a theory of needs that suggested institutions would only change when they ceased meeting such needs and would only be replaced by other institutional arrangements when this occurred. Following this gradualist model of social change, Malinowski was an advocate of the doctrine of association. He favored the idea that peoples ought "to develop along their own lines," that is to say, that they should be ruled indirectly, the colonizer relying, where possible, on "indigenous institutions" to achieve governance.

While in America, however, Malinowski had not yet spelled out his theoretical support for "indirect rule," the generic form of governance in British colonial Africa. He was still concerned about race relations and what was then known in the United States (and still is in Canada) as the "Indian problem." This reflects interest in anthropology's application to public administration.

With growing commitment to the idea that anthropology could aid in developing a rationalized public administration, Malinowski traveled to the American Southwest, intending to visit Hopi and Navajo reservations, as well as the government administrative station at Keames Canyon, Arizona. Explaining that this was a visit and not "even sketchy fieldwork," Malinowski wrote, "The main interest of the visitor lay in assessing the conditions under which American fieldwork was being done; and in studying the relations between the Indian Dept. and its wards." In a section of his report to the Rockefeller Foundation entitled "The Relation between Anthropology and the Practical Aspects of the Indian Question," he stressed the potential or attractiveness that the "ethnological point of view" might hold for the Indian Department. Citing a number of conflicts—from the ban on the snake dance to the forceful enrollment of Hopi children in schools—Malinowski readily acknowledged that American anthropologists would condemn such events as impositions and that a number of aboriginal welfare organizations had been founded. Yet it was his rather bald admission about his then current mandate that should be noted:

> Problems of conflict of culture and race are becoming more and more acute, and it is high time that anthropology should take up more earnestly the economic problems and legal aspects of the present blending of human strains and cultures. I should like to add that this type of anthropology will be, it is hoped, developed at the London School of Economics, where already there are a few research students with a certain practical experience of colonial affairs.

It is impossible to know whether Malinowski, when writing this, knew of the extensive efforts of the Bureau of American Ethnology to apply anthropology to problems of administration. Since 1879 when it was founded, the BAE's director, John Wesley Powell, had frequently spoken of the problems of "contact" and "conflict" to members of the federal government, just as the U.S. Army and white settlers pushed aboriginal peoples into the ethnocidal fringes of the Southwest. Telling Congress, "The Native American is among us, and we must either protect him or destroy him," Powell's answer mirrored Malinowski's almost fifty years earlier, arguing that a "deeper understanding became a matter of public welfare" (Darnell 1998). Again, however, Malinowski stressed culture and race as if they had equivalent conceptual values, all the while pressing an urgency about the problems of culture contact and race relations that could not have gone unnoticed by his Rockefeller benefactors.

It is in Malinowski's travel through the southern United States that race becomes an ever more important focus of his writing. Travel through North Carolina and Georgia was planned in line with J. H. Oldham's interest in education and, in particular, the Negro colleges such as Hampton and Tuskegee, associated with Phelps-Stokes Foundation monies. Oldham was fervently involved in several debates about whether the emphasis on "Negro" education should be academic or vocational. Malinowski's own involvement in such debates was muted until his journey to South Africa in 1934, but he noted the stark social effects of segregation in the American South. In ruminating on experiences he had in the cities and towns of North Carolina and Georgia and those as a child in Cracow, Poland, Malinowski's ambivalence on race swings from "as a fact" to "as a prejudice":

> A few conversations in Pullman Smokers with typical Southerners were enough to give me a clear idea of race prejudice, already known to me from personal recollections of my childhood in Eastern Europe, where a much milder prejudice obtains against the Jewish Ghetto population

Such a "much milder prejudice" would in less than a decade lead to the expulsion, destitution, detention, murder, and genocide of millions of Polish Jews at the hands of the NSDAP and their collaborators. According to Elazar Barkan (1993), the radicalization of NSDAP racist ideology was, in part, a reaction to shifts in the legitimacy of race as a scientific concept in the United States and Great Britain during the interwar period.

Records and correspondence left over from Malinowski's travels through the United States in 1929 are inconclusive as to the effects that debates about the "world race problem" had on his thinking at this time. Yet the trip would be pivotal in his new and reassured position as anthropological authority, particularly within the IIACL where he would play an increasing role through his research students at the LSE. Judged against the historiography of American anthropology, however, his comments are awkwardly ill-informed, particularly with regard to the relationships of anthropologists and the Indian Department (see Darnell 1998). His recommendation to the Rockefeller Foundation regarding the modernization or rationalization of American anthropology boils down to a few practical recommendations about the pressures on young academics in the American university system. He argued that the dearth of opportunity for postdoctoral fellowships dampened promising academic careers, with most American PhD holders being appointed to full teaching positions upon completion of their degrees. Less favorably, however, American anthropology is contrasted with "Functional Anthropology" and found wanting, a strong critique of the discipline in North America that would, in a number of years, be applied by the Rockefeller Foundation to Malinowski's own brand of anthropology. Yet it was not anthropological theory that was the backdrop to Malinowski's visit to the United States so much as the development of his thinking about race and racial policy, especially with regard to segregation or the "color bar" as it was known in South Africa.

Shortly after returning to London from America in early 1930, Malinowski attended a meeting of the Study Circle on Imperial Economic Co-operation about migration in the British colonial sphere. In the minutes of this particular meeting, on January 27, 1930, Malinowski's views of the politics of migration begin to show, in embryonic form, the tensions and contradictions of his understanding of race:

That the economic aspect of migration could not be separated from the biological and political aspects of the question. Migrations were not always beneficial to the country from which the migrants departed. There were the examples of the Jews from Spain and the Huguenots from France to prove that. On the other hand, an exchange of brains was very valuable. Migration from one race to another was almost completely under political control. The Asiatic was not allowed in places outside Asia; the Russian peasant was not allowed to settle in Tanganyika. Practically speaking, the principle was going to be more and more strictly enforced. In regard to the British Empire it was argued that biological mixture of races was a phenomenon we did not wish to encourage and with which we did not want to have to deal. Our problem at present was exclusively a problem of migration within the British Empire. The migrant would not be a peasant, even though it might be the peasant-proprietor who was most needed. But he could not be secured within the Empire. The Chinese would fill Australia in five or six years if they were permitted to do so. Taking all in all, Professor Malinowski thought that it was wise not to open the doors of the Empire widely.

There was still a very strong migration movement to Kenya, and this was to be regretted. The making of parts of Africa into a white man's country was gradually creating for the Empire another such disaster as a South African problem. General Smuts' Oxford speeches were most unfortunate in the way that they dealt with the native question. This question had to be faced; it applied as much to other native races as to white people; the Indians in East Africa should definitely be discouraged. Professor Malinowski concluded with a plea for "the depoliticising of certain human problems in the Empire."

The reference to Jan Christiaan Smuts's Oxford lecture series "Some Problems of World Affairs" shows the degree to which South Africa and other British colonies, such as Kenya, were becoming the central attractions for debates forming out of the "world race problem," namely, that of the native question. In fact, these were separate names for a single generic debate about the suitability of trusteeship and the specter of African nationalism. As will be explored in the following section, the polarization of the native question into debates about plural societies, particularly that of South Africa, led to very different theoretical positions about the object of anthropology and its pragmatic alignment with studies of colonial administration. To turn to this critical moment in colonial policy formation, the question of why Malinowski would be so sternly opposed to the position taken by Smuts sheds light on the growing reservations among anthropologists that their studies were having the intended enlightening effects on colonial administrators.

The "native question" or, alternatively, the "native problem" were generic labels for the political contradictions that colonialization had sprung after centuries of European demands for the land and labor of conquered or capitulated peoples. It was into this "problem" that the first social anthropologists trained in Britain and South Africa threw themselves. The result was a new understanding of social science as empirical, problem-oriented, and practical. This appreciation of social anthropology as being applicable to modern world problems did much to disabuse popular opinion of anthropologists as eccentrics drawn to the romance of primitive societies. Indeed, up until this point, Malinowski was still deeply associated in the British press with his studies of Melanesian sexuality, building a reputation that he had difficulties overcoming. It was certainly an image of the anthropologist that Malinowski consciously sought to transform in Britain, while his contemporary A. R. Radcliffe-Brown attempted the same in South Africa and later in Australia. Despite the sizeable challenges they faced in refashioning anthropology as relevant to world issues, both Malinowski and Radcliffe-Brown struggled to define their answer to the native question against statesmen like General Jan Smuts, whose evolutionary outlook on "natives" painted caricatures of the colonized subject.

Smuts was, for his part, something of a latecomer to the debate. By the time of his speech tour on "world affairs" at Oxford's Sheldonian Theatre on the evening of November 16, 1929, Malinowski, Oldham, and Lugard had already secured significant funding from the Rockefeller Foundation for empirical research in Africa. Yet Smuts was proposing, in essence, a similar project of inquiry into the future of colonialism. On this particular night, his speech touched upon an issue that was fast moving from an ember of concern among the British establishment to a scorching bonfire: native policy in Africa. Although there were no winds of change fanning this fire, discontent was vocal and active throughout British colonies, and there was emerging a generalized debate about what was to be done. As a founding architect of the League of Nations, a prominent ideological thread of Smuts's thought was the right of conquering nations to mandate the form of rule over subject peoples. Everything about Smuts turned back to this jurisprudence. This not only touched upon the fate of the German colonies that had been mandated to the League of Nations and were administered through Britain's colonial office, but also extended deeply into the controversies that rocked his own country, the Union of South Africa. As a combat veteran of the first war against Boer separatists, where he had been a guerrilla commando on the Afrikaner side, Smuts had great respect for the right to rule conquered people: his side had lost, and he had joined the winners' ranks. Only a part of Smuts's lifetime experience of politics was formed by the 1899–1902 Anglo-Boer War that had brought the two Afrikaner republics, the Orange Free State and Transvaal, into the British Empire. By the opening of the Great War, Smuts took South West Africa from the Germans and handed it over as a protectorate to the Union of South Africa as mandated by the League of Nations. Yet there at Oxford in 1929, Smuts was seen as a spokesperson and exemplar for the spirit of the British Commonwealth, itself something of a constitutional compromise on successionist undercurrents everywhere. To the politically informed, perhaps Smuts looked like a surviving King Harold in the court of William the Conqueror.

Four years prior to his lecture tour in Great Britain, following his League of Nations duties in Europe, Smuts had been elected out of power as the prime minister of the Union of South Africa by his rival, General Barry Hertzog, leader of the first Nationalist government in 1924. Hertzog must have been on Smuts's mind the night he spoke to his Oxford crowd, especially so because Hertzog had successfully introduced a bill in 1924 that espoused a policy of segregation between Europeans and Africans everywhere throughout the Union, with the exception of Cape Coloureds, who still had an electoral franchise. As the Nationalist Party consolidated its policies around segregation, then very popular among its Boer supporters, it extended its policies and essentially abolished the right of Cape Africans to vote. While an official declaration of apartheid was still some twenty-two years to follow, segregation had taken root in South African law. There is no doubt, upon reading the published version of Smut's 1929 speech "Native Policy in Africa," that Hertzog's policies were the main tensions prodding his arguments along.

Smuts, for his part, created for his Oxford crowd a caricature of the African colonial subject. Steeped in the kind of evolutionary thinking so dominant among elites of his time, Smuts argued that the only answer to the native question was to impose indirect rule throughout Africa. To him and many of his contemporaries, the native question went something like whether or not Europeans should rule Africans according to universal "natural law" or through "native law." Think of American or French assimilation and you get the first part of the question. Think of South Africa and apartheid and you get the second part of the question. In practice, this meant that European colonizers had a choice of how Africans would be governed. On the one hand, they had to choose between governing Africans as individuals or as communities. On the other, they had to choose whether there should be one law for all colonial subjects or many laws for as many "tribal" groups as could be identified. Here core liberal principles were horn-locked with a communitarian philosophy. The debate took on more serious terms of struggle for those living with its consequences, especially with the later creation of Bantustans and Native Reserves.

The decision to favor a differentiated and decentralized form of governance has largely been called indirect rule when applied to British colonial policy. Although we will see that most colonies practiced a mixed system of direct and indirect rule, it is very common to read that the French colonial policies favored direct rule, where assimilation was a goal of policymakers (cf. Amselle 1998). In contrast British colonial policy was seen to devolve power through indirect rule. This kind of dichotomy, however, conceals as much as it reveals. As Mahmood Mamdani (1996) incisively observes, it matters little what colonial powers called their systems of tyranny. All varieties can still be accurately described as decentralized despotism. Whether French, British, Belgian, Spanish, or Portuguese, all colonial governments confronted a fundamental and pressing question: "How can a tiny and foreign minority rule over an indigenous majority?" (Mamdani 1996:16).

Whether more or less emphasis on indirect or direct rule was stressed is rather moot, Mamdani insists, when political inequality was rooted in legal dualism.

Indirect rule came to dominate colonial policy out of pragmatism. Direct rule was very expensive and demanded that professional administrators be placed as "men on the spot" in many, many spots. The revenue to finance such a venture might be one of the possible reasons why colonial subjects of the German Empire, for example, rose up against their rulers with a resolved commitment to political violence. Another cost of direct rule was the huge budget for military campaigns. Punitive raids were common in all of the colonies, especially during the period of consolidation and annexation that ended around 1920 in the context of the Great War. The sheer cost and the logistical challenges of direct rule prompted a quest for an alternative strategy. In contrast, indirect rule, as conceived by its modern architect, Lord Lugard, in the early 1900s, did not require large investment in personnel or materiel. It was unofficially championed as government "on the cheap" (Berman 1992), but the rationale behind indirect rule seems to have multiple origins beyond the merely pecuniary. To contrast direct and indirect rule further, indirect rule required more investment in terms of recordkeeping, knowledge production, and work from individual colonial officers. It was noted quite early in the colonial encounter that administrators would have to know a society in order to act upon them and that this required some knowledge of their languages, their economics, their social organization, and their laws (see Amselle 1998).This was a need that Malinowski would respond to.

Race and the ideas of the social evolutionists following from Herbert Spencer seem to play important roles in indirect rule's chief proponents. Difference was a key component in the concept of indirect rule. Smuts argued precisely such a racialist point of view to an Oxford colloquium, saying, "It is clear that a race so unique, and so different in its mentality and its cultures from those of Europe, requires a policy very unlike that which would suit Europeans" (Smuts 1930: 76). Upon this racialist argument comes a strict policy: "The British Empire does not stand for assimilation of its peoples into a common type, it does not stand for standardization, but for the fullest freest development of its people along their own specific lines" (78). This idea that peoples who stood at different evolutionary stages, but lived as contemporaries in the new colonial states, had to have different laws was accepted without question by many, including the Judicial Committee of the Privy Council. Upon assessing the question of land alienation in Southern Rhodesia in 1918, the Lordship appealed to evolutionary thinking when they wrote, "The estimation of the rights of aboriginal tribes is always inherently difficult. Some tribes are so low in the scale of social organization that their usages and conceptions of rights and duties are not to be reconciled with the institutions or the legal ideas of civilized society. Such a gulf cannot be breached" (quoted in Buell 1965: 210). As I will explain shortly, Malinowski's functionalist approach would argue that indirect rule was the way to go but that there could be no uniform answer to the native question.

The story could also be picked up later in the debate, before it took the brutal path toward apartheid in 1948. Just ousted from his position as a member of parliament, Jan Hofmeyr spoke to the Bantu Studies Student Society at the University of Witwatersrand on August 13, 1936. Although I do not know from historical sources for certain, these were not Bantu students, since South Africa had already moved to policies of educational segregation at all levels. The absence of African students in South African universities, save Fort Hare at a later period, is mirrored by the presence of African students like Kenyatta, Busia, and Z. K. Matthews at Malinowski's famous seminar at the LSE at the same time. But on that night of August 13 at Wits, Hofmeyr was speaking to a young crowd with very different political views on the native question. He tried to define such divergent perspectives:

> To different people the Native problem quite obviously means different things. It is a problem that arises from the juxtaposition of white man and black man in the same country. That much is common sense. But for some the problem would appear to be how, in such a country—in this case it is South Africa—the white man is to ensure his position of dominance for the future; how South Africa is to be made safe for the European. Those who so view the problem would proclaim their ideal as being that of a white South Africa. For others,

however, the problem is one of the adjustment of the inequalities in the position of the black man conceived as a fellow-citizen along with the white man of a common country—and of these the ideal is rather that of "equal rights for every civilised man." For my part, I can conceive of no better description of the problem than it is an aspect of what Dr. J. H. Oldham has described as the ultimate political problem of the world—"the problem of how the different races which inhabit it may live together in peace and harmony." And, of that description of the problem, the essence seems to be the notion of living together, in joint participation in the life of a single community (Hofmeyr 1937:272–273)

Because he was part of the United Party of the Union of South Africa, but not reelected because of the swing toward Nationalist Party policies on segregation, Hofmeyr was very aware of these diverging views on the growing "color bar" in South Africa. There were, throughout the British colonial world, two basic statements of policy on the native question, although African colonies could in no way be taken as identical in their policies that shaped the political relations between Europeans and Africans.

These divergent policies were spoken of as doctrines. The doctrine of identity would emerge in some colonies, such as Tanganyika, when "decolonization" was seen as inevitable at the end of the Second World War. This doctrine held that, in the words of Lord Hailey, author of *An Africa Survey*, "the future social and political institutions of Africans" were "destined to be similar to those of Europeans" (Hailey 1957:150). It polar opposite, and the girders of apartheid, was the doctrine of differentiation. Again according to Hailey's *An Africa Survey*, which was a voluminous, multi-edition treatise on the native question originally published in 1937 and revised in 1956, differentiation "aims at the evolution of separate institutions appropriate to African conditions and differing both in spirit and in form from those of Europeans." One might see in these doctrines ghostly principles for what was to be assimilationist and segregationist policy, the latter most adhered to in settler colonies, such as the Union of South Africa, Southern Rhodesia, and Kenya. Although both could be thought about in terms of indirect rule, where there were different laws for different categories of people, in Hofmeyr's South Africa the path being taken was toward its most extreme expression: apartheid.

Indirect rule is frequently associated with Lord Lugard's notion of the "Dual Mandate," which he applied firstly to Nigeria, before the governor of Tanganyika, Donald Cameron, applied a variant to East Africa. Ideologically speaking, however, indirect rule was an old stratagem for rule, aimed at differentiating colonial subjects by territorial and ethnic identification. Malinowski found in Lugard's writings something akin to functionalism. According to the historian John Cell, Malinowski's papers contain a note, written after reading *The Dual Mandate* in 1927, that is suggestive of Malinowski's personal stance on indirect rule and the native question. In diary form was written: "If he [Lugard] had wanted to control Scientific Anthrop, so as to fit into his Imp[erial] idea, he couldn't have done anything but to create Functional School. L.L.'s Indirect Rule is a Complete Surrender to the Functional Point of View" (Cell 1989: 483). Not without a little irony, Cell notes that this surrender might be in the reverse direction.

Malinowski's views on indirect rule were political, despite his insistence on the scientific endeavor that was functionalist anthropology (Gellner 1987). His position on cultural change was that it should not be mandated from above, and he was particularly critical of the consequences of direct rule, as could be seen in the settler colonies of Kenya, Southern Rhodesia, and South Africa. He openly wrote, condemning forced labor (then a major reformist issue), harsh taxation, and arbitrary imposition of "European" laws—in effect, anything that threatened the native's own "culture." He was entirely aware of the devastating effects of blackbirding in the Melanesian region where he conducted his major fieldwork and critiqued land alienation in Africa with some vitriol. In this light, Malinowski's politics were very much of his own time. Yet some contradictions in his politics have been noted by observers of his life.

Ernest Gellner, going further into Malinowski's youth in the Hapsburg Empire, even argued that he was not opposed to colonialism, nor did he really think that Africans and other colonial peoples were "fit to rule themselves," a sentiment that had sympathetic assent throughout the British Empire on the eve of the colonial reforms (cf. Matthews).

Gellner argues that the essence of Malinowski's political thought was reducible to a three-part equation: "Hapsburg Empire = League of Nations = indirect rule" (Gellner 1987:557). Although an administrator might champion indirect rule as a "cheap" form of governance, the appeal among people like Malinowski was not that it resolved practical problems facing the colonizers but rather that it offered to preserve the indigenous culture, while direct rule erodes them, as was assumed to happen in the settler colonies. In making the case that anthropologists could work with colonial officials to ameliorate the conditions of colonial rule, he wrote:

> The real difference between "direct rule" and "indirect or dependent rule" consists in the fact that direct rule assumes that you can create at one go an entirely new order, that you can transform Africans into semi-civilized pseudo-European citizens within a few years. Indirect rule, on the other hand, recognizes that no such magical rapid transformation can take place, that in reality all social development is very slow, and that it is infinitely preferable to achieve it by a slow and gradual change coming from within. (Malinowski 1929:23)

This approach to the native question became known in the 1930s as "gradualism." The functionalist bend to this argument is apparent, but it contains something of a moral argument. One of Malinowski's chief concerns in his 1929 paper on practical anthropology was that the object of field studies should be the "changing native." He argued that the erosion or subversion of an "old system of traditions, of morals or laws" would give rise to what he called "black bolshevism," the emergence of some form of African nationalism that was then already in nascent form (Malinowski 1929: 28). In comparing how American anthropologists under Boas practiced salvage ethnography to what he hoped his functionalist anthropology could achieve, Malinowski stressed the importance of studying the here and now of the native: "Even in their study of the fully detribalised and Yankified Indian, our United States colleagues persistently ignore the Indian as he is and study the Indian-as-he-must-have-been some century or two back" (28). It is clear from these statements that Malinowski acknowledged change but was committed to the idea that the best changes were gradual.

Gradualism did not deny that the colonized had been changed by European domination, but it still held out that their proper line of development was along "their own lines" and that the erosion of tradition was lamentable. More worrying, from the point of view of colonial administrators, was the scare that too fast a change would lead to some kind of challenge to colonialism itself. The so-called detribalized "Native" was a threat to the colonial order. In proposing that Africans be ruled through their own institutions—however much under European supervision—Malinowski was supporting a fundamental legal dualism. Gradualism, in turn, suggested the happy thought that when the "native" was ready for "natural law," the time would arrive for an end to "legal particularism." Until that time, however, the best resolution to the native question would be to encourage the development of native administration under the Dual Mandate. Isaac Schapera, in a review of economic change and African laborers, warned in 1929, however, that colonial policies had encouraged differentiation among African subjects, a by-product of indirect rule. Not sharing Malinowski's perspective, Schapera stated, "Any attempt to deal with all these different classes as a single unity is doomed to failure. We must recognize their differences, and approach the particular problems they each present, with no illusion about the uniformity of the native question" (Schapera 1928:188). In anthropological recommendations to colonial policymakers, Malinowski's emergent brand of functionalism would be used to support legal dualism, while still advocating that the real focus of modern anthropological fieldwork would be the "changing native."

The question of how functionalism could have supported legal dualism from a theoretical point of view is critical in understanding anthropology's legacy in contemporary Africa. Malinowski claimed that while the "savage" held his own "criminal" and "civil" codes, these were still very different from European jurisprudence. In reviewing the colonial administration's attempts to codify African systems of land tenure, for example, Malinowski observed that European lawyers were likely to impose their own cultural framework in making their recommendations—a mistake, he argued, that a trained ethnographer would be able to overcome. In making the case for the anthropologist's competence in the analysis and translation of "native law," he warned that the "untrained European . . . uses words such as 'communism,' 'individualism,' 'private property,' 'tribal property' . . . without giving them the slightest intelligible meaning, or understanding himself what he is talking about" (1929: 31). This meant that anthropologists were in the best possible position to comment on colonial policy and the impacts such policies would have for the politics of "race relations" in Africa.

IMPERIAL AIR: MALINOWSKI IN AFRICA

By 1934, Malinowski's grasp on the political situation in colonial Africa was informed by the field reports filed by his numerous students. These were all research fellows of the African Institute or were funded through the LSE with grants administered through the university system by the Rockefeller Foundation. The Laura Spelman Rockefeller Memorial fellowships, awarded through the African Institute, were to mature in 1936, after which anthropological research would need to rely upon other sources of funding. Having never been to Africa for any extensive period, the opportunity to attend the New Education Fellowship Conference, hosted at the University of Witwatersrand in the summer of 1934, was enthusiastically seized by Malinowski. In his travel grant application, Malinowski touted the benefit of being able to visit five research students in their respective field sites in southern and eastern Africa. These were Godfrey and Monica Wilson (Nyakusa), Hilda Beemer (Swazi), Günther Wagner (Maragoli), and Kalvero Oberg (Banyankole). He also endorsed a preliminary survey study of African and European attitudes toward colonial administration, particularly the doctrine of indirect rule.

Most of his students traveled to their African field sites on passenger ships and, depending on the favor of Malinowski's reference letters, secured second or third class passages. Imperial Air, however, was Malinowski's carrier when he flew, circuitously, from London to Cape Town, across a continent he had never set eyes upon. That this trip left an impression there can be no doubt, for it seemed to bring into sharp focus many of the theoretical and ideological arguments he had made over the previous decade. Flying below cloud lines, from one airfield after another, in a constant search for petrol, Malinowski literally "saw" Africa before any other part of the continent's life came to his senses.

Perhaps inspired by the Archimedean vantage point of air flight and the way that life, on the ground, is telescoped into a functional model-like existence, Malinowski would later write something about what he saw: "A Bird's-Eye View of Africa Today" (1938).

The evocation of differing kinds of "Africa" became, for Malinowski, emblematic of much of his rhetoric for studying the "native as he is," the principal tenet of functionalist rhetoric against historicist reconstruction. His students' ethnographic writings from mining camps in Tanganyika to agro-pastoralists in the Gold Coast emphasized the diversity of social organizations and cultures to be found in Africa. Flying over the marshes of the Upper Nile, then refueling at a mining camp, before resting in a Nairobi hotel bed was a pastiche of experiences that represented, to Malinowski, a tripartite division of "old Africa, imported Africa, and the new composite culture" (1938). Fragments of his prose are worth presenting:

> The circular villages built on the old pattern without a single touch of European architecture; the Natives in their old clothes—or lack of them—moving among the cattle penned in the inner enclosure; the obvious isolation of each settlement in what appear to be almost inaccessible swamps—all this gives at least a surface effect of old untouched Africa. . . .
>
> Among the Baganda the houses are new, square, built on the European pattern; even from above, the dress and ornaments of the Natives spell Manchester and Birmingham. Roads and churches, motor cars and lorries, proclaim that we are in a world of change in which two factors are working together and producing a new type of culture, related both to Europe and Africa, yet not a mere copy of either. . . .
>
> And then not far away, in a settler's bungalow or in a small European community, you listen to music from England on the short wave, and enjoy "purely European" song all about "Alabama" and the "Baby" and the "Coon crooning with the crickets"; you can read the latest *Tatler* or *Sketch*, and enjoy a discussion on sport, local or overseas, or English party politics.

In these descriptions of alterity and mimesis, there is a clear division, even a tension, owed to the institutional separation of different categories of people. In a description of a white household in Nairobi, this observed separation is palpable: "This world the African enters only as a shadowy figure: the servant bringing the tray with 'sundowner' drinks" (Malinowski 1938). Here, in the midst of culture contact, racial segregation is institutionalized and hardened but not indifferent.

Malinowski's travels to southern and eastern Africa are important because both race relations and indirect rule seem to dominate his correspondence. Among the various newspaper clippings that he culled from various South African and Kenyan newspapers, two major themes captured Malinowski's imagination. The first are efforts in psychology and, specifically, the application of IQ testing on ascertaining racial differences in mental aptitude between Europeans and Africans. The second and more important was the growing body of press editorials on African self-determination. It is at this point where the native question ceases to be premised on cultural differences alone, hinted at through more and more attention to the detribalized Native, but by officially legislated institutional segregation. There is tension in some of his notes at this time. In handwritten notes, often on the back of mimeographed briefs of conference papers, Malinowski is obsessed by race and indirect rule. On the back of a letter inviting Malinowski to visit Bloemfontein, he scrawled what appears to be the outline of a lecture on indirect rule:

> "'Indirect Rule' the dominant motif in Africa," then "wider" and "develop": effects on African lives (separation/segregation) Why? Hypothesis: "Dual Mandate" to "recognition of rights"—cheaper— less burdensome of all burdens—most educated Africans against /African religion, African schools, African movement—universal clamour for self-determination.
>
> Here's anthros—we can teach you, we can show you the way, we can open your eyes, but thank you? No, for you'll have to pay the price.
> Anthros conservative factors—retribalize, suspend...land hunger.

The notion of "rights" is indicative of Malinowski's increasing attention to the legal difficulties of European trusteeship. He grew more cautious of the rhetoric of terms like "separation" and "segregation," seeing that the real problem in colonial Africa was one of how long

European hegemony would last. Malinowski warned that the costs of failing to adjust to the native question could cost the empire, even though he did not explicitly state such a position. He recognized that the emergent African elite were opposed and even hostile to the idea that there should be separate institutions for Africans, like schools and courts, because they could see the iniquity that this brought in a plural, multiracial society. Finally, Malinowski could see conflict and the implications this held for anthropologists working on the native question: "Here's anthros—we can teach you, we can show you the way, we can open your eyes, but thank you? No, for you'll have to pay the price." What price did Malinowski have in mind?

South African newspapers, of which Malinowski kept clippings, lend some clue as to the political climate in southern African during 1934. Citing his addresses at the Witswaterand conference on education, the *Johannesburg Star*, July 26, 1934, carried the headline "Natives Must Be Given Their Rights: Development to Political Self-Government / Professor Malinowski's View as a Scientist." In the language of "self-determination," Malinowski's shifting views of the native question turned toward the inevitable crisis that institutional and territorial segregation would bring the South Africa. In paraphrasing Malinowski's views on indirect rule, the *Star* quoted the following:

"Sooner or later the Protectorates, too—but I must not speak of these—sooner or later they, too, will receive the rights of indirect rule. Political self-government is the line of development. It is as good to give it as to demand. If we impose burdens and responsibilities we must also grant the privileges and advantages that go with them.

"The native should be given his economic rights and the right to develop along his own lines—his rights territorially, economically, and politically. Sacrifices would be demanded from the white man and the white man must be prepared to make them.

"I believe," concluded Prof. Malinowski, "that as South Africa has led the world in the solution of her own internal problem, so she will also show us the way out here. Anthropologists can help only by showing to the native the value of his own culture and thus revive in him his own faith in himself."

Although Malinowski had still not renounced his belief that racial differences were irrelevant to the actual political realities of racial segregation, his rhetoric takes on a sharper tone from his 1934 visit to Africa.

Malinowski's trip to Africa brought about a change in perspective. In a letter written to Oldham, shortly after returning to London, Malinowski said, "I am back from Africa a wiser and sadder man. There are lots of things—not all of them pleasant—which I have to discuss with you arising out of the trip." Like his 1929 tour of the United States, Malinowski's travels throughout southern and eastern Africa brought about a shift in his political thinking, but also some contradictions.

The most immediate change in Malinowski's thinking was that he grew more openly critical about the "welfare" of colonial subjects. His attitude to colonial paternalism becomes more blunt:

> There is no doubt that the destiny of indigenous races has been tragic in the process of contact with European invasion. We speak glibly about the "spread of Western civilization," about "giving the Natives the benefit of our own culture," about the "Dual Mandate," and the "White Man's Burden." In Reality, the historian of the future will have to register that Europeans in the past sometimes exterminated whole island peoples; that they expropriated most of the patrimony of savage races; that they introduced slavery in a specially cruel and pernicious form; and that even if they abolished it later, they treated the expatriated Negroes as outcasts and pariahs. (Malinowski 1961:4)

Participation in the New Education Fellowship Conference, along with Isaac Shapira and other prominent South African anthropologists, allowed him to deliver at least one critical address that won him scorn in the South African, especially Afrikaans, press. In a speech entitled "African (Negro) Patriotism," Malinowski earned the ire of some Afrikaners whose support for segregation was growing as the political tensions of nationalist party activities found resistance across a wide spectrum of South African society. As contradictory as ever, Malinowski penciled this speech as his "Nig Lecture"!

The impact of Malinowski in southern Africa perhaps should not be overstated. Even with respect to anthropology, his influence was moderate and not always welcome. In visiting his students, however,

Malinowski came into contact with the problematic themes of economic compulsion, labor migration, shifts in domestic life, changes in marriage and bridewealth, and other themes linked to detribalization. His visits to Hilda Beemer, among the Swazi, brought him into contact with the Paramount Chief of the Swazi, Sobhuza II, who, along with his solicitor, was petitioning the House of Commons and the deputation of the Colonial Secretary against the incorporation of Swaziland into the Union of South Africa. In Moshi, Tanganyika, Malinowski sought to investigate conditions of native life, perceived administrative problems, and wanted to speak with members of the "white community," mainly settlers, traders, missionaries, and planters. In his visit to Günther Wagner, among the Maragoli, North Kavirondo, Kenya, Malinowski would come face-to-face with the impact of a newly opened gold mine, seeing for himself some of the effects his students encountered in their fieldwork. With this experience behind him, Malinowski returned to London having formed a critically revised stance on the native question, as it pertained to future colonial rule in Africa.

Malinowski's visit to eastern and southern Africa did, however, strain his relationship with other directors of the African Institute, notably Oldham. His relationships with some of the first Rockefeller fellows, particularly Hofstra and Fortes, were also strained owing to a perceived sleight in their loyalty to Malinowski following their independent communications with other IIACL directors. Oldham criticized Malinowski for not following up his letters while touring his students, chidingly claiming that he had failed to carry his responsibility in choosing "to bury yourself for some months in the wilds of Africa." And, significantly, Oldham had reason to question Malinowski's inaccessibility during his African tour, since the tides had turned against Rockefeller funds and the grant to the African Institute was in its last phases.

CONCLUSIONS

What we now call "functionalism" owes its prominence, in part, to a theoretical tension that existed quite independently from anthropology: the native question. My aim is to show that anthropologists and administrators were compelled to address the question of the colonial subject because it was one of the dominant issues of their day, not a bit unlike our contemporary and contingent concern with human rights, the environment, or indigenous peoples.

The main thrust of my argument is that anthropologists' relationships to colonialism must not be seen as exceptional or particular but rather as a form of governmentality. We should probably retain Foucault's original sense of governmentality as the "conduct of conduct," seen as a way of analyzing power outside of the conventional oppositions of state/civil society, domination/emancipation, government/governed. As Nikolas Rose (1999:3) puts it, this kind of governance "refers to all endeavors to shape, guide, direct the conduct of others, whether these be the crew of a ship, the members of a household, the employees of a boss, the children of a family, or the inhabitants of a territory." This seems perhaps a more promising avenue of analyzing the political stakes of indirect rule, since none of these formal categories really applied to African subjects who were denied any civil entitlements outside of race, tribe, and gender. Under the same notion of governmentality, we can also seek to locate the anthropologist, the missionary, the chief, and the administrator, since all had to define the "conduct of conduct" for each other. Peter Pels and Oscar Salemink (1994:15) make the point that anthropologists were not in a position to examine colonial assumptions, because their contact with a variety of colonial agents "necessarily led to the sharing of discursive patterns." This was especially the case when it came to the native question, because each specific answer to this problem space came from these stakeholders. If anthropologists would like to understand how the personalities and institutions of the past have interrogated the native question, whether in Africa or elsewhere, they must be prepared to treat colonialism not as a past *problematique*, not as an intellectual game, but as an enduring, albeit transformed, form of governance that shapes our conduct and our practice today as it did for past generations of anthropologists.

Contemporary ethnographers cannot sweep the legacies of indirect rule aside. It is fallacious to argue that such legacies no longer bear any relation to those vestiges of the native question that continue to exist. One need only examine the root of the 1994 Rwandan genocide in the policies of Belgium rule to see the long, historical basis that the native question has had for surviving Tutsi, Hutu, and Twa (Mamdani

2001). Justice for working citizens continues to be elusive. In a similar vein, attempts to understand the emergence of "private indirect government" in geographically large and contiguous parts of sub-Saharan Africa points to continuities in policy in the 1930s and today, linkages which frequently take as their starting premise a rather shocking crisis of citizenship among Africans (cf. Mbembe 2001: 66–101). Rather, those working in the present, especially in Africa, must take into account the forms of governmentality that underpin and guide how we accept "political conceptions of human collectivities" (Rose 1999: 5).

Colonialism cannot be seen as a uniform process, spelled out exactly in the same ways all over the world, but its brutality can be stressed whether one is looking at its effects in Soweto or in Kanawake. For quite a number of anthropologists today, the problem really is one of exorcism, in the sense that individual anthropologists erroneously presume that the discipline can be de-colonized. It is an error to proceed with such a project, exactly because de-colonization is a residual concept, resting upon the original and more powerful historical fact of colonialism (I attribute this idea to Mamdani). Coming to terms with the legacy of colonialism means that scholarship needs to identify the impasse reached by questioning colonialism, by stressing its "de-" or "post-" before these have been proven. As Peter Pels (1997:164) frames it, "colonialism is not a historical object that remains external to the observer." Tied to this, Pels reminds us that the "techniques of observation," namely censuses, mapping, travel writing, and ethnography, are still very much with us and still inform what he calls "western governmentality." Scholarship must examine existing forms of such power in all their historical specificity and map out how such forms of governmentality have managed to slip under the radar. Before scholars recognize their political ambitions toward such legacies, the problem of residual concepts must be addressed and their unilinear, evolutionist underpinnings made explicit.

Theoretically, anthropology is rife with such residual concepts, whose epistemological existence owes everything to the root from which they grow. "Non-Europeans" are residual to the already-there category of the European. "Underdevelopment" is seconded to the centrally organizing concept of development. The list of such residual concepts, stemming from core concepts and core identities, seems to dominate much of the literature dealing with the effects of colonialism. Part of our problem today lies in finding a way out of rooting our interpretations of colonialism in a series of ill-conceived temporalities. Hence when we speak about "pre-capitalist" or "pre-colonial," which are the operative and stronger referents? Obviously when anthropologists begin to speak about their place in colonialism, our focus should attempt to break away from the core-residue dilemma. This essay calls for such a break through discussing colonialist ideas before anthropology, before looking at particular anthropologists' relationships to colonial institutions and epistemologies.

NOTE

1. Malinowski, 8/2 Rockefeller Files, LSE.

REFERENCES

Amselle, Jean-Loup. 1998. Mestizo Logics: Anthropology of Identity in Africa and Elsewhere. Stanford: Stanford University Press.

Asad, Talal, ed. 1973. Anthropology and the Colonial Encounter. London: Ithaca Press.

Barkan, Elazar. 1993. The Retreat of Scientific Racism: Changing Concepts of Race in Britain and the United States between the World Wars. Cambridge: Cambridge University Press.

Berman, Bruce. 1992. Control and Crisis in Colonial Kenya: The Dialectic of Domination. Athens: Ohio University Press.

Buell, Raymond Leslie. 1965. The Native Problem in Africa. Vol. 2. London: Frank Cass.

Cell, John. 1982. The Highest Stage of White Supremacy: The Origins of Segregation in South Africa and the American South. Cambridge: University of Cambridge Press.

———. 1989. Lord Hailey and the Making of the African Survey. African Affairs 88 (353):481–505.

Dahrendorf, Ralf. 1995. LSE: A History of the London School of Economics and Political Science, 1895–1995. Oxford: Oxford University Press.

Darnell, Regna. 1982. The Role of History of Anthropology in the Anthropology Curriculum. Journal of the History of the Behavioural Sciences 18:265–270.

———. 1998. And Along Came Boas: Continuity and Revolution in Americanist Anthropology. Philadelphia: John Benjamins.

Fardon, Richard. 1990. Malinowski's Precedent: The Imagination of Equality. Journal of the Royal Anthropological Institute n.s. 26:569–587.

Firth, Raymond. 1988. Malinowski in the History of Social Anthropology. *In* Malinowski between Two Worlds: The Polish Roots of an Anthropological Tradition. Roy Ellen, ed. Pp. 12–42. Cambridge: Cambridge University Press.

Fisher, Donald. 1980. American Philanthropy and the Social Sciences: The Reproduction of a Conservative Ideology. *In* Philanthropy and Cultural Imperialism: The Foundations at Home and Abroad. Robert Arnove, ed. Boston: G. K. Hall.

———. 1986. Rockefeller Philanthropy and the Rise of Social Anthropology. Anthropology Today 2(1):5–8.

Gellner, Ernest. 1986. Original Sin: The Legacy of Malinowski and the Future of Anthropology. Times Higher Education Supplement, October 10, p. 13.

———. 1987. The Political Thought of Bronislaw Malinowski. Current Anthropology 28(4):557–559.

Goody, Jack. 1995. The Expansive Moment: Anthropology in Britain and Africa, 1918–1970. Cambridge: Cambridge University Press.

Gough, Kathleen. 1968. New Proposals for Anthropologists. Current Anthropology 9(5):403–435.

Hailey, Lord. 1957. An African Survey, Revised to 1956: A Study of Problems Arising in Africa South of the Sahara. New York: Oxford University Press.

Hofmeyr, Jan. 1937. The Approach to the Native Problem. Journal of the Royal African Society. Pp. 270–297.

Hymes, Dell. 1974. Reinventing Anthropology. New York: Vintage Books.

James, Wendy. 1973. The Anthropologist as Reluctant Imperialist. *In* Anthropology and the Colonial Encounter. Talal Asad, ed. Pp. 41–69. London: Ithaca Press

Jarvie, Ian. 1964. The Revolution in Anthropology. London: Routledge & Kegan Paul.

Kuklick, Henrika. 1991. The Savage Within: The Social History of British Anthropology, 1885–1945. New York: Cambridge University Press.

Kuper, Adam. 1983. Anthropology and Anthropologists: The Modern British School. 2nd ed. London: Routledge and Kegan Paul.

Loizos, Peter. 1977. Anthropological Research in British Colonies: Some Personal Accounts. Anthropological Forum 4 (2):137–144.

MacMillan, Hugh, and Shula Marks, eds. 1989. Africa and Empire: W. M. Macmillan, Historian and Social Critic. Aldershot: Published for the Institute of Commonwealth Studies by Temple Smith.

Mair, Lucy. 1936. Native Policies in Africa. London: George Routledge.

Malinowski, Bronislaw. 1922. Argonauts of the Western Pacific: An Account of Native Enterprise and Adventure in the Archipelagoes of Melanesian New Guinea. London: Routledge and Sons.

———. 1929. Practical Anthropology. Africa 2(1): 22–38.

———. 1930. The Rationalization of Anthropology and Administration. Africa 3(4): 405–430.

———. 1938. Introductory Essay on the Anthropology of Changing African Cultures. In Methods of Study of Culture Contact in Africa. Bronislaw Malinowski, ed. Oxford: Oxford University Press.

———. 1961. The Dynamics of Culture Change: An Inquiry into Race Relations in Africa. New Haven: Yale University Press.

Mamdani, Mahmood. 1996. Citizen and Subject. Princeton: Princeton University Press.

———. 2001. When Victims Become Killers: Colonialism, Nativism, and the Genocide in Rwanda. Princeton: Princeton University Press.

Mbembe, Achille. 2001. On the Postcolony. Berkeley: University of California Press.

Myres, J. L. 1929. The Science of Man in the Service of the State: Presidential Address to the Royal Anthropological Institute. Journal of the Royal Anthropological Institute 59:38–42.

Oldham, J. H. 1924. Christianity and the Race Problem. New York: George H. Doran.

Pels, Peter. 1997. The Anthropology of Colonialism: Culture, History, and the Emergence of Western Governmentality. Annual Review of Anthropology 26:163–183.

Pels, Peter, and Oscar Salemink. 1994. Five Theses on Ethnography as Colonial Practice. History and Anthropology 8(1–4):1–34.

Radcliffe-Brown, A. R. 1922. The Andaman Islanders. New York: Free Press.

Rich, Paul. 1984. White Power and the Liberal Conscience: Racial Segregation and South African Liberalism, 1921–60. Manchester: Manchester University Press.

Rose, Nikolas. 1999. Powers of Freedom: Reframing Political Thought. New York: Cambridge University Press.

Schafft, Gretchen. 2004. From Racism to Genocide: Anthropology in the Third Reich. Urbana: University of Illinois Press.

Schapera, Isaac. 1928. Economic Changes in South African Native Life. Africa 1(2): 170–188.

Smuts, Jan Christiaan. 1930. Africa and Some World Problems. Oxford: Clarendon Press.

Urry, James. 1989. Headhunters and Body-Snatchers. Anthropology Today 5:11–13

IAN CAMPBELL

4

Radcliffe-Brown and "Applied Anthropology" at Cape Town and Sydney

A. R. Radcliffe-Brown (1881–1955) was one of the founders of modern social anthropology. His published output was not large, but it was influential. His reputation was probably greater through his teaching and personal contacts, for he was a compelling lecturer with an apparently powerful and attractive personality. The extent of his fieldwork is compared unfavorably with that of his contemporary, Bronislaw Malinowski (though Malinowski's only sustained experience of fieldwork was his enforced stay in the Trobriands). Hence Radcliffe-Brown is known mainly as a theorist, not as an ethnographer, and as an advocate of pure research grounded in the scientific method. At the close of his life he was said to be interested only in new insights into anthropological theory (Firth 1956:302). However, for ten years he was engaged in work in which "applied" anthropology featured strongly, and the practical potential of anthropology was a theme to which he returned periodically. Evaluations of his career dismiss or misconstrue this aspect of his work.

A further characteristic of Radcliffe-Brown that distinguishes him from other leading figures of the first half of the twentieth century is that his career was peripatetic. Over a period of less than twenty years he was appointed to and accepted chairs in four universities on four continents—three of them foundational chairs (Cape Town, 1921–25, Sydney, 1925–31, Chicago, 1931–37, and Oxford, 1937–46)—as well as visiting appointments in China and Brazil and after retirement in Egypt and South Africa. This mobility has led to the perception that he was an initiator, not a consolidator, that his ambition was greater than his ability to achieve, and that in the damning words of one university head, he was a "careerist" (Phillips 1993:25), presumably meaning one whose primary motivation was the eminence of prestige positions rather than a lasting contribution to an institution or discipline.

Such strictures echo the faint praise and stern judgments of his successor at the University of Sydney, A. P. Elkin, that Radcliffe-Brown left when he had finished the foundational work to which he was "temperamentally suited," although he took anthropology into an "ivory tower" (Elkin 1956:242, 243). These critical remarks pale in comparison with the trenchant condemnation of Elkin's biographer in whose view Radcliffe-Brown's department in Sydney collapsed as a result of his antagonizing people through duplicitous, spiteful, and vindictive conduct (Wise 1985:97–102). An authority on the history of anthropology estimates Radcliffe-Brown's tenure of the chair as "in the end only just short of disastrous" owing to his "overbearing ways and political maladroitness" (Kuper 1983:46). These judgments cumulatively label Radcliffe-Brown with a damning trinity as a restless egotist who was shy of fieldwork. These assessments, however, contradict the obituaries and appreciations written by those who knew him best and, more to the point, the archival documentation of his work in both Cape Town and Sydney.

FROM FIELD EXPERIENCE TO APPLIED ANTHROPOLOGY

Radcliffe-Brown's career began with two extended periods of fieldwork. The first, 1906–1908, was conducted in the Andaman Islands and formed the basis for his fellowship thesis and later book, *The Andaman Islanders* (1922). On returning to England in 1909 he was appointed to a lectureship at the University of London. He gave this up to undertake his second extended period of fieldwork, from 1910 to 1912, mainly in Western Australia. After a further period in Britain he returned to Australia to attend the 1914 meeting of the British Association for the Advancement of Science and to undertake further research (Schapera 1990:10). The outbreak of the First World War upset his plans, and after being rejected for military service, he taught at Sydney Church of England Grammar School from 1915 to 1917 (Schapera 1990:8). This allowed him little time, opportunity, or surplus income for research or a way to leave Australia, so it is perhaps not surprising that at the end of 1917 he took the conjunct positions of director of education in Tonga and principal of Tonga College (Tonga 1918:21).[1] The prospect of getting close to a society in which a functioning exotic culture was literally on his doorstep was possibly an attraction.

Radcliffe-Brown's tenure was brief. He left Tonga after only one year. The government of Tonga was in a chaotic state at the time. Radcliffe-Brown's predecessor had resigned four years earlier when his attempts at educational reform were frustrated by government lethargy and opposition, and it is likely that Radcliffe-Brown suffered much the same way. The much-needed reforms that he instituted or advocated mainly lapsed after his departure (Campbell 1957:101–108). Moreover, the lung complaint that had troubled him since childhood was probably exacerbated in Tonga's humid climate where tuberculosis was already established (Campbell 2003:138). He explained later that he was invalided from Tonga (Schapera 1990:1). He left Tonga on the same steamer, *Talune*, that had introduced the 1918 influenza pandemic (Herda 1994), and broke his journey in Fiji where the influenza was already raging. There he worked as a volunteer with the sick. His departure was probably on the next monthly circuit of the same steamer. In this way he had the opportunity to visit Samoa before returning to Australia, presumably but not necessarily via New Zealand.[2]

Now unemployed, Radcliffe-Brown's next move was to South Africa where his brother lived and where the dry air of the Transkei was possibly an attraction to improve his health.[3] In 1920 he had temporary work teaching English and psychology with hopes of securing a curatorship at the Pretoria Museum. In June he made inquiries in response to reports of the creation of a chair in anthropology at the University of Cape Town.[4] Any position in anthropology would have attracted Radcliffe-Brown in 1920, but Cape Town had the advantage of being near at hand as well as available. There was a further aspect that may have weighed heavily with him—the potential utility of social anthropology as a practical help in managing social issues. The rationale for the chair was the need in a plural society for expertise in social processes. Since reading Durkheim years earlier, Radcliffe-Brown saw anthropology as the "science of society" and considered it in the nature of a science to enable the manipulation or management of natural phenomena.

Between 1906 and 1920 Radcliffe-Brown had spent perhaps ten years in colonial or semicolonial situations. Perhaps three years qualified as formal field research, and he had opportunities to observe and meet indigenous peoples and those who worked with them. As an anthropologist with a particular interest in theory beyond ethnographic recording—in developing social anthropology into the science of society—it is unlikely that any of these experiences were of no interest or use to him. Indeed, it is likely that his Polynesian experience was more important in his life than has previously been recognized, and it contributed to his choices of how he would spend the next ten years. In three related societies, under related jurisdictions, Radcliffe-Brown had witnessed the inept application of attempts to introduce western education in a British protectorate (Tonga), the ravages of an introduced disease in a British Crown colony (Fiji), and the calamitous effect of administrative failure in a German possession under New Zealand military administration (Western Samoa). Twelve years after his brief visit to Western Samoa, when the territory was embroiled in controversy, he commented:

> I believe that the reason is that no systematic, or at any rate successful, attempt has been made to understand the Samoans and their point of view.
>
> Samoa used to have what I think is one of the most efficient and satisfactory forms of government to be found anywhere in the world.... A proper understanding of it can probably only be obtained by those who have been trained in the scientific study of civilizations. The assistance of a competent anthropologist, or a proper training in anthropology for the administrative officers, would, I fully believe, have saved and could still save much of the existing friction between the natives and those who have assumed control of their destinies.
>
> Australia has recognised the need of assistance from anthropology in the administration of its Mandated Territory. Why does not New Zealand do the same?[5]

By this time Radcliffe-Brown had accumulated eight years of experience in providing the training that he advocated, but the final sentence suggests that this letter was not mere self-promotion or surreptitious advertising for his courses. That his mind had long been turning on these matters is implied by lectures he delivered at the University of Birmingham as far back as 1913 when lobbyists were advocating the establishment of anthropology in British universities for utilitarian reasons.[6] He was still urging the importance of anthropological knowledge by administrators and others at the end of his life (Radcliffe-Brown 1950: 1).

His work for over a decade was to display a commitment to two dimensions of what was coming to be known as "applied anthropology." One was a bureau of ethnology on the American model to be a clearing house for information about indigenous societies; the other was taking the insights of social anthropology to officials and missionaries whose professional lives were spent working with native peoples, for the better management of the latter.

FINDING A NICHE

Pressure had been increasing on the South African government to raise the level of expertise of people working with native South Africans. Industrialization was creating a new class of urban blacks; the effects of labor migration on village communities were visible but not understood. No one could be blind to the "native problem." Anthropological lobbyists had been making this case at least since 1902 when the South African Association for the Advancement of Science was established (Schapera 1990: 2). In 1918 the SAAAS further urged the scientific study of African society; a resolution was forwarded to the Union government by the University of Cape Town Council, urging the importance of research into native languages and society.[7] The government responded by establishing a committee on university grants, the Coleman Committee, the ensuing report of which on the subject of ethnography recommended that the government "establish a school of such strength as will show a real and adequate interest on the part of South Africa in problems whose solution is necessary for the future safe development of a country in which white and black are to live side by side." These were referred to as "the most serious problems of South Africa," and the study of native society was "one not merely for the world of science but peculiarly linked with problems of administration." The Coleman report recommended that a school be established at the University of

Cape Town rather than having the effort dispersed among several universities, and it also suggested the creation of a bureau of information and museum (1919: 7–8). The government responded by offering a grant of £3,000 p.a. for five years, on the condition that the University of Cape Town provide £1,000 p.a., consult the Department of Native Affairs on the formation of the school, and obtain the approval of the minister of native affairs.[8] A bureau of ethnography was referred to by Radcliffe-Brown in a letter (20 March 1920) to his patron at Cambridge, A. C. Haddon, urging him to put the suggestion to Prime Minister Jan Smuts. It is not clear whether Radcliffe-Brown had read the Coleman report at the time, but it is clear from his letter that he had in mind that the bureau be established as part of the Pretoria museum where he was an applicant for the curatorship (Schapera 1990:1–2).[9] In this way, he would be able to turn the museum curatorship away from the care of material objects in which he had little interest and toward the ethnographic work that he wanted to do. Haddon obligingly wrote to Smuts urging an ethnological bureau for both scientific and practical purposes, "since it is well-recognised that the good Government of Native races depends largely upon sympathy based upon accurate knowledge. Ethnology is increasingly recognised as being a science which has very real practical value."[10] The idea traveled with Radcliffe-Brown from Pretoria to Cape Town and thence to Sydney. The amassing and collation of information was important not only for the comparative analysis that was foundational for the framing of laws of social organization but also as a resource for those who would be engaged in applied anthropology.

Radcliffe-Brown began work at the museum in Pretoria in January 1921 (Schapera 1990:6) by which time the chair at the University of Cape Town had been advertised.[11] He was preeminently the most highly qualified candidate. The selection committee (Frazer, Haddon, Marett, and Rivers) clearly expected that field research would be among Radcliffe-Brown's contributions in South Africa, and the tenor of the Coleman report on which UCT acted was clearly in favor of appointments that would add to the knowledge of African societies. It was clear from the circumstances of appointment that both "pure" and "applied" work was intended in the provision for Bantu studies, and that for both intellectual reasons and as a result of experience, this dual role accorded closely with Radcliffe-Brown's outlook. Notwithstanding, he moved on to Sydney after only five years without having undertaken any significant field research, or creating the proposed bureau, or forming a cohort of anthropologically informed civil servants. The reasons were both sound and revealing.

POLITICS AT THE UNIVERSITY OF CAPE TOWN

Radcliffe-Brown took up his appointment at UCT on 1 August 1921, joining W. A. Norton, who had been appointed professor of Bantu philology in April 1920 along the lines proposed in the Coleman report. Radcliffe-Brown's work at UCT was to be framed by his relations with Norton, the tension between research and training, and the fate of the government grant. These were interrelated. As early as May 1922, it is evident that there were tensions developing. Norton was an Anglican clergyman and former missionary with an apparently intimate knowledge of several Bantu languages. However, he was unimaginative, an uninspiring teacher, and highly sensitive about questions of status and the value of his work. Rather than being a builder of the school, he was a drag on its progress. Norton's insecurities evidently made him a difficult man to work with, but the suggestion that Radcliffe-Brown undermined him and manipulated his removal is incorrect (Phillips 1993:22–24).[12] Norton could not attract students, and his research was not considered of much merit. Within two years, his competence and productivity were in question.

Radcliffe-Brown chafed at being harnessed with a man who shared neither his energy nor his outlook. Whereas anthropology was off to a good start, the languages were not, and Radcliffe-Brown was anxious even at that early time of the need to show results if the school were to continue. He urged Norton in May 1922 to collaborate in establishing the Bureau of Ethnology within the school of African Life and Languages to justify the government grant and demonstrate their value. To that end, Radcliffe-Brown had laid aside his former interests and begun looking into Bantu law. Evidently Norton chided Radcliffe-Brown with not being interested in fieldwork. Radcliffe-Brown's response is important in understanding his future career choices: he pointed out that he had a track record in fieldwork but could do more to advance the state of knowledge by training others to do fieldwork than to attempt to do it alone, and that the immediate need was to organize existing knowledge. Their school had two masters to satisfy, the university and the government, and he pleaded for an agreed strategy for the school.[13]

By late 1922 Norton, despondent at attracting not students but criticism from the university principal, was already hoping for a job elsewhere. By June 1923 relations were strained over Norton having failed to collaborate with Radcliffe-Brown and having unwittingly undermined the latter's attempts to induce the government to recognize that public servants in native affairs should take courses at UCT. Norton had also disparaged Radcliffe-Brown's work at a senate meeting, presumably in justifying their lack of collaboration. As early as April 1923, the future of Norton's chair came under consideration, but Norton preempted discussion by announcing his intention to resign at the expiry of the five-year funding arrangement with the government in April 1925.[14] Later he attempted to withdraw his resignation, but it was too late to retrieve the position because his student enrollments continued to be negligible and he had alienated the people whose support he most needed. This included the principal, J. C. Beattie.[15]

Norton had difficulty settling into any situation. A former mission superior chastised him for his restlessness and impatience with authority. He had been anxious to get the appointment at Cape Town and then anxious to get an appointment away from there. At the end of 1924 he went as principal to a theological college in Mauritius.[16]

Norton's unhappy experience at the university cannot be laid at Radcliffe-Brown's door. Whereas Norton had neither the aptitude nor the charm to build on his opportunity at UCT, Radcliffe-Brown was amply equipped with both. He quickly took the initiative in planning, organization, and strategy, for it was only after he joined the university that the development of the school seriously began.[17] He soon became an influential member of the university senate. Eventually he was a member of six out of eleven senate committees and chair of two. At only his second senate meeting a resolution was adopted to recommend to the government that all native affairs officers be required to study native languages, laws, and customs and that it accept a certificate from UCT attesting qualifications in those areas. He cultivated government in order to create a demand for courses in African Life and Languages, and he strove to establish the Bureau of Ethnology in order to launch a program of compilation and research. Clearly he could be an effective academic politician, but his talents were unequivocally employed in the interests of his discipline.

In April 1922 Radcliffe-Brown wrote a detailed memorandum to the senate on the proposed activities and scope of the school. It was evident that the initiative was coming from him, and his energy and strategic thinking reflected badly on Norton, his senior in tenure by more than a year. This memorandum was in effect a plan for what Radcliffe-Brown hoped to achieve at UCT, and he argued that because the subject matter of anthropology was rapidly disappearing, a team of researchers was necessary to gather data that should be organized on the model of the U.S. Bureau of Ethnology beginning with the compilation of available published data. The collection and collation of new information systematically should begin through informants using questionnaires to be followed by targeted research by trained field ethnologists. The necessary research, which could not reasonably be done by professors because of the lengthy residence in milieu required, needed additional staff. Provision should also be made for the publication of data, and finally the UCT should assume control over the ethnological collections of the South African Museum.[18]

By implication, Radcliffe-Brown's role would be the direction of an ambitious, coordinated program. The senate endorsed the proposals and observed in addition that although the university had conformed to the requirements of the Coleman report and government in designing the School of African Life and Languages, the government had cut the annual grant from the original £3,000 to £1,500.[19]

Meanwhile, the Public Service Commission, following a meeting with Radcliffe-Brown and two other professors, acknowledged the importance of qualifications for native affairs officers, but found the practical difficulties insuperable.[20] This meeting was vital. There was the material consideration that the viability of the school required students, and if students could be induced to enroll because of an official requirement or incentive, it would enhance the viability of the entire program. Not less important in Radcliffe-Brown's view was his conviction that people who were engaged in the management of a subordinate society should understand the consequences of their practices, appreciate the native outlook, and be acquainted with the dynamics of the native social system. He was in the position of offering a product capable of benefiting a discrete target market, and the market was failing to respond. If this aspect of the work should prove futile, his disappointment might be expected to be proportionate to the high value that he placed on it. Indeed, the work was urgent. As the Coleman report stated, issues to do with race were the most pressing ones facing the Union at the time. Unfortunately for Radcliffe-Brown's plans and for the school, the Public Service Commission concluded eventually that the public service was too small to allow either study leave or the specialization that recognition of qualifications in anthropology would imply.[21] In effect, this cut away much of the rationale for the school and the government subsidy.

Radcliffe-Brown's position on this was coherent and consistent. Personal field research was driven into the background by the sheer magnitude of what needed to be done to retrieve knowledge of rapidly changing societies. His proposals represented the way to accomplish comprehensive results in creating an informed administration to respond to the perceived urgency of managing racial and cultural contact. They would also be the most cost-effective way of adding to scientific knowledge and providing the basis for theoretical considerations.

TEACHING AT UTC

Radcliffe-Brown arrived at UTC with clear plans for the program he wanted to implement. Degree courses began in 1922.[22] Before he left Cape Town he instituted the diploma in anthropology for graduates, consisting of the undergraduate anthropology courses and a research dissertation. Radcliffe-Brown taught all courses himself. In addition to that he arranged vacation courses in the summer for people unable to attend university. The target audience included missionaries and native commissioners. The first was held in six weeks during February and March 1923. The *quid pro quo* for this extra work was to have his second term (the winter term) free for field research of his own, but

Radcliffe-Brown's term off did not eventuate. He handed the opportunity to a new colleague. The program was ambitious: Norton would give eight lectures on Bantu comparative philology and four on tribal histories. Dr. C. T. Loram would deliver nine lectures each on native education and native law and administration. The remaining lectures were Radcliffe-Brown's on principles of social anthropology (eighteen lectures), African ethnology (six), Bantu social systems (eight), and field methods (four).

The program was the subject of a very favorable testimonial endorsed by those who attended, expressing deep appreciation and judging it as meeting an urgent need. The letter also pointed to a fundamental difficulty that had already been the subject of attention: the low enrollment, which was attributed to the fact that the intended audience generally could not get leave from their various employments to take it.[23] The course underwent extensive revision for offering again in 1924. Radcliffe-Brown delivered a course of lectures for magistrates in the Transkei that similarly attracted a glowing letter of appreciation from those who attended.[24]

SOUTH AFRICAN DISAPPOINTMENT

The inescapable impression drawn from Radcliffe-Brown's activities in South Africa is of a determination to establish social anthropology both as a field of intellectual inquiry and as a profession with a constituency and a role. Considerable thought and effort went into establishing the School of African Life and Languages, the host for social anthropology, on a sound footing. It was Radcliffe-Brown, not the ineffectual Norton, who secured the appointment of a senior lecturer in phonetics (Dr. D. M. Beach)[25] and a research assistant (A. J. H. Goodwin, who later turned to prehistory, contributed to the archaeology of South Africa, and remained at UCT until retirement),[26] groomed them for future work in anthropology, created research opportunities, and in the case of Goodwin (who was apparently expected to teach) supplied lecture notes to tide him over the initial learning period. He also arranged research leave for Beach, Norton, and Goodwin each for a term during the academic year 1924.[27] One can see his hand behind the institution of prizes for the collection of "native lore," guaranteed funds for publication, a proposed degree course in phonetics, and a proposed university press.

In May 1924 the senate established a committee to report on the reorganization of the School of African Life and Languages.[28] The need arose from its never having been formally constituted as originally recommended, the failure of the plans for Bantu languages, and the halving in 1921 of the government grant. As 1924 was the fifth year of the five-year grant, the future of the entire program was at risk. The committee's recommendations were characteristic of Radcliffe-Brown's thinking and parallel proposals that he later made elsewhere. These included a school board and a formal head responsible directly to the senate, but with funding directly from the university council and the immediate appointment of additional teaching staff. Its role should be "organized and systematic research" into native life. In addition, the senate adopted a recommendation that the university should enable Radcliffe-Brown to lecture to future conferences of the Transkei magistrates as in 1924. A further recommendation was for the appointment of an editorial committee for a projected publications series of the School of African Life and Languages. These were necessary steps toward the larger goals that Radcliffe-Brown had in mind, and it may be concluded that he had succeeded at least in laying the groundwork.

However, in November 1925, Radcliffe-Brown announced his resignation. The senate resolution on the occasion urged the continuation and extension of the work of the school in words that reveal continuing frustrations and probable motives for resignation: "To urge upon the council the necessity of making such financial provision as would secure the adequate staffing and equipment of the school and enable the staff to do the necessary fieldwork, while also carrying on the purely teaching duties of the University." A subcommittee was appointed to draft a submission, and Radcliffe-Brown was a member of it. The resulting report—the third attempt to induce the university to follow through on its intentions of 1920—was a detailed document recommending provision for both BA and MA degrees in anthropology and a postgraduate diploma course. The emphasis was to be on social anthropology, with linguistics as an integral part, not particular languages but (and here again is a recurrent Radcliffe-Brown theme) comparative linguistics, and scientific methods for studying and learning languages. The proposed program spread over two years would be:

1st year: Social Anthropology I, Psychology I, Phonetics I

2nd year: Social Anthropology ii, a special history course (including South African history, method, comparative study of native administration), a special psychology course (including general social psychology and the psychology of language), linguistics (including general comparative morphology of language, genetic classification of languages, the phonetics of African languages), and physical anthropology.

The MA would be a purely research degree. The school's research goals should be resourced by provision for fieldwork by staff and advanced students, the coordination and direction of research in South Africa by non-university personnel, and the compilation of information. Further recommendations referred to staffing, salaries, a scholarship for field research, and publication grants. The report concluded:

If the scheme suggested above is carried out it would be advisable to take steps to bring before the notice of Governments and missionary bodies of Africa the fact that the University of Cape Town is providing a course of training specially adapted for the needs of missionaries and officials dealing with natives.[29]

It is evident from this document what Radcliffe-Brown had been trying to achieve since his appointment in 1921. It is equally evident that the reasons for his resignation may be read in this manifesto: he had taken to heart the recommendations of the Coleman report which accorded with the outlook that he had developed in the previous decade; neither the government nor the university council had followed through on funding, staffing, or structure. An opportunity had been proffered but the means withheld. He had thrown himself energetically into doing what he could with slender resources, and when in the end he was enticed away, it was to a university similarly placed, offering almost identical opportunities, but with a promise of funding on a more secure basis than the capricious promise of 1920. Funding, however, was not the only issue. Radcliffe-Brown wanted to impart the insights of anthropology to people whose daily work was with Africans. The government failed to deliver these employees to him, whereas in Australia it was guaranteed, the training of administrative cadets for New Guinea was of "central importance," and the design of the training program was his.[30] In Sydney, the battles that he had had to fight in Cape Town had already been fought and won.

It is evident from the senate minutes that in his closing work at UCT Radcliffe-Brown attempted to ensure that the work he initiated would continue and that the project that he planned might yet be implemented. However, the soundness of his decision to go was justified by the sequel. The School of African Life and Languages languished for some years further, but there is no basis for saying in the words of the university historian that he left his school in "acute disarray" (Phillips 1993: 25). The school was merely Radcliffe-Brown and Goodwin in anthropology, plus Dr. D. M. Beach, the senior lecturer in phonetics, and Miss Bleek, the honorary reader who taught Bushman languages.[31] Any "disarray" was on the part of the government and the university. The tenure of Thomas Barnard, Radcliffe-Brown's successor, was disastrous because he was so indolent and indifferent that he apparently delivered his lectures from notes left for him by his more capable predecessor (Phillips 1993: 25). Assessments of Radcliffe-Brown should not be tainted by Barnard's failure to match him.[32] Phillips's judgment on Radcliffe-Brown echoes the despondent, retrospective comment made by the university principal almost eight years later and which was inevitably colored by the failure of Radcliffe-Brown's successor:

At present I look upon the school [of African Life and Languages] as our worst effort. We were unfortunate in a way getting Radcliffe-Brown—a careerist—and Norton—a fool.... One of my objects will be to pull the school together or get rid of it. Barnard ... is as charming as ever, but I don't know that he is any more effective than he was.

The same letter grumbled about Beach as well.[33]

In January 1926 the council was informed that the government grant for 1926–27 of £1,500 p.a. for the School of African Life and Languages would terminate in three months, to be replaced by one of £950 under different conditions.[34] These were that the grant was on a "£ for £"

basis, with an additional £100, also £ for £, for a vacation course in Bantu studies for officials. An identical grant was offered to the University of Witwatersrand.

Subsequently, the Universities of Stellenbosch and Pretoria also wanted to share in the money. Indeed, one of the issues that the Coleman report in 1919 had dealt with was the argument that any grant money for Bantu studies should be shared. Coleman had recommended it be concentrated at UCT, but evidently the question had not been allowed to rest. The new formula therefore was to be a £ for £ grant of up to £800 to be divided: £250 for UCT, £250 for Witwatersrand, £150 for Stellenbosch, and £150 for Pretoria.[35] Even by the currency values of the time, this sum amounted to no more than grants-in-aid. Government had retreated from its earlier determination, but it was no longer the same government: Smuts's liberal South Africa Party had lost the 1924 election to Hertzog's Nationalist and Labour coalition. Support for Bantu studies was not the only thing that changed. It is small wonder that Radcliffe-Brown should have been attracted to Sydney away from this frustration and disappointment.[36] His undertakings at Sydney evince the same consistent planning and line of thinking as at Cape Town and the same energetic eagerness. But ultimately he resigned his second chair for the same reasons as he had his first.

HOPES IN SYDNEY

Anthropology was established at the University of Sydney under much the same circumstances as in Cape Town. The same academics and the same academic bodies, including the British Association for the Advancement of Science and the Royal Anthropological Institute and finally a resolution of the Pacific Science Congress that met in Melbourne in 1923, put the same arguments to the Australian Federal government as they had put to the Union government in South Africa: the urgency of studying human society as a scientific, humanitarian, and practical necessity. In addition, the lieutenant governor of Papua, Sir Hubert Murray, made his own representations to the same effect. What gave these appeals particular force at the time was the desperation of the administration of the Mandated Territory of New Guinea for field staff of higher caliber. Various proposals were made in the early 1920s for recruiting a better type of patrol officer for New Guinea, and eventually the proposal was made for a hybrid program of practical orientation in New Guinea with university study in anthropology adopted (Campbell 1998). At the request of the Commonwealth government, the University of Sydney agreed early in 1924 to establish a chair subject to funding from government. The estimated cost of the chair with necessary support staff was £2,500 p.a. By the middle of 1925, commitments from Commonwealth and State governments totaling £2,270 p.a. had been made, whereupon the university proceeded with the proposed appointment.[37]

There was a further attraction. Australia had a National Research Council to advise government and disburse funds for research. In February 1925 the Rockefeller Foundation of New York, responding to news of the proposed establishment of anthropology, offered the Australian National Research Council a sum of $10,000 to $20,000 p.a. for five years to fund fieldwork and publication,[38] and when Radcliffe-Brown's appointment was announced, the foundation invited him to New York for discussions about the grant.[39] By the time he arrived in Sydney (assuming duty on 30 June 1926) he had a guaranteed source of research funds and a multilateral guarantee of funding for the department and a commitment that certain government servants would be required to take his courses. The prospects for his being able to implement the project that he had envisaged in South Africa seemed bright.

Things began well. There was no political obstruction in the university senate, no troublesome colleague such as Norton, and the funding was secure. Relations with colleagues who were teaching aspects of anthropology (in geography and anatomy) were cordial and cooperative.[40] Radcliffe-Brown had a free hand and took to the work with vigor and enthusiasm. He had an early meeting with members of government in Canberra and had his training plan for the New Guinea cadets accepted. After a year of training and field experience in New Guinea, cadets would come to the university for a year where they would take both the first and second years of the anthropology program simultaneously, supplemented with classes on colonial administration. Further, they would be eligible to complete a diploma in anthropology by dissertation after their return to the territory. He also offered and had approved a concentrated form of these courses whereby serving officers could complete the same lectures in three months during their periodical long leaves. They too could qualify to proceed to the diploma. In this way Radcliffe-Brown could reach not only senior officers in the New Guinea administration but also senior officers in Papua and the Western Pacific High Commission and missionaries.[41]

J. H. P. Murray, lieutenant governor of Papua and later Sir Hubert, declined to join the cadet scheme for practical reasons,[42] but he remained supportive of Radcliffe-Brown's program and released his senior officers for the short course. The first three came from Papua in December 1927 and January 1928. The first six cadets came in 1928, followed by five in 1929. But by then recruitment had faltered, and no more cadets came until 1931, and then only three. The second short course for serving officers was run from mid-May to mid-August 1929 and was taken by two officers from New Guinea, seven from Papua, and one from the British Solomon Islands Protectorate.[43] These numbers were not regarded as viable, and given the smallness of the territorial services, officials alone could not sustain the program. Radcliffe-Brown had always intended that the courses would be attended by missionaries as well, and he negotiated with mission bodies to that end. Fifteen attended the 1929 course.[44] From the beginning, he also tried to attract public servants in Aboriginal administration within Australia, but it took until 1929 for Home Affairs to agree. Inevitably, given a small and scattered staff, the numbers that could take advantage of the opportunity were few, and the only such official to take the course in Radcliffe-Brown's time was Dr. Cecil Cook, the Northern Territory Protector of Aborigines, who attended in 1930.[45]

Undergraduate courses were well received. Courses began in 1926 notwithstanding Radcliffe-Brown's midyear arrival. Whereas his years at Cape Town produced one anthropologist of distinction, Isaac Schapera, who succeeded to his old chair in 1935, there were several future "names" in his Sydney classes. In 1927 twenty-four students passed Anthropology 1 (a second-year degree course), one completed the diploma in anthropology, and one (Ralph Piddington, later foundation professor of anthropology at the University of Auckland) graduated with first class honors in anthropology (1928 Calendar, p. 549).[46] In 1928, thirty-eight passed Anthropology I and ten passed Anthropology II (1929 Calendar), which was also the year that the first batch of cadets came to him. In 1929 Radcliffe-Brown's best student in Anthropology I was W. E. H. Stanner, later professor of anthropology at the Australian National University. In the same year, two MAS graduated including H. Ian Hogbin (later reader in anthropology at the University of Sydney), and one diploma in anthropology (Leo Austen, the first Papuan officer to so qualify) (University of Sydney Calendar 1930). In 1930, Radcliffe-Brown's last year at Sydney, enrollments were forty to fifty in Anthropology I and twelve to fifteen in Anthropology II.[47] In a small university and for a new discipline, these numbers were creditable. Each undergraduate course had ninety lectures and was repeated for the short courses. Until 1928 all of this teaching fell to Radcliffe-Brown, as well as lectures elsewhere in the university on ethnology and physical anthropology. Bernard Deacon, a Cambridge graduate then engaged in field research in the New Hebrides, was appointed to a lectureship to share this load at the end of 1926,[48] but he died before taking up the appointment. Camilla Wedgwood was found as a temporary replacement, but she could not come until February 1928,[49] so it is little wonder that Radcliffe-Brown described 1927 as "one of the busiest years of my life."[50]

SPONSORING RESEARCH

Contrary to Kuper's view that Radcliffe-Brown "organized a little— surprisingly little—research" (Kuper 1983: 48), he used the Rockefeller research fund effectively. In June 1928 he had five field workers busy in Australia, two in New Guinea, and two in the Solomons.[51] The beginning of sustained and systematic work in Aboriginal anthropology can truly be said to begin with Radcliffe-Brown's Rockefeller–ANRC grants. Research into Aboriginal Australia included work by himself, W. Lloyd Warner, A. P. Elkin, Ursula McConnel, Donald Thomson, C. M. W. Hart, B. Davies, S. D. Porteus, Ralph Piddington, A. Wallace, and V. Laves. Between 1927 and 1931, Radcliffe-Brown sponsored, funded, or otherwise facilitated work in Papua and New Guinea by Margaret Mead, Reo Fortune, Hortense Powdermaker, Gregory Bateson, Geza Roheim, Felix Speiser, Beatrice Blackwood, and elsewhere in Melanesia by W. G. Ivens, Ian Hogbin, and Raymond Firth. He also tried to get Richard Thurnwald back to resume the New Guinea work interrupted by the war in 1914 and Maurice Leenhardt to visit from New Caledonia. By the time the five-year grant agreement expired in 1931, over £15,000 of Rockefeller money had been spent on these activities, sending students to European and North American universities, and bringing European and American scientists to Australia.[52]

Other projects included a Bureau of Ethnology that he had been wanting to create since before his museum appointment in Pretoria. At Sydney he came closest to achieving this. He made a specific proposal in April 1927,[53] and although nothing formal eventuated, he began its work by arrangement with the government anthropologists and administrators of Papua and New Guinea. Extracts of patrol reports—those sections incorporating ethnological observations—were sent to him for collation and filing.[54] Complementary to the proposed bureau was the idea of a national ethnological collection. At Cape Town he had wanted to bring the ethnological specimens at the museum under his control; in Australia, correspondence on a national museum began in 1926 about specimens lodged at the university.[55] He put a proposal to the Commonwealth government in August 1927, wanting to know whether he should initiate the appropriate training for a curator and whether he should devote energy to building a collection. He regarded this and related matters of sufficient importance for the advancement of science to seek an interview with the prime minister. The government agreed in principle but pleaded poverty.[56] Another idea that he had offered in South Africa and tried again in Australia was a gazetteer of Papua and New Guinea, modeled on the gazetteer of India, providing a comprehensive description of the social landscape, with the identity, characteristics, and locations of the many tribes.[57] In 1930 he expressed hope of support from the League of Nations for a sociological survey of New Guinea.[58] One may say in retrospect that these suggestions were premature, even naïve, but a start had to be made some time, and they are indicative of Radcliffe-Brown's strategic linking of pure research and practical application.

Complementing the research and information collection, Radcliffe-Brown pursued another objective that he had initiated in Cape Town:

publication. There he had been frustrated by the shortage of funds, but at Sydney he had the Rockefeller money. This time he proposed not a press but a journal, and he founded *Oceania*, the first issue of which appeared in 1930, publishing the work of the researchers whom he had trained and sponsored.

Ultimately, the activities of Radcliffe-Brown at Sydney and Cape Town conform to a single program of establishing the discipline through an intense program of teaching, research, and publication and active campaigning to show that the study of anthropology was not an idle matter of merely intellectual interest but a practical subject of urgent social needs and national priorities. The unity of his thought and its continuity is evident from the fact that all his initiatives while at Sydney were foreshadowed in a meeting with J. G. McLaren of the Prime Minister's Department within three months of his arrival.[59] His achievements and failures in both places should be understood in terms of available resources. In Cape Town he was starved of funds and of government and mission enrollments; in Sydney until 1930 he had all. The opportunity was well used in Sydney, and the money was well spent. His achievement there fully justifies his decision to leave Cape Town, which could promise him only further frustration.

APPLIED ANTHROPOLOGY

At both Sydney and Cape Town, Radcliffe-Brown was expected to meet a demand for applied anthropology. His special courses for magistrates, missionaries, and administrators may be understood in such a light, but it was part of his conception of social anthropology as a science, closely analogous to the natural or inductive sciences in methods and theory, that there should be both practical and pure aspects. He did not regard these as separate or antithetical. He wrote to R. H. Lowie in California in 1927 that training cadets "will be one of the most important activities of this Department in the future. My plan here is, as in South Africa, to make Anthropology a practical subject fitted to the needs of those who have the task of educating and administering to native people."[60]

After cadets left Sydney to return to New Guinea, Radcliffe-Brown corresponded with them, encouraging their research, asking for information, and answering their questions. Far from being interested in applied anthropology for mercenary purposes, it was a theme to which he returned repeatedly. He broached the issue in an early paper during his Cape Town years; dealt with it directly in 1929 while at Sydney, again after he left Sydney, and yet again when, close to retirement from the University of Oxford, he made a statement which virtually summarized his lifelong stance:

> The recognition of applied social anthropology has certain very definite advantages and certain equally definite disadvantages. To mention only one of the latter, theoretical social anthropology is still in the formative stage. The demand on social anthropologists to spend too much of their time on practical problems would inevitably reduce the amount of work that can be given to the development of the theoretical side of the science. But without a sound basis in theory, applied anthropology must deteriorate and become not applied science, but merely empirical practice. (Radcliffe-Brown 1958d)

His continuing interest in applied anthropology was noticed during his years at the University of Chicago, where he gave attention to the program of Indian reform undertaken by the commissioner of Indian affairs (Eggan 1991:407).

One of Radcliffe-Brown's persistent criticisms of the ethnology and historical anthropology of his youth was that it did not lead to an understanding of the mechanics of society, that is, of how institutions worked. By implication, it was incapable of being of any use either in understanding what might be happening in society or informing how society might be deliberately changed. His scientific comparative sociology, however, would provide such understanding. It was potentially practical, whereas older anthropology was not. He was equally insistent, however, that it was not for the social anthropologist to attempt to solve practical problems of society. The application of laws discovered by the scientist of society was the role of the teacher, magistrate, and administrator (Radcliffe-Brown 1958a). One of the merits of functionalism as he developed it was that it allowed one to "foresee what will be the results of any influence, intentional or unintentional, that we may exert upon it" (Radcliffe-Brown 1958b:41). He expressed satisfaction in real progress having been achieved with the Sydney university courses: "The result of this arrangement will be that in a certain number of years all the administrative officers of the territory will have a sound knowledge of the principles and methods of Comparative Sociology, and by its means will have acquired a considerable knowledge of New Guinea institutions and customs and their meaning, and will have made a systematic study of administrative problems and methods" (Radcliffe-Brown 1958c).

A SECOND BETRAYAL

Unfortunately, after five years in Sydney, the Cape Town history was to be repeated. The onset of the Great Depression after 1929 eliminated the States' contributions to his department. The Commonwealth grant was reduced and threatened with termination; the Territory of New Guinea, faced with declining revenues and an expanding frontier, wanted to reduce or eliminate the cadet training program on which Radcliffe-Brown had worked so hard, and the Rockefeller grant that had been for only five years was soon to expire. Its renewal could not be expected partly because it had been intended that Australian sources should assume sponsorship after Rockefeller money got the work started, but also because Foundation funds were conditional on equivalent Australian grants. Papua was never a source of funds, and the flow of senior officers from there to take Radcliffe-Brown's courses ceased, not because, as Elkin says in his obituary, Murray was "frankly disappointed" (Elkin 1956: 243), but because of the penury of the territorial government, most of whose senior officers had already taken the course.[61] Murray lent his support to Radcliffe-Brown's desperate attempts to extract continued funding from the Australian government, but by November 1930 he had no reason to expect success[62] nor, as a consequence, any further Rockefeller money. It seemed by then that he had no choice but to resign because the University of Sydney could not afford his department with the loss of the subsidy.[63]

As in Cape Town, Radcliffe-Brown continued to campaign for his project up to and beyond his decision to resign.[64] Ironically, after he had formally resigned, he was able to inform the Commonwealth government that a Rockefeller grant would be forthcoming if Commonwealth grants could continue.[65] During Radcliffe-Brown's last week in Sydney, the Commonwealth provided a grant to keep the department going for one year,[66] and the Rockefeller made a further large grant in response to his submissions and the support he mustered from influential anthropologists elsewhere. Others picked up the benefit thereof, while Radcliffe-Brown went to a one-year appointment at the University of Chicago that, although subsequently extended, initially offered neither long-term prospects nor any opportunity to continue the work for applied anthropology that had absorbed ten years of his life and his entire professorial career up to that time.

EPILOGUE

In Sydney as in Cape Town, the department was able to continue because of the success of Radcliffe-Brown's representations for continued support and not because his successors resuscitated something that he had fumbled and abandoned. Raymond Firth was appointed acting professor after Radcliffe-Brown's departure, and he declined the substantive position in favor of a lectureship at the University of London. He cited the difficulty over government funding as the reason.[67] His career had been launched by Radcliffe-Brown, whose Rockefeller money funded his first fieldwork on Tikopia and had appointed him to a lectureship. A. P. Elkin came in after Firth's departure and inherited the editorship of *Oceania*, which gave him both patronage and influence in shaping Australian anthropology. He was able to draw on the money that Radcliffe-Brown had secured and continue his program including the applied anthropology thrust and the training of cadet patrol officers for New Guinea. Elkin subsequently had to fight his own battles for subsidies, which continued until 1938, and this and his own achievements as academic activist and authority on Australian Aboriginal society were substantial on their own terms. But until his retirement, much of the work of his department was an echo of Radcliffe-Brown's monumental five years.[68]

Far from being a careerist in the sense defined above, from having a disastrous record at either university, or being a restless dilettante, or leaving his departments in disarray, Radcliffe-Brown's final acts in both places ensured their survival, the continuation of his work, and a durable achievement, if not appropriate posthumous and scholarly recognition. His eclipse could hardly be more complete or ill-founded than the journal that he established declaring on its web site that its founder was A. P. Elkin.[69]

NOTES

1. Primary sources cited are mostly from the archives of the University of Cape Town (cited as UCT) or the University of Sydney (cited as SU). Neither has a Radcliffe-Brown collection. At Sydney University, citations prefixed "Elkin" are to the A. P. Elkin Personal Archives, which include the correspondence and other files of the Department of Anthropology from its beginning. Thus citations to the Elkin collection are generally to correspondence that was part of the departmental record. In addition, there are notes by Elkin that he made of files now housed in the National Archives of Australia. I have checked these notes against the originals, but have generally given the citation to the Elkin collection. Grateful acknowledgment is made to the archives staff at both universities and the Australian Archives for their helpful assistance. With effect from 19 December 1917.

   As Schapera points out, both Fortes and Firth in their obituaries of Radcliffe-Brown date his appointment in Tonga as 1916–1919, and these are presumably the reason that Kuper made the same error.

2. Radcliffe-Brown to *Sydney Morning Herald*, 15 April 1929. Newspaper cutting in Elkin P130/41/26.

3. It was from this time that he began using the double surname Radcliffe-Brown (Schapera 1989:10).

4. Letter to Beattie 18 June 1920. File on Chair of Social Anthropology, 1921, UCT. Also Schapera 1990:4–5.

5. Radcliffe-Brown to *Sydney Morning Herald*, 15 April 1929. Newspaper cutting in Elkin P130/41/26. For New Zealand's attempts to do the same, see Campbell 2000.

6. Meyer Fortes's obituary of Radcliffe-Brown credits Sir Richard Temple, a notable scholar-administrator of India, with having urged the establishment of anthropology in British universities because of its usefulness for colonial government (Fortes 1956). Temple made such a call at the 1914 meeting of the British Association and was the author of *Anthropology as a Practical Science.* See J. L. Myres 1929:49. Sir Richard

Temple was half-brother of C. L. Temple, colonial administrator and theorist of colonial government and author of *Native Races and Their Rulers*.

7. University of Cape Town Council Minutes for 27 December 1918, UCT.

8. Council Minutes, 25 May 1921, UCT.

9. The idea of such a bureau had a long history. Radcliffe-Brown referred at various times to the U.S. Bureau of Ethnology as a model, and the idea was advocated in British circles at least as early as 1896. See Myres 1929:38–41.

10. A. C. Haddon to J. C. Smuts, 16 April 1920. Chair of Anthropology 1921, UCT.

11. Advertisement 6 November 1920. File on Chair of Social Anthropology 1921, UCT.

12. Professor G. H. T. Malan to Norton, 6 August 1923, refers to an unnamed colleague, overseas at the time of writing, as being responsible for a move against Norton. Norton Papers, M&A, UCT.

13. Radcliffe-Brown to Norton, 4 May 1922, Norton Papers, M &A, BC40, UCT.

14. Senate minutes, 10 July 1923, UCT.

15. Beattie to Loram, 16 August 1933, Principal's Out-Letters, vol. 2, UCT.

16. Norton to Loram, 6 November 1922, Norton Papers M&A, BC40, UCT.

17. Senate Minutes, 20 September and 4 October 1921, UCT.

18. Senate Minutes, 18 April 1922, UCT Archives.

19. Senate Minutes, 20 June 1922.

20. Senate, 21 March 1922, in Senate Minutes, 20 May 1924, UCT.

21. Letter from the Secretary of the Public Service Commission, 27 April 1923. Copy in Norton Papers, BC40, UCT.

22. The syllabus for Social Anthropology I was summarized as "general social anthropology, and the races and cultures of Africa, especially South Africa." Prescribed texts were by Tylor, Marett, Junod, and Lowie. Social Anthropology II was "General Social Anthropology, the Social System of the Bantu." Prescribed texts were Tylor, *Primitive Culture*, Smith and Dale, *The Ila-Speaking People of Northern Rhodesia*, Durkheim, *The Elementary Forms of the Religious Life*, and McDougall, *Introduction to Social Psychology*. University of Cape Town, Prospectus, 1923.

23. Senate Minutes, 22 March 1923. Letter from A. A. Louw on behalf of those who took the vacation course, UCT.

24. Senate Minutes, 10 June 1924, UCT. Letter from the Chief Magistrate of the Transkei, 6 May 1924, Council Minutes, 6 May 1924, UCT.

25. Senate Minutes, 22 October 1922 and 19 April 1923, UCT.

26. Senate Minutes, 11 July 1922, UCT. The appointment was to be effective from March 1923.

27. Senate Minutes, 22 October 1922, 19 April 1923, UCT.

28. Membership: the Principal (Beattie), Professors Clarke, Reyburn, and Ritchie, Dr. Beach, the new senior lecturer in phonetics, and Radcliffe-Brown.

29. Senate Minutes 4 December 1925, addendum, UCT.

30. Radcliffe-Brown to McLaren (head of the Prime Minister's Department, Australia), 21 December 1926, Box 197, File 4/2/576, Elkin Papers, University of Sydney Archives.

31. Appointed in May 1923. Senate Minutes, 15 May 1923, UCT.

32. Thomas T. Barnard was professor of social anthropology from 1926 until 1933. He subsequently made a name for himself as a botanist in South Africa.

33. Beattie to Loram 16 August 1933. Principal's Out-Letters, vol. 2, UCT.

34. Council Minutes 26 January 1926, UCT.

35. Memorandum on the method of reallocation of the Government Research Grant for Bantu Studies [n.d]. Department of African Studies, UCT.

36. There is no evidence that national politics influenced Radcliffe-Brown's decision to resign, but it must have been evident that the more severe attitude toward racial questions of the Labour and Nationalist Parties would be a less fertile context for what he was trying to achieve.

37. Senate Minutes, 3 March 1924, 1 June 1925, SU. The breakdown of annual contributions was Commonwealth £1000 (for five years), New South Wales £577; Victoria £425; Queensland £212; South Australia £137; Western Australia £93; Tasmania £56. Contributing governments were entitled to one free place per £100 or part thereof. None appears to have taken full advantage of this entitlement. Minutes of the Permanent Advisory Committee to the Chair of Anthropology, March 1927, Elkin P130/41/576.

38. Senate Minutes, 2 February 1925, SU.

39. Thus it is incorrect to assert that the chair was "Rockefeller Foundation funded" (Bashkow 1995: 3). The chair was funded by state and federal grants; the Rockefeller Foundation grant was actually to the Australian National Research Council and was to be used to support research in Australia and Melanesia. The money was administered by a board of the ANRC and of which Radcliffe-Brown was a member—indeed, the only expert member of it.

40. Physical Anthropology was accepted as a course for the bachelor of science degree at the senate meeting of 11 April 1927.

41. Proposals 1926, Elkin P130/41/40.

42. Murray to Minister of Home & Territories, 24 September 1926. An annotation made in the Minister's Office on this letter pointed out that the cadet scheme had not been intended for Papua, but was designed for New Guinea. Elkin P130/41/576. Also Murray to Minister for Home & Territories, 29 June 1927, excusing Papua from joining the New Guinea cadet scheme but suggesting that his officers be permitted to attend Radcliffe-Brown's courses. Elkin P130/41/576.

43. Radcliffe-Brown to Lord Lugard, 10 September 1930, Elkin P130/41/17.

44. Radcliffe-Brown to Millicent Herring, 31 July 1929 and 23 May 1930, and other correspondence of the same period. Elkin P130/41/5.

45. Letters from Radcliffe-Brown to the Secretary of Home Affairs, 8 February 1929, 30 May 1929 in Elkin P130/41/45, and 11 April 1931, 23 April 1931 in Elkin P130/41/46.

46. Radcliffe-Brown to Lowie, 28 June 1927—forty students in course 1 and twenty in course 2. "My plan here is, as in South Africa, to make Anthropology a practical subject fitted to the needs of those who have a task of educating and administering to native people." Elkin P130/41/67.

47. Radcliffe-Brown to Secretary Prime Minister's Department, 26 February 1931, Elkin P130/41/46.

48. Registrar to Radcliffe-Brown, 10 December 1926, Elkin P130/41/40.

49. Report to the Chair of Anthropology Advisory Committee, January 1928, Elkin P130/41/576.

50. Radcliffe-Brown to Lowie, 3 July 1928, Elkin P130/41/17.

51. Radcliffe-Brown to Lowie, 28 June 1927, Elkin P130/41/17.

52. Radcliffe-Brown to secretary Prime Minister's Department, 26 February 1931, Elkin P130/41/46.

53. April 1927, Elkin P130/41/40.

54. Correspondence various dates 1927–28 between Radcliffe-Brown and Hubert Murray and Leonard Murray, Elkin P130/41/21 and correspondence with the Home & Territories Department, 1 September 1927, 4 April 1928, in Elkin P130/41/44.

55. Elkin P130/41/18.

56. Elkin P130/41/44. Correspondence of Radcliffe-Brown dated August 1927, 7 October 1927, 19 March 1928, 30 November 1928, and folder 4/2/45, 20 February 1929. Reply from Secretary of Home Affairs, 9 April 1929, Elkin P130/41/45.

57. Radcliffe-Brown to Home & Territories, 16 November 1926, 15 September 1927, 16 November 1927, and 30 November 1927, Elkin P130/41/44.

58. Radcliffe-Brown to Chinnery, 22 July 1930, Elkin P130/41/48.

59. "Chair of Anthropology (Sydney University) in its relation to Cadets and Officers of the Territorial Services." McLaren's report of his discussion with Radcliffe-Brown on 19 August 1926. A1 1924 / 26997, Australian Archives.

60. Radcliffe-Brown to Lowie, 28 June 1927, Elkin P130/41/17.

61. Murray to Prime Minister, 9 February 1931, A518 N806/1/1 Australian Archives. This dispatch gives Murray's assessment of Radcliffe-Brown's courses based on reports from his officers. At this time Murray was especially concerned to make no financial commitments for his impoverished territory.

62. In his application for leave from August 1931, he stated that he would return to the university in February 1932 "unless it had become clear by then that the Department had come to an end." Radcliffe-Brown to Vice Chancellor, 20 October 1930, Elkin P130/41/42.

63. Vice Chancellor to Prime Minister (draft nd, filed with April 1931 correspondence) stated that the university would have been in a "very awkward situation" financially had Radcliffe-Brown not resigned. Elkin P130/41/46.

64. Correspondence and submissions at Elkin P130/41/46.

65. Radcliffe-Brown to McLaren, 23 March 1931. A518. P806/1/1, pt. 1. Australian Archives.

66. Secretary Prime Minister's Department to Radcliffe-Brown, 22 May 1931, Elkin P130/41/46.

67. Firth to Masson, 10 August 1932, Elkin P130/41/577.

68. For example, in 1955 on the eve of his retirement, Elkin was still offering a course called "Native Administration and Applied Anthropology: Training for Administrative Officers and Missionaries' Course," description in Elkin P130/41/581. This entry or one similar to it continued to appear in the University Calendar until 1961. The thread of continuity with Radcliffe-Brown's program three decades earlier is clear, although by 1955 the training of administrative officers for Papua and New Guinea had been located for ten years in a purpose-designed college independent of the university.

69. "*Oceania* began in 1931 when A. P. Elkin, Professor of Anthropology, University of Sydney founded the journal. . . . Elkin died in 1979, having edited *Oceania* for 50 years." http://www.arts.usyd.edu.au/publications /oceania/about.htm [accessed 27 March 2009]. In fact, *Oceania* began

in 1930, and Elkin did not become professor of anthropology and editor of *Oceania* until 1933.

REFERENCES

Australian Archives. Various dates. Records series A1, A257, A518.

Bashkow, Ira. 1995. Clio's Fancy: Documents to Pique the Historical Imagination. History of Anthropology Newsletter 22(2):3–14.

Campbell, I. C. 1998. Anthropology and the Professionalisation of Colonial Administration in Papua and New Guinea. Journal of Pacific History 33:69–90.

———. 2000. Staffing Native Administration in the Mandated Territory of Samoa. New Zealand Journal of History 34:277–295.

———. 2003. Island Kingdom: Tonga Ancient and Modern. 2nd ed. Christchurch: Canterbury University Press.

Campbell, S. J. 1957. A History of the Development of Education in Tonga. MEd thesis, University of Queensland.

[Coleman, P.] 1919. [Report of] Committee of Inquiry into University Grants. Copy among Council Minutes, UCT Archives. Schapera 1990:12 gives the full reference as Union of South Africa, Report of the Secretary for Education for the year ended 31 December 1919 (UG57-'20), appendix A.

Eggan, Fred. 1991. A. R. Radcliffe-Brown. *In* Remembering the University of Chicago: Teachers, Scientists, and Scholars. Edward Shils, ed. Chicago: University of Chicago Press.

Elkin, A. P. 1956. A. R. Radcliffe-Brown, 1880–1955. Oceania 26:239–251.

Firth, Raymond. 1956. Alfred Reginald Radcliffe-Brown. Proceedings of the British Academy 42:287–302.

Fortes, Meyer. 1956. Alfred Reginald Radcliffe-Brown, FBA, 1881–1955: A Memoir. Man 56:149–153.

Herda, Phyllis. 1994. The 1918 Influenza Pandemic in Fiji, Tonga, and the Samoas. *In* New Countries and Old Medicine, Auckland. Linda Bryder and Derek A. Dow, eds. Pp. 46–51. Auckland: Medical History Society.

Kuper, Adam. 1983. Anthropology and Anthropologists: The Modern British School. 2nd ed. London: Routledge and Kegan Paul.

Myres, J. L. 1929. The Science of Man in the Service of the State. Journal of the Royal Anthropological Institute of Great Britain and Ireland 59.

Phillips, Howard. 1993. The University of Cape Town, 1918–1948: The Foundation Years. Cape Town: University of Cape Town Press.

Radcliffe-Brown, A. R. 1922. The Andaman Islanders. Cambridge: Cambridge University Press.

———. 1950. Introduction. *In* African Systems of Kinship and Marriage. A. R. Radcliffe-Brown and Daryll Forde, eds. London: Oxford University Press.

———. 1958a. The Methods of Ethnology and Social Anthropology. In Srinivas 1958: 3–32. Original publication South African Journal of Science 20 (1923):124–147.

———. 1958b. Historical and Functional Interpretations of Change. In Srinivas 1958:41. Originally published as abstract of a paper read before the fourth Pan-Pacific Science Congress at Java, 1929.

———. 1958c. The Present Position of Anthropological Studies. In Srinivas 1958:90–91. Originally Presidential Address to Section H of the British Association for the Advancement of Science, Centenary Meeting in London, 1931.

———. 1958d. Meaning and Scope of Social Anthropology. In Srinivas 1958:105–106. Originally in Nature 154 (26 August 1944): 257–260.

Schapera, I. 1989. A. R. Brown to Radcliffe-Brown. Anthropology Today 5(5):10.

———. 1990. The Appointment of Radcliffe-Brown to the Chair of Social Anthropology at the University of Cape Town. African Studies 49(1):1–10.

Srinivas, M. N. 1958. Method in Social Anthropology: Selected Essays by A. R. Radcliffe-Brown. Chicago: University of Chicago Press.

Tonga. 1918. Government Gazette, no. 5.

University of Cape Town. 1921–1927. General prospectus.

University of Cape Town Archives. Various dates. Files consulted include Minutes of Council, Minutes of Senate, A. J. H. Goodwin Papers (file BC290), W. A. Norton Papers (file BC40), Principal's Out-Letters, vol. 2. Department of African Studies; Chair of Social Anthropology 1921.

University of Sydney. 1921–62. Calendar.

University of Sydney Archives. Senate Minutes 1924–1931.

University of Sydney Archives, A. P. Elkin Personal Archives.

Wise, Tigger. 1985. The Self-Made Anthropologist: A Life of A. P. Elkin. Sydney: George Allen and Unwin.

GEOFFREY GRAY AND DOUG MUNRO

5

"The Department Was in Some Disarray"

The Politics of Choosing a Successor to S. F. Nadel, 1957

It was clear . . . that the needs for the development of the Department made it essential not to miss such an opportunity for a permanent appointment as had been presented.

ELECTORAL COMMITTEE MEETING for the chair of anthropology, August 20, 1957

Curious, isn't it: where in the anthropology we write do we deal with those high realities of academic actuality: the smear, the careful silences, the well-placed knife, the packing of panels of selectors, and the arts of prearranged judgement?

W. E. H. STANNER to Raymond Firth, October 15, 1958

On the unexpected and sudden death of S. F. Nadel in January 1956, at the comparatively young age of fifty-two, the Australian National University (ANU) needed to find a new professor of anthropology in the Research School of Pacific Studies (RSPacs).[1] It was keen to find someone of similar international standing and distinction and quickly drew up a list of possible candidates, settling on the British anthropologist Edmund Leach and, in the event of Leach's refusal, the American anthropologist Douglas Oliver (Gray and Munro 2012). Both were unable to accept the offer; consequently, the ANU decided to delay making an appointment until a suitable candidate was found or offered himself. In the interim Derek Freeman, a senior fellow, was acting head of department, relinquishing this to W. E. H. Stanner, the senior member of the anthropology staff, when he returned from study leave and fieldwork (Port Keats) at the end of August 1956. Stanner then prevailed upon the ANU's academic board, known as the Board of Graduate Studies (BOGS), that he be appointed head of department for at least two years so he could revitalize the department and thus salvage what he declaimed was "the sadly depreciated value of the Chair."[2] Only then, Stanner declared, would the chair regain its former international stature and attract a strong field of applicants. Five months later, this arrangement was abruptly reversed and the search reactivated. It was a messy and makeshift affair in which the university adhered loosely, at best, to its own procedures.

In the nature of academic appointments there are winners and mostly losers. The annals of university life are replete with disappointments. Nonetheless it is useful, on the basis of detailed documentary evidence, to show how this particular senior academic appointment was handled—the vagaries, the quirks and processes, questions of good faith and bad faith—and how the urgency to fill the chair brought in wider academic networks as senior figures within the anthropological fraternity became involved as referees for the various candidates, not to mention the lobbying for a preferred candidate or on behalf of one's self. Appointment decisions are also important in terms of their consequences, whether it be to continue a line of descent, theoretical orientations, or being the catalyst for change, as well as in terms of relationships within a department. It is, however, more than a matter of personal alliances and enmities, although these are integral. Rather, we are mindful of what David Mills calls the interplay of the four *i*'s: individuals, ideas, identities, and institutions (2008:3, 11). That is to say, academic networks and the relationships between individuals are mediated through institutional prisms that, in turn, have a bearing on the directions and orientations of an academic discipline (see Gray 2000, 2007; Stocking 1995). The appointing of senior academics brings these interrelationships into sharp focus.

As well as epistemological and institutional issues, there is a methodological question. The present study is firmly based on the documentary record, with a leavening of oral testimony, although we recognize that memory fades and transmutes with the passing of time (see Alden 2001:473, fn.10; Haslam 1999:xii.). We are also aware that documentary evidence has its own problems, not least in creating an illusion of fixed evidence. In short, no single set of documents and no single memory concerning a university appointment is likely to yield other than a partial and sometimes misleading version because even those most closely involved will necessarily have an incomplete (and sometimes mistaken) understanding of events, or repeat a trope generated by stories within a department often favorable to a failed candidate, or perhaps simply being deceitful, or any combination of these things. Our initial reading of the appointment file in the Davidson Papers,[3] which provided the impetus to write this paper, led to understandings that were continually modified as we consulted the Firth Archive, the Gluckman Papers, and sundry other sets of personal and institutional records. It thus follows that a plausible reconstruction of an academic appointment is contingent upon recourse to a broad archive of contemporary evidence.

PRELIMINARIES

From its establishment in 1946 the ANU had been beset by teething problems. The professors arrived in dribs and drabs, often dismayed by the unattractiveness of Canberra, the undeveloped state of the university campus, and the sometimes ambivalent attitude of the federal government toward its own creation. Unsurprisingly, some of the academics made speedy exits. Walter Crocker, the professor of international relations, was the first to come and the first to go, thereby confirming a habit of disaffectedly leaving employers at an early juncture and thereafter denouncing them (Crocker 1981). Crocker's defection underlined not so much "the extreme shortage of good men" to creditably fill positions at the new research university as the difficulty in retaining them.[4] By the time of Nadel's death, finding suitably qualified scholars continued to be a struggle, although many positions had been filled (Cornish 2007). Another departure involved Raymond Firth, who had been one of ANU's four academic advisors during the formative stages. It was hoped that he would remain as professor of anthropology and director of RSPacs, a position he accepted temporarily in 1951, but the cultural pull of the Old World saw him return to the London School of Economics (LSE).[5]

Nadel's death created more than one problem of succession. He had succeeded Crocker as dean of the RSPacs, and that position had to be filled, too. Briefly ANU originally had four research schools, each headed by a director (with executive powers) or else a dean (with more consultative powers). There was not much to pick from in RSPacs, which had four academic departments and was now down to only three professors: O. H. K. Spate (geography), J. W. Davidson (Pacific history), and C. P. Fitzgerald (Far Eastern history). Spate was appointed dean for two years when he returned from study leave in late 1956, but he soon resigned following a serious dispute with the vice chancellor, L. G. Melville. Davidson was then appointed for twelve months from mid-March 1957.[6] One of Davidson's duties as dean was to preside over the Electoral Committee for the vacant chair of anthropology.

A second development was the appointment of W. K. Hancock as professor of history and director of the Research School of Social Sciences (RSSS). As one of ANU's four academic advisors at the formative stage, Hancock was no stranger to the university; he arrived back in Canberra within days of Davidson assuming office as dean of RSPacs. Hancock is still widely regarded as the greatest historian Australia has produced (Low 2001; Davidson 2010). Conscious of his standing and status, he had a deep-seated urge to dispense patronage. Before accepting ANU's offer of employment, he had sought and received the assurance that he would be involved in the appointment of Nadel's successor and that he would be consulted about other professorial appointments in RSPacs, including potential directors of the school.[7]

STANNER'S PROPOSAL

W. E. H. Stanner, reader in comparative institutions, suggested to Melville a way out of the impasse created by the rejection of the chair by Edmund Leach and Douglas Oliver; this was to delay the appointment of a new professor and to give Stanner authority to get the department "back into a strong working condition" and regain its international stature.[8] His argument was that by withholding the chair "from the market for some time" it would "increase [its] sadly depreciated value" as well as give Stanner time to "reconstruct the department and set it on a new path of work."[9] He would then step aside, having not declared any interest in the chair for himself. In January 1957 Melville "regulariz[ed] the *de facto* arrangement" and confirmed Stanner's position as head of the Department of Anthropology and Sociology, adding, "It is not anticipated that any further move towards filling the Chair will be made for some time."[10] BOGS made Stanner's appointment conditional on his remaining in Canberra "most of the time, even though this is likely to involve his giving up field work which he had hoped shortly to undertake in connection with his own research."[11] Melville, however, had made a separate arrangement with Stanner the previous year, which enabled him to go to Port Keats from late June to the end of August 1957.[12] Stanner made a compelling argument, as 1957 would be a comparatively light year with only one new scholar arriving. The other students were in the field or near completion: "Until about mid year, therefore, things will be pretty quiet, not much more being required than routine supervision." Mid year was the best time to do fieldwork in northern Australia; added to this was an imperative: "It is a matter of getting some work done in North Australia in 1957, or postponing everything to an indefinite future."[13] Spate, as dean of RSPacs, supported Stanner.[14] Melville then approved Stanner's trip conditional that Spate made sure "Freeman was a willing party to the plan."[15] This appears to be a contravention of BOGS deliberations and conditions of appointing Stanner to head the department for two years. Notwithstanding, Spate and Melville were satisfied Freeman could run the department for those months Stanner was in the field.

Davidson believed Melville's loosely worded assurance resulted in Stanner regarding a delayed appointment "as his opportunity to demonstrate that he could make a real success of running the department. He had hoped, as he has told me several times, that in a few years he would be accepted as the natural person to continue to run the department on a permanent basis."[16] Stanner claimed to have another outcome in mind, namely, that of creating the circumstances in which Firth could be tempted back to the ANU as both professor of anthropology and director of RSPacs. He told Firth that he had "observed your wish that I should not introduce your name, but I can tell you now (I suppose far too late) that the whole rationale of my effort to keep things open in the department for a few years was an idea that if I could prevent a premature appointment of anyone to this Chair I might be able to fix things so that you would again have to be asked."[17]

As part of his strategy Stanner rejected visiting professorships, which ran the risk, he believed, that one such appointee might be invited to become a permanent professor.[18] He forcefully declared that "in due course, I shall make my own proposals about visiting Professorships. The first year I shall make them for is likely to be 1959, when I hope there will be a concentration of people returned from the field."[19] This caused Spate to comment to Melville:

> As you will see, it is unfortunately completely *non possumus*. Some of his arguments seem rather obscure, but his general line is quite clear. This was of course to be reckoned with. I do not know whether any useful purpose would be served by discussing it further with Dr. Stanner. His general views on the development of the Department's work in the near future are I think sound on the whole.[20]

Like Davidson, Spate remained skeptical, reckoning that Stanner "may not be entirely disinterested." Melville himself was having second thoughts, wondering whether "we must take some action now or lose our opportunities."[21] There seems little doubt that Stanner's rigid manner and his curt dismissal of the possibility of visiting professors for the foreseeable future did not endear him to Melville and some in the BOGS. As a result Melville may have lost confidence in Stanner's ability to make a balanced assessment. Moreover, Stanner's approach to visiting professors may have been a factor in accounting for Melville's secrecy when he found a possible candidate for the chair in mid-1957.

J. A. BARNES

John Barnes was the successful candidate for the chair at the University of Sydney in 1955 (the unanimous choice of the selection committee) with Stanner ranked second (Gray and Munro 2011). His credentials were undoubted, as he had worked on Max Gluckman's Rhodes-Livingstone Institute team in the 1940s, written two books on the Ngoni tribes of Northern Rhodesia (Zambia) and Nyasaland (Malawi), and conducted fieldwork in a fishing village in western Norway.[22] At the time of his appointment he was reader at the LSE. He had been tempted to Sydney quite simply because he could see no prospects for advancement in Britain; "all the professors of anthropology were hale and hearty, and none were near the retiring age" (2007:246).

Arriving in Sydney in May 1956, Barnes was soon disillusioned.[23] Unsurprisingly, Barnes was dismayed by the "hordes" of undercommitted pass students who had no interest in "a broad learning for its own sake." Nor was it much better on the postgraduate front. Sydney had just started to supervise anthropology at the PhD level, but only one of the six doctoral students gave cause for confidence. His own departmental staff had a bearing on the unsatisfactory "pedagogic environment," as he called it. The two other senior members of the department, Ian Hogbin and Arthur Capell, were too entrenched and were not interested in change. Happy to continue delivering the same lectures year in year out, they resisted the mounting of new courses. Such was the state of the university's finances that no new positions were on offer (as had been promised), thus adding to the burdens of teaching.

These financial and academic problems at Sydney caused Barnes to wonder if he had made the right decision, and his misgivings were compounded by what he regarded as the generally undistinguished anthropological fraternity in Australia. Nor could he see himself as being able to effect any changes in courses offered or teaching. There were no funds for new appointments, and his ability to influence the research agenda was hindered by his predecessor, A. P. Elkin, reneging on an understanding to hand over the editorship of the journal *Oceania* (2007:142–143).

Barnes feared that the aggravations might distract him from his academic calling. He explained to Gluckman:

> I have to guard against becoming a reformer! I can see it happening already with people who came out at about the same time as I did, or a little before it. One gets so frustrated at the short-comings of Australian life, and so little encouragement to persue [sic] learning and truth that one abandons scholarship and the ivory tower and tries to change the world. I don't suppose that Elkin needed much encouragement to follow this course; but this is certainly the line he followed, and this is why he has this extremely high reputation among the public generally here and is more or less unknown outside Australia. I hope this won't happen to me.[24]

Keen to fill the professorial positions vacant in RSPacs and aware that Barnes was unhappy at Sydney, Hancock suggested to Melville that Barnes should be sounded out for the chair.[25] Contrary to Stanner, Hancock took a view that leaving the chair unfilled diminished the ANU internationally. The search had dragged on for almost eighteen months, and Barnes was an elegant way out of this stalled situation. Hancock had known Barnes for some years, even recommending him for a position at Rhodes University in South Africa in 1949, and Barnes had been a participant in Hancock's Tropical Dependencies seminar in London a few years later.[26] Hancock had also been one of Barnes's referees for the Sydney position, describing him as "completely first rate.... He is lively, friendly and a man of the most cheerful good humour. He is very hard working and well disciplined and has, I believe, as well, a strong vein of personal originality."[27]

In June 1957 Stanner left for three months of fieldwork at Port Keats (Wadeye) in the Northern Territory in a Land Rover that had been purchased with departmental funds earmarked for the 1956–57 professorial salary. On or near the day Stanner departed, the university registrar advised Melville that it was difficult to interpret the ambiguous passage, assuring Stanner that there was no intention of filling the chair "for some time." In spite of this ambiguity he advised Melville that he didn't think it precluded the ANU "from accepting someone who let us know he was anxious to come," despite being unsure as to "what interpretation to put on" the arrangement with Stanner.[28] Consequently an appointment was made for Melville to meet with Barnes when the latter was in Canberra attending a meeting of the Social Science Research Council.[29]

Barnes was asked if he was interested in moving to Canberra. "Attracted by the idea," Barnes wanted to seek the views of his wife, Frances, before making any commitment.[30] In the meanwhile Melville asked him to keep their conversation confidential. The immediate upshot was an awkward meeting later that day with Davidson, who was an old friend of Barnes. It was evident to Barnes that Davidson had been sidelined, hence his discomfiture. When John and Frances Barnes visited Canberra two weeks later, "surveying the schools and talking to the University's architects," Davidson was in Noumea on university business; he had still not been informed of these developments.[31] Of course, as Barnes wrote to Gluckman, "Fran's sudden and unexplained appearance in Canberra with a curious interest in visiting schools and looking at university houses in the company of the Deputy Registrar must have made things obvious to anyone with half an eye open."[32]

One can understand Barnes's surprise at being headhunted for the chair at ANU. When Davidson asked Barnes in late March whether he had any suggestions for the chair, should the committee wish to reopen the search, he suggested his close friend and colleague Max Gluckman, professor of anthropology at the University of Manchester, whose presence in Canberra would have made his life at Sydney bearable. Freeman, too, on a visit to Sydney in late May, enthusiastically discussed with Barnes the possibility of tempting Gluckman to Canberra. Barnes too had been urging Gluckman to make himself available to ANU, and now he was being sounded out by Melville for that very position. The speed with which the ANU acted and the secrecy must have been somewhat bewildering for Barnes, but it was a way out of Sydney.[33]

Even Derek Freeman, who went out of his way to find out what was going on, was caught out by what transpired, explaining to Gluckman that he was greatly surprised because Barnes had recently agreed that Freeman and he should persuade Gluckman to apply. Davidson, who had returned from Noumea, was also surprised, "for he had not heard the news himself until earlier the same day." That Melville "had acted without conferring with the Electoral Committee *in any way* . . . annoyed Davidson; and . . . also annoyed the other members of the Committee with whom I have discussed it."[34] Davidson believed that Hancock and Melville were undermining his position as dean,[35] and he complained that Hancock was interfering in the affairs of RSPacS, one of several episodes that led to the estrangement between Davidson and his former patron.[36]

THE APPOINTMENT (PROCESS)

Davidson was somewhat mollified when he realised Melville had not intended to bypass the usual appointment procedures and that an orderly process would go ahead.[37]

But what was proper process? What were the ANU's own rules? In successive letters, Melville provided Hancock with information regarding appointments, which had altered since the latter's involvement as academic adviser in 1949, when ANU appointed by invitation:

The Appointments Process
The de facto position is that [BOGS] makes the appointments and the de jure is the Council. In actual fact, the Electoral Committee makes a nomination and the Board's only concern in reviewing that nomination has been to establish the overall standards to be observed. Lately we have added to the stature of the Electoral Committees by having a senior representative of each school included in the membership so that the recommendation comes to the Board with a greater unanimity of understanding of the standards adopted. The Electoral Committees have fairly wide discretion on the procedures to be followed and, if delay would prejudice the best appointment, can even issue an invitation.[38]

Advertising Vacancies
There is stronger tendency to her to make vacancies known, usually through press advertisements . . . than prevails elsewhere. This in part reflects our special situation as a National University with perhaps more than ordinary responsibility to give any possible candidate a chance to apply, both to ensure the best appointments and to prevent any suggestion of patronage. . . . There is also much to be said for the Board's [Board of Graduate Studies] procedure as a means of protecting standards in a young and rapidly growing university. . . . However, the policy is not immutable, and I am sure the Board would be willing to listen to arguments for any other methods of filling posts within the University.[39]

Paradoxically, the ANU was relaxing its appointment procedures in practice even as they were being tightened up on paper. What transpired was only a veneer of proper process as the formalities were followed rather than respected. It shows that Melville confidently anticipated a simple process that would result in the appointment of Barnes. When the Electoral Committee met on June 24, the chairman reported in wording that implied that Barnes had approached the university, not the other way around:

> The university had received information that Professor J. A. Barnes might like to be considered for appointment to the Chair of Anthropology at a fairly early date. He reminded the Committee that Professor Barnes's name had been frequently mentioned during earlier consideration by the Committee but had not been seriously considered owing to his recent acceptance of the Chair at the University of Sydney. It was clear, however, that the information now received made it necessary to consider whether Professor Barnes should now be invited to accept the Chair.[40]

The Electoral Committee also considered that the

> proposed appointment of Professor Barnes might be in conflict with the understandings entered into with Dr. Stanner when he was asked to act as Head of the Department [of Anthropology]. The Vice Chancellor's letter to Dr. Stanner on this point . . . was read and it was agreed that the proposed appointment was not in conflict with the terms of that letter, though it was clear that he would necessarily be disappointed at this new development. It was clear, however, that the needs for the development of the Department made it essential not to miss such an opportunity for a permanent appointment as had been presented.[41]

The Electoral Committee agreed that the external assessors—E. E. Evans-Pritchard, Meyer Fortes, and Robert Redfield—should be asked for "their opinions of Professor Barnes's qualifications for the Chair and his suitability for appointment in relation to the present senior members within the Department," namely, Stanner and Freeman. Having dismissed the possibility of approaching Raymond Firth for the chair, the committee decided to request his services as an external assessor.[42]

Melville and Davidson wrote individually to Stanner. As acting head of the Department of Anthropology and Sociology, Stanner should have been informed (if not consulted) that the Electoral Committee was reopening the question of an appointment to the chair and that Barnes had been approached. Melville was conscious that Stanner would be upset and disappointed, and his letter was carefully crafted but hardly truthful. Melville assured Stanner "that no decision has been reached and your own position is not being overlooked. It may well be some time before I can let you know the outcome of the present consideration, and I see no reason why you should let it interfere with your present arrangements."[43] Davidson, as chairman of the Electoral Committee, wrote in "long hand to emphasize the fact that this was a private and personal communication," a puzzling decision seeing as he had been asked to formally advise Stanner. It was, he told Stanner, "the possible availability of Barnes which had led to the re-opening of the question"; he also inquired "whether [Stanner] wished to do anything to support his own claim to consideration as a candidate for the Chair."[44]

Stanner did not receive this mail until 23 July. It is likely both Melville and Davidson were aware of the unpredictability of the mail service to Port Keats. Whether or not this was a deliberate tactic on their part is unknown, but Davidson or Melville could have cabled Stanner, as Freeman had over another matter concerning a graduate student in the department. The decision to write rather than cable (or do both) suggests that both men knew that Stanner had been deceived—a view Stanner certainly held, telling Davidson that the Electoral Committee reconvening to consider the appointment of Barnes told him "nothing about the most important things: what urgencies were felt, or what pressures were used, and by whom, to start this affair in my absence, without my knowledge, and in disregard of an agreement about the Department."[45]

There had been one unexpected problem, not anticipated by either Melville or Hancock. As we have seen, Barnes and Freeman had attempted to persuade Max Gluckman to apply for the chair. Freeman forced the issue, beseeching Gluckman that he was the "person best qualified to . . . promote the development of anthropology in Australia generally"; if it were a choice between "you and John there could be no question at all as to which should fill the ANU Chair of Anthropology."[46] Freeman then sent Davidson an extract of a personal letter from Gluckman in which the latter had expressed that he "would certainly . . . consider the possibility of going [to ANU]." For good measure Freeman appended a copy of Gluckman's CV and his entry in

Who's Who, 1955.[47] Davidson passed this information to Melville, saying that there was no point in the Electoral Committee reconvening until Gluckman had responded, and adding the rebuke that "I hope that from this point on we shall be able to proceed to a decision in an orderly and constitutional way."[48] Davidson's pitch to Gluckman was that if "one could plan for an ideal world, one would hope to see you in Canberra and John Barnes . . . in Sydney. Then, anthropology in Australia would be in a really flourishing condition. Unfortunately, things are not so simple." Because Barnes's position and working conditions were far from ideal, to build up the struggling Sydney department would "take years . . . if it could be done at all; and John Barnes is somewhat repelled by the unpromising prospect."[49] The year before, he had alluded to this elsewhere.[50] Such a view that Gluckman needed some wooing was supported by Firth, who told Davidson that Gluckman "may well have wanted to be asked, especially in view of the earlier request to Leach."[51] In rejecting the overtures of Freeman and Davidson, Gluckman saved the Electoral Committee the problem of challenging Melville and Hancock.

With Gluckman out of consideration and no other external prospects, there was a need nonetheless to create the artifice of a selection process; the inclusion of Stanner and Freeman only illustrates the farcical nature of the process. Stanner did not know he was being considered, and Freeman likewise was enlisted to give the process a veneer of legitimacy, although he told one of us that his sole motivation was to thwart Stanner (interview, 3 February 1993). Freeman had limited experience, although he had been acting head after Nadel's death and was highly thought of both by Nadel and others at the ANU and the LSE. The external assessors, by contrast, took the process more seriously, unaware it was a fait accompli.

REFEREE REPORTS

Firth provided the most detailed report. He prefaced it by expressing respect for Stanner's "intelligence and insight and admired his grasp of broad subjects," and he paid tribute to Stanner's "strong interest in politics and his training in economics as well as anthropology."[52] The most damning statement was his assessment that Stanner "has been his worst academic enemy. Essentially he has seemed unwilling to face responsibility. His refusal of the directorship of the East African Institute of Social Research was symptomatic of his tendency to dwell upon the difficulties inherent in the situation rather than the possibilities of what can be made out of it. His desire for a really worthwhile achievement sometimes makes him over-elaborate his argument." He continued: "While I respect his capacity and achievement I recognise his defects, which are much more obvious than those of the other two men. How far complete responsibility for a Research Department would settle and strengthen him as an administrator I do not know."

Firth also raised a question mark against Barnes; he wondered whether Barnes "would supply the drive and theoretical distinction needed in a Research Professorship." On Freeman he expressed more certainty, confident that he "would . . . supply the drive and his theoretical potential [is] at least Barnes' equal . . . a reservation is whether the mould he would supply would in the end turn out to be cast-iron." Firth, not sure that any of the candidates were suitable, suggested that "if there is a possibility of any other major candidate being in the field, then I think it would be well to look more widely before coming to a decision."

Meyer Fortes dismissed Stanner's claims, stating that he did not "feel that Dr. Stanner is a suitable person for this Chair." He declared that Stanner's interests, judged from his publications and from "talks with him when he was over here last year, are not primarily anthropological and sociological." In his opinion, for all of Stanner's "ability, charm, and versatility," he did not think Stanner was "likely to give any impetus to a department or to maintain a high level of research in it." He saw it as a choice between Barnes and Freeman. He favored Freeman, whom he described as "one of the two or three outstanding Social Anthropologists not yet in professorial positions in the British Commonwealth." Freeman's fieldwork was "superb," "rich, and penetrating, in quality, . . . a man with original ideas . . . and a meticulous respect for scientific accuracy. . . . [Combining] patient and acute analysis of detail with theoretical judgment of a high order . . . I can only say he would add distinction to any department in which he held a post." The American anthropologist and ethnolinguist Robert Redfield knew little about Barnes and made no reference to Freeman; on the basis of Barnes and Stanner holding similar qualities, he pumped for Stanner, a "very good man, an able anthropologist, and an excellent personal and academic associate." Evans-Pritchard did not respond to the ANU's request to provide a report on the candidates.[53]

MAKING THE APPOINTMENT

Ignoring Firth's suggestion that the decision be delayed, Fortes's support for Freeman, and Redfield's preference for Stanner, the Electoral Committee went ahead and recommended the appointment of Barnes as was always planned. In providing its recommendation to BOGS, the Electoral Committee advised it had received "information . . . that Professor J. A. Barnes . . . would consider an offer of appointment to the Chair of Anthropology," as though Barnes had initiated proceedings. The Committee duly recommended Barnes stating that his work "shows originality, intellectual power, and unusual breadth of interest . . . a freshness and originality of approach." Aware that he was "not primarily a theorist in the sense that Professor Nadel was in his later years," the Committee was confident that his approach to empirical studies "is of a kind which has made them (and will continue to make them) of considerable significance in the development of theory." Moreover, Barnes had reached a stage in his career "at which he both sees clearly the role of the head of a research department and is prepared fully to carry out the duties which the role involves." As for future research Barnes prepared a statement, at the University's request, where he indicated "generally the type of research he would like to see the Department undertake—particularly in New Guinea—and . . . it would be his intention to keep in close touch with field work, by visits to the field, while avoiding any prolonged absence from Canberra . . . till he was sure that others could carry out his duties toward junior staff and students."[54] And finally, "on grounds of personality . . . Barnes would be an admirable choice."

A final matter for BOGS to consider was whether or not to promote Freeman to a readership. He had originally applied for the position of reader, but Nadel was prepared only to make him a senior fellow. Nadel wrote at the time of Freeman's appointment that "on the grounds of capabilities and research" he had no "hesitation in recommending his appointment to a Readership. On the other hand, his publications are at the moment insignificant," and Nadel subsequently recommended Freeman be appointed as a senior fellow. He intended to "keep him on and offer him the chance of a Readership in due course." In the discussion it was noted that the Committee placed Freeman slightly below Barnes on two grounds: "his keen . . . interest in theoretical questions leads him to a certain rigidity in his approach to empirical studies," and he "is in the middle of a period of most valuable work upon the Iban, which would make it difficult (and perhaps undesirable) for him to assume the duties of a Head of Department." The Committee recommended and BOGS agreed that Freeman be promoted to reader. In his autobiography, Barnes expresses annoyance that he had been presented with a fait accompli over Freeman's promotion to a readership. In fact, Barnes was consulted beforehand and had given his distinct approbation.[55] Freeman, of course, was "entirely happy" with the Electoral Committee's decisions, telling Firth, "It's a huge relief to know that the long, difficult, and profitless interregnum that has followed Nadel's tragic death is at last at an end."[56]

In later life Barnes memorably said that he "jumped at the possibility of moving from an impoverished teaching department to a well-funded research school" (2007:143). Actually, he had to overcome a number of misgivings. It seemed that he would be swapping one unsatisfactory department for another. Before becoming a contender he had written to Gluckman that "there are several people at ANU who would be quite pleased to see the anthropology department run downhill for a while, and who don't want to see the chair filled in a hurry, and certainly not with someone as forceful as Nadel was."[57] He predicted that "in two years' time the [ANU] will be quite dead, so anyone who goes there then will have to start from scratch, with a rather sour Freeman and Stanner as a legacy from the past."[58] His professional qualms mainly centered on having to work with Stanner and Freeman and the poor relationship between the two. He also had to consider the upheaval of yet another relocation and Frances's medical career being put on hold. But he overcame his concerns, and all that remained was for Barnes to stay at Sydney until his two years were up and thereby avoid the necessity to repay his fares and removal expenses to the university—but at the cost of having to administer two departments until his arrival in Canberra in May 1958 at the age of thirty-nine (2007:273–274).

Barnes got the chair; Freeman got a readership; Stanner got nothing. From the moment Stanner heard that the search for the chair had been reopened, he realized that he had been duped. His disappointment and anger were palpable as he saw his best-laid plans disappear, compounded by the duplicity of Melville (and Hancock) and the apparent connivance of Davidson. Stanner was furious with Davidson's part in the process: "As far as I am concerned, what you and my other colleagues are now doing rests on a breach of faith. There was an agreement, and you would know it. I recall that, before leaving Canberra, I asked you as Dean to watch for and delay until my return any attempted changes of policy." Stanner felt badly let down by Davidson. It was, Stanner declared, an absurd situation in settling on three candidates: "one of whom did not ask to be considered [himself], and one of whom [Freeman] assured me not long since that he would ask to be considered if only a junior person (such as [Cyril] Belshaw) were being thought about seriously.... These methods may fill the Chair, though not too gloriously; but they will not earn the ANU much respect. I can only ask: WHY do things in this way?"[59]

The burden of Stanner's recriminations, however, centered on Melville and Hancock. Stanner's understanding of events, what he called "the odd affair at Canberra," was correct: the decision was "cut and dried before I left, and was under way within a week of my departure. By the time I heard, it was just a matter of signatures. There was nothing I could do except go on with what interested me. So I came back [to Port Keats]—digging out a cave, and finishing off an organizational study." He saw Hancock as the primary instigator: "in essence, it began with Hancock, who swung Davidson into line, and Davidson and Freeman worked together, Melville condoning."[60] Realizing that the Sydney Chair, the only other chair of anthropology in Australia, would again be vacant, he expressed some misgivings about its future. He argued that Barnes resigning from Sydney "will wreck that unhappy

Department; and make us some justified enemies, if the outcome of solicitation by the ANU. . . . [H]is appointment will look ramp. I only hope you [Davidson] have taken this into good account. Surely, if you were determined on making an appointment, you should either have advertised or widened the field of consideration."[61]

Notwithstanding, several questions remain largely unanswered. Despite denying any interest in the chair, was Stanner's primary motivation to keep the department in limbo while waiting to seize his chance to implement his plan for succession? We have to take his word that he hoped for Firth to return as professor and director. But there is a more pressing question raised by the selection process: Why was Stanner treated so shabbily? A concomitant question: Why was he deemed unsuitable for senior positions, not only at the ANU but elsewhere? We will consider these questions on another occasion.[62]

AFTERMATH

The process of finding a successor to Nadel, protracted as it was, was not without its aftershocks. First, Davidson was mistaken in thinking that Stanner, although "bitterly disappointed," seemed "determined to accept the situation."[63] To the contrary. Stanner returned to Canberra briefly at the end of 1957 before heading off again to Port Keats (Wadeye). As it was, Stanner made four trips, spending twenty of the next twenty-four months using Port Keats as a respite from the politics and hurt of the ANU.[64] In a talk delivered at University House in September 1959 Stanner said, "Sometimes when I am in that northern country, where the Dreaming stands for—all the ultimate meanings which the human intuition finds in life—take on a very great power. Then I have to resume diplomatic relations with the ANU. Sometimes this is quite hard."[65]

Stanner poured his heart out to Firth in letters that are full of recrimination and forecasts of doom for Australian anthropology: "Well, me, I am out of it, and not ungladly so; I like little of what I see and hear; and if it were not that the School, and anthropology in Australia, were in such a bad way, I should have thoughts only for what I am doing which interests me."[66] In the months since the appointment of Barnes, Stanner had lashed out at various members of the Electoral Committee, but he reserved his severest comments for Hancock, with devastating clarity and insight. In Stanner's opinion, Hancock's

> form becomes increasingly clear: much protestation that he does not want power and responsibility, together with a slow acquisition of both. I should guess that when the time comes he will with the utmost reluctance allow himself to be persuaded that it is his duty to look after [RSPacs] as well as [RSSS]. Meanwhile, with much pretty play on the disabilities of age ("after all, I'm going on for sixty") and on the joys of other times ("there was no snobbery at All Souls") and of things foregone ("I have been too long away to understand the modern Australia") he proceeds to dominate.[67]

The following year Stanner added to his disappointments by applying for the chair of anthropology at Sydney that had been vacated by Barnes. He was careless enough to submit his previous application, which contained the names of two deceased referees, Nadel and Radcliffe-Brown. Whereas he was ranked second in 1955, on this occasion he failed to reach the short list. The chair went to W. R. Geddes (Gray and Munro 2011:363–364). Marie Reay recalls meeting Stanner in the University House car park soon after the decision was made, when he broke down and wept. He was devastated and wondering whether he should remain in anthropology (interview, 3 February 1993). This was probably as bleak as it got for Stanner.

Overall the process of making the appointment led to a rupturing of relations: Hancock and Melville's secrecy and duplicity overshadowed the deliberations, and Stanner blamed Hancock, seeing him as the instigator. Barnes was both a willing and unwilling participant in the secrecy and machinations of Melville and Hancock. Relations between Stanner and Davidson never quite recovered.

The aftermath of Barnes's appointment revealed a pattern of fracturing relations centered on Derek Freeman. What started off on a promising note progressively soured. Soon after Freeman's arrival, Stanner told Firth, "Freeman has settled down happily: he will be a strong addition to the staff, and is already well liked."[68] In spite of his early assessment, relations steadily worsened and were ruptured after the appointment of Freeman to a readership. When Gluckman declined to be considered, Freeman then said that he was "entirely happy with what has now happened," not simply his promotion to a readership but the appointment of Barnes to the chair. He was confident that he and Barnes "would work together extremely well."[69]

There was a steady deterioration of working relations over time between Barnes and Freeman, what Barnes later described as his "long and troubled relationship" with Freeman (2007:345). Confrontational, disputatious, and unyielding, prone to deracination, and convinced of having ultimate answers, Freeman taxed the abilities of his head of department. Barnes found it unpleasant dealing with Freeman's overpowering personality and occasionally bizarre behavior. He was, said Barnes, "the major disruptive element" in the department (2007:356). An unintended consequence was an uneasy détente between Barnes and Stanner, ironically given that Barnes had previously expressed his disdain of Stanner, on one occasion saying that "Derek has his limitations, but at least he is an anthropologist, which is more than one can say of Stanner."[70]

CONCLUSIONS AND DÉNOUEMENT

When the search for Nadel's replacement began, it was hoped that the appointee would be suitable as dean, if not director, of RSPacS. With the appointment of Barnes, these plans were shelved. Barnes was the antithesis of Nadel in personality and manner. Nadel was irked by the limitations on his power as dean, whereas Barnes expressed no interest in higher office. The overriding motivation of the ANU was to fill the chair, which had been vacant too long, giving the department a direction and leadership that had been lacking since Nadel's death.

The situation found by the young British anthropologist Jeremy Beckett, who arrived at ANU two weeks before Nadel's death, recalls that it "coincided with the departure of a number of . . . people in the department, and within a few weeks we were reduced to a small group under the acting headship of Derek Freeman, the only member above the level of research scholar." Nadel's "death left a vacuum, intellectually and politically. There was an expectation that he would be replaced quite soon, but by whom? . . . It was a difficult period for everyone, since major decisions were on hold" (2001:90). Twelve months later Robert Glasse, a doctoral student, made a similar observation when he returned from the field, commenting that the department was "in some disarray." Six months into Stanner's time as acting head and just as the endeavors regarding Barnes were gathering steam, he was offered a temporary lectureship at the University of Sydney. He notes the contrast: the appointment was a "godsend"—the "presence of Ian Hogbin, Mervyn Meggitt, and D'Arcy Ryan on the faculty led to many helpful discussions," unlike the situation at the ANU (Glasse 1992:243–244).

The ANU anthropologist Michael Young, in an obituary for Barnes, stated that his "theoretical contributions were to fields as diverse as kinship and social organization, political and legal anthropology, network analysis, the sociology of knowledge, historical demography, colonialism and post-colonialism, and the study of professional ethics" (2010:2–3). He also ensured the continuity of Nadel's broader research agenda by the continuing interests of the department to center on twelve specified topics, all of which dealt with social organization, politics, economics, and exchange (Hays 1992:33–34). Barnes, on the other hand, claims to have "resisted pressure to produce a detailed plan for departmental research. . . . I was lucky in being able to maintain intellectually flexible parameters for our departmental research activities, and although I often reported of our research that it conformed to our department's strategy, I escaped having to disclose exactly what that strategy was" (2007:143–144).

Barnes continued Nadel's research focus on Papua New Guinea, writing a seminal paper, "African Models in the New Guinea Highlands" (Barnes 1962; see also Barnes 2007:331; Beckett 1999; Hays 1992). He also appointed, in 1958, his former Manchester colleague A. L. "Bill" Epstein, who "brought more African research experience to bear on New Guinea, notably among the Tolai of New Britain" (Young 2010: 4). One difficulty of an anthropology department within RSPacS was in defining the limits of "the Pacific." In Barnes's time it extended as far as northern Afghanistan, but he drew the line at Madagascar (2007:293–294). The broadening of social science research in Australia also led to the occasional "turf war" with other departments as the anthropology department redefined its disciplinary span and its interdisciplinary linkages. Linguistics and prehistory were taken on board, under the umbrella of the anthropology department, but eventually they went their separate ways.

As part of his strategy, Barnes put high priority on postgraduate supervision and enforced the maintenance of standards. On one occasion he refused to accept any of the doctoral candidates on offer because he felt none was sufficiently equipped for the rigors of fieldwork (2007:281, 294–295). He was a supervisor who encouraged his students to work out their own research objectives, which "must have been a somewhat traumatic initiation process for new arrivals to the department." Although socially welcoming, intellectually he "preferred to neglect, or even ignore, newly arrived students in the hope that they would learn to work on their own and would discover what their own anthropological interests really were. I think this policy worked reasonably well; the department had a good success rate for doctoral dissertations that were substantial contributions to our understanding of the societies in our region" (2007:143).

The department expanded both in spatial range and in scholarly output. Beckett had noticed a change when he returned from his second stint of fieldwork in the Torres Strait; he felt that

> the Anthropology department's character had changed considerably . . . in particular, the Highlands no longer dominated the discussion. We got to see a rather different side of British anthropology, particularly during the visit of Max Gluckman, whom Barnes had invited. . . . [I] found it refreshing to have conflict brought into focus, since I had so much of it in my notebooks. . . . I tried to incorporate some of these ideas, along with John Barnes's work on networks in Norway. (2001:95)

The intellectual energy and scholarly collegiality missing for Glasse in early 1957 was back. Barnes brought a stability, direction, and intellectual vigor to the department. Barnes moved Australian anthropology into the mainstream of social inquiry (Hiatt 1965:ix), giving the department "the international reputation that it had gained under Fred Nadel."[71]

Stanner's standing was diminished; he had been placed third behind Barnes and Freeman, illustrating the lack of faith BOGS had in him. In the brief period Stanner headed the department, with the support of BOGS and Melville, he had made only negative decisions, most notably rejecting visiting professors. This had the potential to isolate the department internationally and to underpin the potential for intellectual and scholarly sterility inherent in a new university like ANU and alluded to by both Beckett and Glasse.

Stanner would not have made a good fit. Referee reports from other senior positions he applied for suggest he was a man unwilling to take on responsibility, with a tendency to dwell upon the difficulties inherent in the situation rather than the possibilities of what could be done. Firth, for example, alerted the Electoral Committee of the risk if Stanner was made department head: "How far complete responsibility for a Research Department would settle and strengthen him as an administrator I do not know."[72] Elkin in turn had described Stanner as a person "apt to dissipate his energy in various directions, and finds it hard to decide just what he wants to do";[73] "He is a little unsure of himself . . . and prone to let circumstances beat him."[74] In retrospect, the ANU got it right: he was not the person to head a research department. Stanner had offered to remake the department, but he showed interest in his own work above that of revitalizing the department.

Given the humiliation and rejection, Stanner wondered whether remaining in Canberra was possible: "I could get along very well with Barnes, but I do not think it would be a good thing for me to stay on. Throat-cutting of that order leaves a lot of blood lying around."[75] Stanner also retained an ambition for a chair. Aware that he was courting a "second failure," he applied halfheartedly (as we have seen) for the Sydney chair left vacant by Barnes's departure but did not reach the short list. He remained at the ANU until his retirement. He was appointed to the second chair of anthropology in 1964, almost a consolation prize, as he believed the chair was earmarked for F. G. Bailey, a British social anthropologist who was part of Gluckman's Manchester School. Bailey was unavailable.

Barnes left ANU in 1969 to become foundation professor of sociology at Cambridge. There are complex reasons for his departure, but a large part of the explanation was a desire to "avoid spending the next decade being administratively responsible for Freeman."[76] Dissatisfaction had brought him to the ANU, and it accompanied his departure.[77] A final twist to the tale is that Freeman was appointed professor and head of the department after the departure of Barnes and Stanner.

1. While noting the death of Nadel, the official history of the ANU (Foster and Varghese 1996:110) is silent on the succession, not even mentioning the name of eventual appointee J. A. Barnes.
2. Stanner to Spate, 11 February 1957, ANUA 53/1114/6.5.2.1, Part 1 (Anthropology Department, RSPacS).
3. Davidson Papers, ANUA 57/30 (RSPacS, Chair of Anthropology, 1957–1958).
4. Firth to Hancock, 25 March 1949, Hancock Papers, ANUA 77/15.
5. Firth 1974, 1996: 7; Firth to Copland, 11 February 1952 (copy), Crocker Papers, Series 9, vol. 1.2 ("The basic reason is that my roots in Europe go too deep").
6. Spate to Melville, 13 February 1957, ANUA 19/6/6.2.1.2, Part 3 (O. H. K. Spate); Hohnen to Davidson, 21 March 1957, ANUA 19/87/6.2.1.3, Part 1 (J. W. Davidson); Spate 2006: 27.
7. Hancock to Melville, 24 February 1956, ANUA 19/18/9.2.1.7(c), (W. K. Hancock); Melville to Hancock, 16 March 1956, ANUA 19/18/9.2.1.7, Part 1.
8. Melville to Hancock, 21 November 1956, ANUA 19/18/9.2.1.7(c); BOGS Minutes, 28 September 1956, 26 October 1965, ANUA 193; Barnes to Gluckman, 25 March 1957, Gluckman Papers; Gray and Munro 2012.
9. Stanner to Spate, 11 February 1957, ANUA 53/1114/6.5.2.1, Part 1.
10. Melville to Stanner, 11 January 1957, ANUA 53/1114/6.5.2.1, Part 1.
11. BOGS Minutes, 23 February 1957, ANUA 193.
12. Stanner to Melville, 3 December 1956, Spate to Melville, 14 December 1956. Stanner had previously sought permission from Melville to accept a position as visiting professor at Harvard and Cornell Universities in the belief that a new professor would take up duties in the first term of 1957. If Leach had accepted, he would not have been available until July 1957. Stanner to Melville, 16 April 1956, Melville to Stanner, 26 April 1956, Stanner to Melville, 4 June 1956, Melville to Stanner 13 June 1956, ANUA 19/82/6.2.2.1, Part 2 (W. E. H. Stanner).
13. Stanner to Melville, 3 December 1956. ANUA 19/82/6.2.2.1, Part 2.
14. Spate to Melville, 14 December 1956; Spate to Melville, 9 January 1957, ANUA 19/82/6.2.2.1, Part 2.
15. Notation by v-c (4 January 1957) on Spate to Melville, 14 December 1956, ANUA 19/82/6.2.2.1, Part 2.
16. Davidson to Firth, 10 June 1957, FIRTH7/3/39; also Freeman to Gluckman, 7 June 1957, Gluckman Papers.

17. Stanner to Firth, 15 October 1958, FIRTH 8/2/13.

18. There had been several candidates proposed as visiting professorship, including potential contenders for the chair, namely, Meyer Fortes at Cambridge and Isaac Schapera of the lse. See Barnes to Gluckman, 25 March 1957, Gluckman Papers.

19. Stanner to Spate, 11 February 1957, ANUA 53/1114/6.5.2.1, Part 1.

20. Spate to Melville, 25 February 1957, ANUA 53/1114/6.5.2.1, Part 1.

21. Melville to Spate, 5 March 1957, ANUA 53/1114/6.5.2.1, Part 1.

22. Barnes 1951, 1954a, 1954b.

23. The remainder of this section is drawn from Barnes's autobiography (2007:256–268); Barnes to Firth, 25 January 1957, FIRTH 8/1/3; Barnes to Gluckman, 25 March 1957, 28 June 1957, Gluckman Papers.

24. Barnes to Gluckman, 25 March 1957, Gluckman Papers.

25. The other vacant chairs within RSPacS were international relations and economics.

26. Barnes 2007: 199; Davidson 2010: 267. Barnes was repelled by the apartheid regime in South Africa and declined to pursue the matter.

27. Hancock to Registrar, 27 June 1955, "Chair of Anthropology 1955," University of Sydney Archives, g3/190.

28. Notation (6 June 1957) on Melville to Stanner, 11 January 1957, ANUA 53/1114/6.5.2.1, Part 1 [Department of Anthropology, RSPacS, ANU file 6.5.2.1].

29. Barnes to Gluckman, 28 June 1957; Freeman to Gluckman, 15 July 1957, Gluckman Papers. Some of the details concerning Barnes being sounded out by ANU (2007:269–270) do not square with the contemporary documentation. For example, Barnes recalls that he went to Canberra on that occasion to examine a PhD candidate.

30. Barnes to Gluckman, 28 June 1957, Gluckman Papers.

31. Davidson to Melville, 10 May 1957, ANUA 19/87/6.2.1.3, Part 2; Davidson to Firth, 10 July 1957, FIRTH 7/5/39.

32. Barnes to Gluckman, 28 June 1957, Gluckman Papers. It was during this visit that Barnes told Freeman of the vice chancellor's approach.

33. The paragraph is drawn from Barnes to Gluckman, 25 March, 28 June 1957, and Freeman to Gluckman, 7 June, 8 July, 15 July 1957, Gluckman Papers; Barnes 2001:143; Barnes 2007: 269.

34. Freeman to Gluckman, 15 July 1957, Gluckman Papers. Emphasis in original.

35. Hancock's biographer (Davidson 2010:407) agrees that he interfered in the affairs of RSPacS: "He enjoyed a wide ambit, for as director of the

[Research] School of Social Sciences he could effectively impose a protectorate over the [Research] School of Pacific Studies, led as it was by a
mere dean."

36. Davidson 2010: 385–86, 414; Foster and Varghese 1996: 134; Lal 2006:5,
13; Munro 2005–2006:50–56; 2009:102–109. Davidson's relationship
with Hancock deteriorated almost from the moment Hancock set foot
on campus. Hancock had supported Davidson's appointment to the
ANU and was aggrieved that Davidson had published so little in the
intervening years. Nor did it help that Davidson and Melville had no
respect for each other.

37. Davidson to Firth, 10 July 1957, FIRTH 7/5/39.

38. Melville to Hancock, 19 March 1956, ANUA 19/18/ 9.2.1.7(c).

39. Melville to Hancock, 25 May 1956, ANUA 19/18/9.2.1.7(c).

40. "Dean's Draft of Report of the Electoral Committee [for the Chair
of Anthropology]" (527/1957), Davidson Papers, ANUA 57/30.

41. "Electoral Committee [Meeting] for the Chair of Anthropology," 20
August 1957, Davidson Papers, ANUA 57/30.

42. "Dean's Draft of Report of the Electoral Committee [for the Chair
of Anthropology]," (527/1957), Davidson Papers, ANUA 57/30; BOGS
Minutes, 27 August 1957, ANUA 193.

43. Melville to Stanner, 28 June 1957, Davidson Papers, ANUA 57/30.

44. We only have Stanner's reply to Davidson, indicating what Davidson
wrote. Stanner to Davidson, 15 August 1957, Davidson Papers, ANUA 57/30.

45. Stanner to Davidson, 15 August 1957, Davidson Papers, ANUA 57/30.
Davidson assured the ANU Deputy Registrar (on 26 June) that he had
already told Stanner that he had sent a handwritten letter to Stanner
(and therefore did not have a copy) to emphasize the personal nature of
the case (Davidson to Deputy Registrar, 26 June 1957, Davidson Papers,
ANUA 57/30). In fact, Davidson's letter to Stanner (according to the latter's response) is dated 27 June.

46. Freeman to Gluckman, 8 July 1957, 15 July 1957, Gluckman Papers.

47. Freeman to Davidson, 11 July 1957, Davidson Papers, ANUA 57/30.

48. Davidson to Melville, 16 July 1957, Davidson Papers, ANUA 57/30.

49. Davidson to Gluckman, 15 July 1957, Davidson Papers, ANUA
57/30; see also Davidson to Firth, 10 July 1957, FIRTH 7/5/39.

50. Copy of extract of Emrys Peters (senior lecturer in anthropology at the
University of Manchester) to Ralph Bulmer (Auckland University College), 14 July 1957, Davidson Papers, ANUA 57/30. We have not been
able to discover how this extract came into Davidson's possession.

51. Firth to Davidson, 8 October 1957, FIRTH 8/1/18 see also Gluckman to Freeman, 8 August 1957, Davidson Papers, ANUA 57/30.

52. See BOGS Minutes, 27 August 1957, ANUA 193. Unless indicated otherwise all quotes from the referees' reports are in "Electoral Committee [Meeting] for the Chair of Anthropology," 20 August 1957, Davidson Papers, ANUA 57/30.

53. An explanation may be that Evans-Pritchard was not supportive of the Manchester school under Gluckman: "He describe[d] the enterprise as 'a public menace–cheapening anthropology.'" Goody 1995: 73.

54. See J. A. Barnes, "Some Comments on the Work of the Department of Anthropology and Sociology," 18 August 1957 (652/1957), Davidson Papers, ANUA 57/30 (also in ANUA 53/1114/6.5.2.1, Part 1).

55. Barnes 2007: 271–72; Davidson to Barnes, 24 July 1957, Barnes to Davidson, 26 July 1957, Barnes to Davidson, 30 August 1957, Davidson Papers, ANUA 57/30; BOGS Minutes, 27 September 1957, ANUA 193.

56. Freeman to Firth, 28 August 1957, FIRTH 8/1/33, Part 1.

57. Barnes to Gluckman, 25 March 1957, Gluckman Papers. See also Reay 1992: 138–140.

58. Barnes to Gluckman, 25 March 1957, Gluckman Papers.

59. Stanner to Davidson, 15 August 1957, Davidson Papers, ANUA 57/30.

60. Stanner to Firth, 24 February 1958, FIRTH 8/1/121.

61. Stanner to Davidson, 15 August 1956, Davidson Papers, ANUA 57/30. On the other hand he was not enamored with the situation at Sydney. He was critical of both the journal *Oceania* (edited by Elkin) and the department, pointing to a lack of interest in theory and the "thin sociological studies of the Middletown type" pursued by the department. He told Firth that "since you and Radcliffe Brown left I can't find one theoretical gleam." Stanner to Firth, 6 April 1946, FIRTH 7/7/31.

62. We plan to write a follow-up paper on the breaking and (re)making of Stanner's reputation.

63. Davidson to Firth, 2 October 1957, FIRTH 8/1/18.

64. Between July 1956 and October 1959, Stanner was absent from Canberra for twenty-three months and in Canberra for sixteen months. Davidson to Melville, 29 July 1959, Davidson Papers, 57/49.

65. W. E. H. Stanner, 30 September 1959, Stanner Papers, Australian Institute of Aboriginal and Torres Strait Islander Studies, ms485 (11).

66. Stanner to Firth, 15 October 1958, FIRTH 8/2/13.

67. Stanner to Firth, 15 October 1958, FIRTH 8/2/13.

68. Stanner to Firth, 1 April 1955, FIRTH 8/1/121.

69. Freeman to Gluckman, 15 July 1957, Gluckman Papers; also Freeman to Firth, 28 August 1957, FIRTH 8/1/33, Part 1.

70. Barnes to Gluckman, 28 June 1957, Gluckman Papers. Although Barnes, Freeman, and Stanner lived nearby in Canberra, they never socially fraternized, except at Christmas barbeques when it would have been churlish to have done otherwise. Information from Rory Barnes (John Barnes's son), Adelaide, 20 October 2011.

71. Freeman to Gluckman, 15 July 1957, Gluckman Papers.

72. Firth to Registrar (ANU), 25 July 1957, FIRTH 8/1/3.

73. Elkin to Firth, 3 August 1936, FIRTH 8/2/3.

74. "Resume of Elkin," University of Sydney Archives, "Chair of Anthropology 1955," g3/190.

75. Stanner to Firth, 24 February 1958 (Port Keats nt), FIRTH 8/1/121

76. Barnes 2007:368. It is somehow fitting that Stanner, "In a disconsolate mood one day . . . predicted to me that sooner or later Freeman would force me out of the department" (Barnes 2007:357).

77. Barnes was quickly dissatisfied at Cambridge and within two years of his arrival he was attempting to return to the ANU, even applying for the position of director of RSSS in 1979. See variously in ANUA 19/8/5 (J. A. Barnes). Rory Barnes recalls that "there was a huge amount of ill-feeling at Cambridge towards Sociology, which was seen as the Trojan horse of anarchy." Telephone discussion, 4 January 2012.

REFERENCES

Alden, D., assisted by J. S. Cummins and M. Cooper. 2001. Charles R. Boxer: An Uncommon Life. Lisbon: Fundacao Oriente.

ANUA 19: Australian National University, staff files, Australian National University Archives, Canberra. Series 19.

ANUA 53: Australian National University, records of the Department of Anthropology, Research School of Pacific Studies, Canberra. Series 53.

Barnes, J. A. 1951. Marriage in a Changing Society: A Study in Structural Change among the Fort Jameson Ngoni. Manchester: Manchester University Press for the Rhodes-Livingstone Institute.

———. 1954a. Politics in a Changing Society: A Political History of the Fort Jameson Ngoni. London: Oxford University Press for the Rhodes-Livingstone Institute.

———. 1954b. Class and Committees in a Norwegian Island Parish. Human Relations 7:39–58.

———. 1962. African Models in the New Guinea Highlands. Man 62:5–9.

————. 2001. Looking Back and Hardly Believing. *In* Before It's Too Late: Anthropological Reflections, 1950–1970. Oceania Monographs no. 51. G. Gray, ed. Pp. 138–51. Sydney: Oceania.

————. 2007. Humping My Drum: A Memoir. www.lulu.com 2007. [Available by print-on-demand, and each copy is dated by the year it was printed.]

Beckett, J. 1999. Social Organization in the New Guinea Highlands: The Problem of Terms. Australian Anthropological Society Newsletter 76:12–18.

————. 2001. Against the Grain: Fragmentary Memories of Anthropology in Australia, 1956–1970. *In* Before It's Too Late: Anthropological Reflections, 1950–1970. Oceania Monographs no. 51. G. Gray, ed. Pp. 82–98. Sydney: Oceania.

Board of Graduate Studies (BOGS) Papers: Minutes of the Board of Graduate Studies, Australian National University, Australian National University Archives, Series 193 (ANUA 193).

Cornish, S. 2007. The ANU's First Professor of Economics. History of Economics Review 46:1–18.

Crocker Papers: Papers of Sir Walter Crocker, Special Collections, Barr Smith Library, University of Adelaide, MSS 327 C938p.

Crocker, W. 1981. Travelling Back: The Memoirs of Sir Walter Crocker. Melbourne: Macmillan.

Davidson Papers: Papers of J. W. Davidson, Australian National University Archives, series 57 (ANUA 57, followed by file number).

Davidson, J. H. (2010). A Three-Cornered Life: The Historian W. K. Hancock. Sydney: University of New South Wales Press.

Firth Papers: Archive of Sir Raymond Firth, British Archive of Political and Economic Science, London School of Economics (FIRTH, followed by series, box, and file numbers).

Firth, R. 1974. Interview by Margaret Murphy (7 June 1974), Oral History Section, National Library of Australia. ORAL TRC 283. http://nla.gov.au/nla.oh-vn613496.

————. 1996. The Founding of the Research School of Pacific Studies. Journal of Pacific History 31(1): 3–7.

Foster, S. G., and M. M. Varghese. 1996. The Making of the Australian National University, 1946–1996. Sydney: Allen and Unwin.

Glasse, R. M. 1992. Encounters with the Huli: Fieldwork at Tari in the 1950s. *In* Ethnographic Presents: Pioneering Anthropologists in the Papua New Guinea Highlands. Terence E. Hays, ed. Pp. 232–249. Berkeley: University of California Press.

Gluckman Papers: Papers of Max Gluckman, Royal Anthropological Institute, London MS 450 (unsorted).

Goody, J. 1995. The Expansive Moment: Anthropology in Britain and Africa, 1918–1970. Cambridge: Cambridge University Press.

Gray, G. 2000. Managing the Impact of War: Australian Anthropology, WWII, and the Southwest Pacific. In Science and the Pacific War: Science and Survival in the Pacific, 1939–1945. R. M. MacLeod, ed. Pp. 187–210. London: Kluwer Academic.

———, ed. 2001. Before It's Too Late: Anthropological Reflections, 1950–1970. Oceania Monograph no. 51. Sydney: Oceania.

———. 2007. A Cautious Silence: The Politics of Australia Anthropology. Canberra: Aboriginal Studies Press.

Gray, G., and D. Munro. 2011. Australian Aboriginal Anthropology at the Crossroads: Finding a Successor to A. P. Elkin, 1955. Australian Journal of Anthropology 23(3):351–369.

———. 2012. "Leach would be first rate—if you could get him." Edmund Leach and the Australian National University, 1956. History Compass 10(11):802–811.

Hancock Papers. Australian National University Archives, series 77, folder/file 15.

Haslam, J. 1999. The Vices of Integrity: E. H. Carr, 1882–1982. London: Verso.

Hays, T. E., ed. 1992. Ethnographic Presents: Pioneering Anthropologists in the Papua New Guinea Highlands. Berkeley: University of California Press.

Hiatt, L. R. 1965. Kinship and Conflict: A Study of Aboriginal Community in Northern Arnhem Land. Melbourne: Cambridge University Press.

Lal, B. V. 2006. The Coombs: Journeys and Transformations. In The Coombs: A House of Memories. B. V. Lal and A. Ley, eds. Pp. 1–20. Canberra: Research School of Pacific and Asian Studies, Australian National University.

Low, D. A., ed. 2001. Keith Hancock: The Legacies of an Historian. Melbourne: Melbourne University Press.

Mills, D. 2008. Difficult Folk? A Political History of Social Anthropology. New York: Berghahn Books.

Munro, D. 2005–2006. J. W. Davidson and W. K. Hancock: Patronage, Preferment, Privilege. Journal of New Zealand Studies 4–5:39–63.

———. 2009. The Ivory Tower and Beyond: Participant Historians of the Pacific. Newcastle upon Tyne: Cambridge Scholars.

Reay, M. 1992. An Innocent in the Garden of Eden. *In* Ethnographic Presents: Pioneering Anthropologists in the Papua New Guinea Highlands. Terence E. Hays, ed. Pp. 137–166. Berkeley: University of California Press.

Spate, O. H. K. 2006. The Salad Days. *In* The Coombs: A House of Memories. Brij V. Lal and Allison Ley, eds. Pp. 23–33. Canberra: Research School of Pacific and Asian Studies, Australian National University.

Stocking, G. W., Jr. (1995) After Tylor: British Social Anthropology, 1888-1951. Madison: University of Wisconsin Press.

Young, M. 2010. John Arundel Barnes (1918–2010). Australian Anthropological Society Newsletter 120:2–6.

6

An Elegy for a Structuralist Legacy

Lévi-Strauss, Cultural Relativism, and the
Universal Capacities of the Human Mind

Structuralism, whatever that term may mean over a decade into the twenty-first century, is overdue for reassessment. The death of Claude Lévi-Strauss in 2009 provides the obligation as well as the opportunity to engage in such an exercise of historical retrospect. Lévi-Strauss moved with characteristic creative aplomb across a remarkable range of potential disciplinary homes, but anthropology remained his home base, the place of comfort from which to discomfit other disciplines. The history of anthropology therefore has a particular claim to the movement he founded and popularized beyond its origins in Saussurean linguistics despite the fact that French structuralism has ranged widely outside anthropology and reinvented itself in poststructuralist positions far beyond the intentions of its progenitor.

Albeit with the somewhat jaundiced eye of the disciplinary historian, I want to assess the ongoing utility of (my version of) Lévi-Strauss's version of structuralism for the contemporary theoretical and ethnographic practice of anthropology. Although Lévi-Strauss would doubtless disagree with all of what I suggest in making him out to be something of a Boasian (Darnell 1995, 2001, 2004), he was sufficiently aware of the inevitable evolution of theory in the human sciences to have appreciated his own undeniable stature as a monumental and perhaps even immovable baseline. His structuralism has provided a constant in the recent architecture of the human sciences. In fact, my argument suggests an inversion by way of contrast to conventional histories of anthropology with their silos of discrete national traditions: if Lévi-Strauss was a Boasian as well as a theorist, then Boas was a theorist as well as an ethnographer. I want to explore the misreadings that might undermine such a syllogism and emphasize commonalities in the positions of Boas and Lévi-Strauss on relativism and relationality.

I'm old enough to remember the slow percolation of structuralist perspectives into North American anthropology. Canada was perhaps a tad more progressive in that we had a Francophone scholarship, thus ensuring that many Canadians did not have to wait for the English translations of Lévi-Strauss (which appeared increasingly close to the date of their French publication as his reputation burgeoned). The less felicitous inverse of this proposition, however, is that over the long term Anglophone Canada effectively relegated Lévi-Strauss to Quebec and thus did little to nurture the internationally acclaimed insight arising during the heyday of his structuralism. As a panel discussant at a Canadian Anthropology Society session in his honor not long before his death, I delighted my Francophone colleagues by highlighting the importance of Lévi-Strauss for Anglophone Canada; sadly, the point was fairly moot in that I was virtually the only Anglophone in the room.

I scarcely heard the name of Lévi-Strauss as an undergraduate, but at the University of Pennsylvania in the late 1960s, some of the faculty embraced his work as an important challenge to the comfortable habits of Anglo-American anthropology. The primary enthusiasts were the linguistic anthropologists Dell Hymes and J. David Sapir, who traced the roots of his thinking to Saussure and Herder. The structuralist method or model was no more abstracted from everyday life than the componential analyses of kinship that were even more the rage at Penn in those days (under the aegis of A. F. C. Wallace, Ward Goodenough, and Hymes). The postwar positivism of descriptive ethnography was undergoing a strong lurch toward both mentalism and formalism that brought it closer to the French tradition that had coalesced around Lévi-Strauss. Ethnoscience, in this period, was moving away from the perceived ambiguities of a psychological approach that provided no mechanism to distinguish adequately between the individual and culture. In this context, Lévi-Strauss's early lack of interest in psychological aspects for the individual of the universal human capacity for abstract thought and his lack of reliance on conscious agency in the course of history may have provided a welcome corrective.

Nevertheless, the tenor of the initial American assessments, like many arising out of British social anthropology, deemed Lévi-Strauss's project to be fundamentally alien to the tradition of an empirical ethnography seeking substantive, deductive laws of human social order. Even in those days, I stubbornly plowed my way through the texts in French, because a translation by Rodney Needham did not seem to me to capture the deliberate ambiguity, stylistic play, and sly (or perhaps wry) humor that leavened Lévi-Strauss's data-heavy analyses of so-called primitive thought. The quintessential French intellectual seemed to me then, as Derrida does in a more contemporary theoretical climate, to be something of a trickster, and I read him with an eye attuned by my undergraduate double major in anthropology and medieval English literature. This rather haphazard early engagement with Lévi-Strauss has since led me to wonder why his work, after a brief flurry of enthusiasm, was tidily filed as structuralist whereas other French structuralists of the same era (Foucault, Barthes, Althusser, and Lacan, for example) are now assessed as poststructuralists and therefore deemed contemporary in a way that Lévi-Strauss himself has not been. To be sure, Lévi-Strauss's conservative response to student activism in 1968 severely damaged his iconic stature in France and abroad. In retrospect, however, there is a continuum in the evolution of structuralism. In reciprocal fashion, the deconstructive poststructuralism of Derrida and Deleuze retains much that is clearly structuralist.

The disconcerting element of my first encounters with the emergent structuralist tradition was its lack of attention to what Franz Boas called "the native point of view." The late Bob Scholte, a Hymes PhD from Berkeley, wrote a fascinating dissertation on Anglo-American interpretations of Lévi-Strauss, arguing that few had seriously addressed the implications of the French anthropological savant's unfamiliar inductive starting point in philosophy. Most Anglo-American scholars had simply adopted structuralism as a method to be applied to the analysis of empirical data—without all that extraneous theorizing about the universal products of the human mind.

In contrast, I argue that the challenge Lévi-Strauss poses is indeed a theoretical one that we ignore at our peril. It is an invitation to seek generalization or abstraction, not only in our ethnographic interpretations but also in the thought-worlds of those we study. Lévi-Strauss was far closer to Boas's maverick student Paul Radin's *Primitive Man as Philosopher* (1927) than to the disquieting drifts into mysticism of Lucien Lévi-Bruhl's "primitive mind." Radin wanted to talk about the conscious thought of some members of some Native American cultures—their biographical experiences, the direct transmission of cultural knowledge in oral tradition, and the transmission across generations of what western philosophy calls "history."

I have written about the Americanist theory of culture and its characteristic cultural relativism on several occasions over the last few years. I concluded, originally somewhat whimsically (Darnell 1995, 2001, 2004), that Lévi-Strauss was a Boasian (although he was, of course, other things, too). This claim became more serious as I realized that Lévi-Strauss had a way of repeatedly inserting himself into the Americanist story, with his insistence that the anthropologist's job is not finished when she or he has recorded the facts of a traditional way of life, with or without the opinion of members-of-culture on the meaning of the ethnographic facts. Rather, it is the relationship among the facts that is of interest, as well as the recurrence of similar structures in this relational sense across the domains of a given society or culture. The ability to formulate relationality, whether indirect or not, whether conscious or not, entails abstract thought wherever it is found. Indeed, Lévi-Strauss and Boas were in fundamental agreement that conscious thought might involve what the former sometimes called "false consciousness" and what the latter eschewed as "secondary rationalization." The less direct generalizations about culture, history, and identity to be found in myth were potentially more reliable, in Lévi-Strauss's view, by virtue of their abstraction from everyday understanding.

Much has been made, especially outside France, of the hierarchical, evolutionary, even ethnocentric entailments of the binary opposition of hot and cold societies or the distinction between the engineer or scientist and the *bricoleur* (despite the fact that Lévi-Strauss explicitly specifies that these are typological discriminations and that actual societies combine and transform the distinctive features that he isolates for analytic attention). Like Saussure, Jakobson, or Chomsky, he is prepared to dismiss the fascinating messiness of cultural description in favor of "*langue*," "structure" or "competence."

The universal claims of structuralism in Lévi-Strauss's version thereof have been critically significant in juxtaposing, without comment or methodological quarter, "myths" from western tradition and from so-called primitive societies. When I teach the structuralist method, usually as symbolic anthropology or language and culture, I encourage students to read the Oedipus analysis from volume 1 of *Structural Anthropology* (1963), which already incorporates native North American exemplars, alongside the Asdival story from Edmund Leach's ASA collection in 1967. From a methodological standpoint, these exemplars are interchangeable. Similarly, I offer my students their choice of domains—kinship, totem-ism, or myth—though I often fail to persuade them that this choice doesn't change the methodological argument. Today's students almost always choose myth; the other two domains are sadly out of fashion.

On the surface, the methodological apparatus of Oedipus and Asdi-val, for Lévi-Strauss, is the parsing out of plot events and motifs to facil-itate two discrete readings: a paradigmatic, metaphoric, or thematic one and a syntagmatic or metonymic ordering of narrative that implic-itly juxtaposes the biography of a particular narrator and the history of her/his community (*langue* and *parole* recapitulated).

For those of us who are interested in *parole* as the language behavior arising from the structure of language in the context of local norms of society/culture, this contrast compels us to go beyond merely retelling the story. The very process of lining up the categories of events across multiple versions of the "same" myth or myth cycle forces attention to what at least some members of a given culture know—and whether or not it matters for anthropological purposes. Lévi-Strauss concludes that it doesn't matter and that members-of-culture do not need to ana-lyze myths in order to take solace from their encoded experience. He is certainly correct that many people do not think about the stories they tell each other, perhaps not even much about what the stories mean. Nonetheless, the storyteller qua mythographer qua philosopher who chooses among sources and motifs to assemble a particular narrative will necessarily be aware, whether explicitly articulated or not, of which things go together—of which things always stand in relationship to one another. The abstract or structural corollary is that not everything can be combined with everything else. A similar train of thought is found in Roman Jakobson on near-universals and in Edward Sapir on "the psychological reality of the phoneme." The capacity of storytellers to use myth templates to convey both historical narratives and personal experience reveals the complexity of conscious construction on the basis of myth structures, whether it be achieved in the manner of an engineer or a *bricoleur*.

The question of multiple versions cannot help but arise here. The paradigmatic axis may be elaborated as a form of redundancy useful to memory in an oral tradition. In an oral tradition, people value the hearing and rehearing of "the same" stories over a lifetime. But these stories are both the same and not the same—their audiences, contexts, expressive features, and moral implications vary with the occasion of telling. Nonetheless, folklorists and descriptive ethnographers have diligently sought origins and type forms of widespread myths, albeit without much in the way of persuasive results. Because every rendition is tailored to context and draws on multiple forms, events, and experiences in the repertoire of the narrator, the storyteller assembles his or her offering on a given occasion as an artist. Although Boas may have chosen to consider that the Oedipus cycle works this way because it, like the myth cycles of the Northwest Coast, initially grew by accretion within an oral tradition, this does not necessarily invalidate Lévi-Strauss's claim that structures of relationality are the universal building blocks of human meaning-making.

Lévi-Strauss's method takes us well beyond the compositional options open to the myth-teller and the interpretive ones available to his or her audience, both at the time of telling and as variegated tellings are remembered and reworked over time. He aspires to compile all of the possible versions, not just the ones that could conceivably have been available to a given teller. It is not a condition of possibility for relational thinking to identify any single individual who actually links all of the elements in particular versions of a myth. It merely strengthens the argument when hearers know what has to come next, by familiarity with the stories themselves but also with their underlying coherence. Again, some people in every society are more interested in such matters than others. Radin argues that we need only accept that some people think about such things.

In any case, this is where Lévi-Strauss fully parts company with the emic perspective. Only he as analyst has access to the potential range of versions and ways of hanging them together. His logic parallels that of Boas with regard to diffusion; the member-of-culture lacks the information to trace the movement of folklore, art, and other cultural forms within a broad region beyond personal experience or direct report. Lévi-Strauss takes for granted that there is no finite number of possible combinations, but he also assumes that the relationships among cultural elements cannot be random. Therefore, only he (or another analyst with training and access to texts) can ascertain how the versions are related. Lévi-Strauss's adoption of the Boasian areal or geographical perspective takes him even further away from member-of-culture understandings, whether conscious or implicit. He turns to versions found among related tribes. While it is certainly the case that stories were told regularly across tribal boundaries in contexts of warfare, captive adoption, intermarriage, and trade, it is also true that the ethnographer with access to a good library of entextualized materials will amass a database of versions far beyond that accessible to any member-of-culture based on culture-internal experience alone. Indeed, Lévi-Strauss spent much of his career assembling and analyzing just such a database. That he did so without a computer makes his commitment to generalizing the underlying, purportedly universal structural pattern(s) all the more remarkable. He saw no particular need to return repeatedly to "the field," where he acknowledged at a conference in his honor in Paris several years ago that he was more voyeur than investigator (Mauzé, Harkin, and Kan 2004). The four volumes of *Mythologiques*, published in English between 1967 and 1981, as well as *The Way of the Masks* (1982) demonstrate how far afield particular motifs and themes have been known to travel. At least some people shared their stories widely and adapted them for local consumption back home, although they would presumably not have been aware of other stories shared widely with other potential narrators across a "vast region" of the Americas.

We might conclude that the Anglo-American critique was well taken and that Lévi-Strauss was not interested in ethnography for its own sake. He largely reserves his sense of ethnographic wonder for this structural process of diffusion and reinterpretation; his appellation of "vast region" recurs frequently. Alternatively, I conclude that Lévi-Strauss was fascinated by its details and reveled in the satisfactions of ethnographic verisimilitude. More pertinently, however, his move to geographical and historical context outside the experience of members-of-culture is precisely the move that Boas himself made. In both cases, it is a theoretical move.

Boas's own methodological position distinguished between historical particularism that modeled the details of a given cultural system in relation to their diffusion and intersection across a cultural region—the Northwest Coast for most of his career—and "the native point of view," which he understood to be interpretive and accessible through the recorded words of native speakers of native languages. Meaning, for him, resided in the things people said about their cultures and in their accumulated cultural knowledge; it was quintessentially linguistic. Boas provided minimal commentary, though his long-term correspondence with George Hunt and other assistants in the field makes it clear that his questions were theoretically motivated to fill gaps in intelligibility as well as substance. In some sense, the documents spoke for themselves and in their own terms.

Parenthetically, there is an odd sense in which, for different reasons, neither Boas nor Lévi-Strauss considered language to be theoretically interesting. For Boas, language was primarily a means of accessing "the native point of view." His obsession with phonetic detail precluded appreciation of phonemic, relational, or structural patterning as developed by Sapir and others in the interwar years. For Lévi-Strauss, language was a methodological toolkit for relational thought. He characteristically treated language as metaphor, the language of x (e.g., music, art, or myth), rather than exploring its structure qua language. From a linguistic standpoint, language was etic, a way to get at the universal.

We now return to the question of the commensurability of a Lévi-Straussian universalist approach to the products of the human mind with Boasian cultural relativism. Both are based in antiracist assumptions that go back to a much older western tradition of the "psychic unity of mankind." Although Boas was a prominent physical anthropologist in his generation, he did not pursue the neuropsychology of cultural variability (and probably would not have done so even if the tools had then been available). Similarly, Lévi-Strauss has been profoundly uninterested in the biological questions about language raised by recent cognitive science. Like Lévi-Strauss in the 1950s, Boas attacked questions of racism on cultural grounds rather than those of race based on physically differential capacities. Like Dewey and other American pragmatists, Boas sought social rather than biological or eugenic amelioration of social problems, largely through pedagogical methods based on cultural relativism.

REFERENCES

Darnell, Regna. 1995. The Structuralism of Claude Lévi-Strauss. Historio-graphia Linguistica 22:217–234.

———. 2001. Invisible Genealogies: A History of Americanist Anthropology. Lincoln: University of Nebraska Press.

———. 2004. Text, Symbol, and Tradition from Franz Boas to Claude Lévi-Strauss. *In* Coming to Shore. Mauzé et al., eds. Pp. 7–29.

Lévi-Strauss, Claude. 1963. Structural Anthropology. Vol. 1. New York: Basic Books.

———. 1982. The Way of the Masks. Vancouver: Douglas and McIntyre.

Mauzé, Marie, Michael E. Harkin, and Sergei Kan, eds. 2004. Coming to Shore: Northwest Coast Ethnology, Traditions, and Visions. Lincoln: University of Nebraska Press.

Radin, Paul. 1927 [1957]. Primitive Man as Philosopher. New York: Dover.

ABRAHAM ROSMAN AND PAULA RUBEL

7

Lévi-Strauss's Approach to Systems of Classification

Categories in Northwest Coast Cultures

Lévi-Strauss, in the first paragraph of *The Savage Mind*, refers to Franz Boas's discussion in the *Introduction to the Handbook of American Indian Languages*. Though many scholars once maintained that native people lacked the capacity for "abstract thought," Lévi-Strauss agreed with Boas that the systems of classification found in the languages and cultures of "native peoples" were indeed examples of abstract thought.

Much of Boas's *The Mind of Primitive Man* deals with the question of race and its relationship to language and culture and the question of what constitutes "primitiveness." However, in the latter part of the volume, in the chapter entitled "The Mind of Primitive Man and the Progress of Culture," Boas attempts to "reconstruct the forms of thought of primitive man" (1963:187). He sets out the way in which language orders systems of classification and points out that "an extended classification of experience must necessarily underlay all articulate speech" (Boas 1963:189). According to Boas, classification is based upon similarities so that different experiences are representative of the same category of thought. He further notes that these systems of classification never rise to consciousness. He provides examples of several systems of classification. Societies classify colors in different ways, using a different number of terms, though the color spectrum is universally recognized. Tastes may also be classified in different ways. Kinship terminology is still another area in which cultures have different systems of classification, so that as Boas notes, "it is hardly possible to translate a term belonging to one system into that of another one" (1963:191). The Eskimos use many terms for snow, water, and seals, which represent systems of classification more extensive than those found in other cultures for similar phenomena. Boas points out that in western societies we see sickness as an attribute of the body while many "primitive societies" see it as an object that enters the body and may be removed. These represent two systems of classification of illness. There are a variety of classifications of illness. Numerical systems also vary in terms of how many numbers are included, from languages in which numerical systems use numbers up to three, to our much more elaborate system of numerical classification. Grammars as systems of classification are obligatory in every language. For example, in European languages, it is obligatory to include time in every statement. In Kwak'wala, the source of information must be included in every sentence (evidentials). What is obligatory varies from one language to another. Boas saw all systems of classification as forming part of the underlying structure of language and culture.

Lévi-Strauss's discussion of the presence or absence of abstract thought among "primitive" people in *The Savage Mind* is a direct continuation of the topic discussed by Boas in the *Handbook of American Indian Languages* and in *The Mind of Primitive Man* (1963:196). In *The Savage Mind*, Lévi-Strauss demonstrates how systems of classification organize the abstract thought of "primitive peoples." He compares Boas's approach with Malinowski's "mistaken" view that native peoples' totemic classification of plants and animals reflects the need to satisfy hunger (1966:3). Totemism as a system of classification is a topic which Lévi-Strauss has examined in great detail. Cultures use distinctive features to distinguish animal species from one another. Societies with unilineal descent systems differentiate one clan from another clan in the same way that species are different from one another. They use species terminology to mark this distinction. In such societies, clans and species are classified by the same logic, so that clan A is to clan B as Ravens are to Wolves or Eagles are to Bears. Lévi-Strauss argues in *The Savage Mind*, "Examples like these may be drawn from all parts of the world and one may readily conclude that animals and plants are not known as a result of their usefulness; they are deemed to be useful or interesting because they are first of all known" (9). This is the opposite of Malinowski's approach. Classification has a value of its own, whatever form the classification takes.

But the real imaginative power of *The Savage Mind* emerges when one system of classification is placed on top of another, creating a homologous structure. Members of Clan A are metaphoric Bears, and Clan B are metaphoric Eagles. Here totemism and social structure represent homologous structures. Things "go together" in metaphoric ways. In totemic societies, marriage, sex, exchange, and eating define relationships between clans. There is a system of classification within a clan system that designates with whom one can have sexual intercourse—from close relatives like sisters to whom incest taboos apply, to suitable partners like cross-cousins but not parallel cousins, to forbidden possible partners like foreign outsiders.

Elsewhere, Lévi-Strauss contrasts this type of structure with another structure having a different series of systems of classification—that of castes, bound to one another by economic specialization, endogamy, and eating taboos. In the caste system one is forbidden to eat with or have sexual relations with members of other castes or other religions. This contrasts with the clan system, where the relationship is characterized as one between metaphoric species (see Lévi-Strauss 1963). Eating is often a metaphor for sexual relations (as in "to hunger for"). There is a relationship between eating as a system of classification and with whom you may or may not have sexual relations, another system of classification. In totemic societies, you may not have sex (or marry) someone classified as a "sister," with whom you share a totemic animal. You may marry anyone outside of your clan. Eating your totemic animal is also forbidden. Similarly, in societies that practice cannibalism, you may only eat members of "enemy" clans, but not members of your own clan with whom you share a totem, that is, your own classificatory brothers. In caste societies you can only marry and eat with someone of your own caste. In both types of societies, totemic and caste, we find a metaphoric relationship between sex and eating.

These topics are discussed throughout *The Savage Mind* as Lévi-Strauss explores how relationships between structures sometimes are homologous, as in the relationship between clan structures and totemic structures, and sometimes not. In fact, one can say that Lévi-Strauss sees culture as no more than a system of homologous structures. That is, systems of classification are linked to one another by metaphoric logic: eating is like sex, parts of the body indicate directions, the day and the year indicate past and future, etc.

We will now explore the various systems of classification in Northwest Coast societies and their relationship to one another as they existed in the early twentieth century. These societies all had potlatch exchange, flexible rank that was determined by potlatching, and a distinctive art style that had many shared characteristics. Northwest Coast art was quite different from the art styles of other Native American areas. Most of these societies had kin groups that were associated with totemic classification. Despite these similarities, there were also many differences. For example, the societies on the Northwest Coast belonged to different language families. They had differences in descent systems, in marriage systems, in kinship terminology, and in the frequency and occasions for potlatching.

The totemic system and its associated mythology found expression in the art of Northwest Coast societies. Boas, in *Primitive Art*, treats the art of this area as a single symbolic system. Lévi-Strauss was extremely interested in the meanings of Northwest Coast art, and he wrote about it in articles as well as in *La Voie des Masques*.

The representations in the art form a taxonomy within which the first distinction was between animate and inanimate. The animate category included humans, plants, animals, insects, sea mammals, and even forces of nature, such as sun, moon, echo, wind, and earthquake, as well as mythological creatures such as sea bears. Since everything in the animate category was considered to be a living thing, they were all represented with faces with human facial characteristics in the art, whether they really had faces or not. Even snails, cockles, and mosquitoes are represented with faces. The eyes, nose, mouth, and ears of each animal form, including insects, mammals, birds, etc., are depicted in different ways, and together they form paradigmatic sets—a set of ears, a set of eyes, a set of appendages—fins, wings, arms and legs. What is represented in the art is what is most distinctive about the "animal" form from the native point of view, so that a hawk is portrayed with a beak different in shape from that of an eagle, raven, or flicker.

Within the animate category, human beings and animals have a special relationship to one another. Humans can be transformed into metaphoric animals by putting on masks that represent animals. Further, in the Kwakiutl Family Histories, the totemic ancestors of some of the Kwakiutl cognatic kin groups, the *numayms*, are described as birds or animals who take off their masks and become humans. Animal masks used in potlatch ceremonies represent these ancestors. These paired relationships all represent reversible transformations.

The distinctive feature in art that differentiates humans from animals is the placement of ears. The ears of humans are on the side of the head, and those of animals are on top. This presents a problem with regard to masks. Sometimes humans are portrayed wearing animal masks, and other times animals are portrayed wearing human masks. In *Primitive Art* Boas gives an example of a hawk portrayed on a carved spoon and a rattle (Boas 1955: figs.166, and 167: 191), and a man wearing a hawk mask that has human ears (Boas 1955: fig. 207: 217). Killer whales do not have ears and would not normally be portrayed in art as having ears. However, in Figure 252 (Boas 1955:243), a painting for a house front, the killer whale is given animal ears on top of the head. This is to symbolize that the killer whale portrayed here is an animal, not a human wearing the mask of a killer whale. By putting on and taking off masks, humans are transformed into animals and animals become human. Throughout the Northwest Coast, masks represent spirits. Sometimes totemic ancestral spirits are represented, and at other times supernatural shamanic spirits are represented. When an individual puts on a mask, he is transformed into the spirit of the mask.

Within the animal category in the Northwest Coast there are two additional systems of classification. One system separates totemic animals that individuals cannot eat, such as beaver, bear, killer whale, wolf, raven, and eagle, from those animals that one can eat, including salmon, herring, cod, deer, elk, and porpoise. The totemic animals are portrayed in the art, and those that can be eaten are not. Among the Kwakiutl, the meat of animals that are eaten is divided according to rank. In the recipe for seals provided by Boas, only chiefs are given the insides. The flippers are divided among chiefs of lower rank, and the blubber is given to common people (1921:457ff.). Seals are not portrayed in Kwakuitl (Kwakwaka'wakw) art. The second system of classification among the Kwakiutl separates totemic animals used in potlatch masks from their supernatural versions used in the Winter Ceremonial and that are often referred to as cannibal masks.

Kwakiutl culture has other systems of classification in addition to the system of classification in art. One of these is that associated with the yearly round. A sharp distinction is made between winter, *tsetsequa*, and summer, *baxus*. This distinction and its systems of classification were associated with two forms of social organization and rituals (Rosman and Rubel 1990). Summer was the time during which most potlatches took place. Summer potlatches were associated with the incremental passage of names and property rights within the *numaym*, the cognatic descent group, until one assumed the most important chiefly name. For each family there was "A Family History," which combined myth and history from mythological times up until the nineteenth century. The histories often begin with an eponymous ancestor who was a bird or an animal and who, in the myth, is transformed into a man, the family totemic ancestor. Among these ancestral animals and birds were Raven, Eagle, Bear, and Wolf. The Family Histories also contain the names and rank positions that are passed down from one individual to another during potlatches.

For the Kwakiutl, winter, *tsetsequa* was the sacred time during which the elaborate Winter Ceremonial took place. According to Boas, "During this period, the place of clans is taken by a number of societies, namely, the groups of all those individuals upon whom the same or almost the same power or secret has been bestowed by one of the spirits" (Boas 1897:418). The Winter Ceremonial was introduced by a liminal period during which whistles representing the voices of the supernatural spirits sound closer and closer to the village. All must be cleansed, and abstention from sexual intercourse is observed. When those to be initiated are captured by the supernatural spirits and disappear, the liminal period has ended and *tsetsequa* has begun. The spirits are members of the secret societies, a different form of organization than the *numayms*. They include *Baxbakualanuxswae*, who seems to be the chief of the spirits, *hamatsa*, a cannibal spirit, *nulmal,* the cannibal grizzly bear, and the cannibal raven. These supernatural spirits and their secret societies and members are ranked with respect to one another, and the latter sit at ceremonies according to their rank, in the same manner as *numayms*. The origins of the secret societies are embedded in a set of myths that tell about the acquisition of supernatural powers by ancestors. These myths are different from the myths about the origins of *numayms*. The supernatural powers, descended through the generations, are acquired through initiation into the secret societies. Since they are based on different principles of organization, membership in the secret societies cross-cuts that of the *numayms*.

During the Winter Ceremonial, supernatural beings are present in Kwakiutl villages. Since the boys to be initiated are taken away by these supernatural beings, the Winter Ceremonial is clearly associated with shamanism. In fact, among the Bella Bella, shamans and the Winter Ceremonial are designated by the same term (Boas 1966:172, 173). The novices or initiates in the Winter Ceremonial disappear into the world of the supernatural, being taken by the supernatural beings who are in fact members of the ranked secret societies. In one of the accounts of the Winter Ceremonial, which Boas witnessed, he refers to those present when the initiates are taken away as "shamans" (Boas 1966:262). In another account, the initiates are referred to by the same term that the Kwakiutl use for shamans. Boas states that "the initiation of the shaman is analogous in all details to that of participants in the Winter Ceremonial" (1921:741).

Among the Kwakiutl as well as in other Northwest Coast societies, becoming a shaman is based upon the attainment of supernatural power. Once this power is acquired, the shaman can cure diseases. (The most powerful Kwakiutl shamans can cause disease as well.) Just as the initiate in the Winter Ceremonial disappears into the supernatural world, the shaman acquires his power by undertaking a journey to the land of the dead, where he meets supernatural animals who become his helpers or familiars. He finally returns as a shaman.

In one account given by Boas, the Kwakiutl shaman-to-be describes his death and his accompanying the howling wolves surrounding his corpse to their village. When he returned, he described how the great shaman, the chief of the Wolf village, carried a rattle with a wolf carving on its back. The great shaman, after holding his sickness in his hands four times and throwing it upward, "asked his people to put on their wolf skins, and they ran back to the village" (Boas 1966:130). This story relates how humans can be transformed into wolves, and vice versa.

There are two important differences between shamanism and the

Kwakiutl Winter Ceremonial. The curing shaman operates as an individual. In contrast, the Kwakiutl Winter Ceremonial is a group phenomenon in that individuals belong to secret societies. Second, the animal spirits at the Winter Ceremonial, depicted in masks, are supernatural versions of totemic animals (eagles, ravens, bears, and wolves), while the spirit helpers of the curing shaman are different, tending to be frogs, toads, and mice, along with wolves and bears. Boas notes that "each shaman is subordinate to the chief of his *numaym*" (Boas 1966:145). The initiates at the Winter Ceremonial are also ranked.

The two forms of shamanism among the Kwakiutl are reflected in two forms of shamanic art. In the art employed during the Winter Ceremonial, totemic animals, important in *baxus*, are portrayed in grotesque ways. This is associated with the supernatural and the distorted vision of the shaman. The straight beak of the raven becomes the enormous beak of the *hamatsa* cannibal raven. The curved beak of the eagle becomes the crooked beak of heaven, the grizzly bear becomes the cannibal grizzly, and the wolf mask turns into the *Walasaxa* wolf mask worn at the Winter Ceremonial. All of these are distortions of the totemic masks associated with the ancestors of the *numayms*.

Animals associated with the curing shamans—his spirit helpers and "familiars"—are largely a different set of animals. These are portrayed on the shaman's costume and paraphernalia: his crown, his drum, and his rattle. The crown was made of grizzly bear claws or mountain goat horns. This constitutes shamanic art.

The larger system of animal classification has two subordinate systems: the system of totemic animals who are not eaten and those that are eaten, and the system of supernatural totemic animals associated with the Winter Ceremonial and portrayed in art and that of shamanic "familiars." The latter are primarily anomalous animals: mice, frogs, land otters, and mountain goats. For the Tlingit, these helpers or familiars of shamans are animal spirits and are portrayed in their art (Wardwell 1996:82, 100). Certain animals do not appear in the shamanic art of the Tlingit. These are all animals that were eaten, such as deer, porcupine, marmot, some birds, and fish. Emmons notes that they "were regarded as possessing harmless spirits of no strength" (1991:373). Animals eaten by the Kwakiutl are also not portrayed in the art.

Following Boas, Lévi-Strauss sees the abstract thought of indigenous populations as organized by systems of classification, which may be related to one another as homologous structures. We have followed Lévi-Strauss's focus in *The Savage Mind* upon societies in which totemism is important, and we have examined Northwest Coast societies with particular emphasis on the Kwakiutl. We described various systems of classification and their relationship to one another. The system of classification of ranked cognatic kin groups, *numayms*, was paralleled by a totemic structure of classification in which the totem was a spiritual animal ancestor who became a man, as described in mythological family histories and as depicted in animal masks worn during the summer, *baxus* ceremonies. Kin groups, totems, mythologies, and masks, manifested in art, formed homologous structures, along with what one can and cannot eat and with whom one can and cannot have sexual relations. The animals and humans were part of an elaborate hierarchical taxonomy whose distinctions are also paralleled in the art. Animals that are normally eaten are not part of the totemic or shamanic classificatory systems and are not depicted in their art.

The homologous structures of classification of *baxus*, the summer, are part of the larger structure of classification of the Kwakiutl yearly round, which distinguishes *baxus* from *tsetsequa*, winter, the sacred time of the year. The Winter Ceremonial during *tsetsequa* has its own structure of secret societies. "Supernatural spirits" are members of these societies. This system of classification is paralleled by a system of myths about the acquisition of these supernatural spirits by ancestors and a system of "supernatural" masks. The latter are grotesque and exaggerated versions of the masks used during *baxus*. The various systems of classification of the Winter Ceremonial are in turn related to and paralleled by the structure of classification of shamanism to the point where Boas uses the word "shaman" in talking about people initiated in the Winter Ceremonial. Shamans are initiated by being spirited away to the supernatural world by supernatural spirits, as are the initiates of the Winter Ceremonial. However, the system of classification of art of these two structures is different

A pervasive feature among all the systems of classification of the Kwakiutl, which we have enumerated, is ranking. Individuals are ranked within *numayms* by virtue of their inherited names and ranked seats.

Numayms and their chiefs are ranked with respect to one another, as exemplified by the ritual, the masking, and seating in the potlatch. In the Winter Ceremonial, secret societies are also ranked with respect to another as exemplified by the masks that they wear. Though shamans act in their curing as individuals, they are also ranked in groups

Systems of classification provide an underlying grid that draws together symbols and the things they are associated with—"things that go together." These systems place the individual within a larger framework—within an "animal" world, within the world of ancient mythological ancestors, and within a complex rank system that competition in the potlatch can alter. Other classificatory systems provide him with "others" whom he marries, with whom he fights, and against whom he potlatches.

REFERENCES

Boas, Franz. 1897. The Social Organization and Secret Societies of the Kwakiutl Indians. Report of the U.S. National Museum for 1895. Washington DC: Smithsonian Institution.

———. 1911. Introduction to Handbook of American Indian Languages. Part 1. Bulletin 40. Washington DC: Bureau of American Ethnology.

———. 1921. The Ethnology of the Kwakiutl. 35th Annual Report of the Bureau of American Ethnology for the Years 1913/1914, parts 1 and 2. Washington DC: Smithsonian Institution.

———. 1955 [1927]. Primitive Art. New York: Dover.

———. 1963 [1911]. The Mind of Primitive Man. New York: Free Press.

———. 1966. Kwakiutl Ethnography. Helen Codere, ed. Chicago: University of Chicago Press.

Emmons, George Thornton. 1991. The Tlingit Indians. Frederica de Laguna, ed. Seattle: University of Washington Press.

Lévi-Strauss, Claude. 1963. The Bear and the Barber. Journal of the Royal Anthropological Institute of Great Britain and Ireland 93(1):1–11.

———. 1966 [1962]. The Savage Mind. Chicago: University of Chicago Press.

Rosman, Abraham, and Paula G. Rubel. 1990. Structural Patterning in Kwakiutl Art and Ritual. Man 25(4): 620-639.

Wardwell, Alan. 1996. Tangible Visions: Northwest Coast Indian Shamanism and Its Art. New York: Manacelli Press.

MICHAEL ASCH

8

Lévi-Strauss on Theoretical Thought and Universal History

Today we know that the archaic nature of the material culture of the Australian aborigines has no correspondence in the field of social institutions. By contrast, their social institutions are the result of a long series of deliberate elaborations and systematic reforms. In short, the Australian sociology of the family is, as it were, a "planned sociology."

CLAUDE LÉVI-STRAUSS, *The Elementary Structures of Kinship* (1969)

Claude Lévi-Strauss is often accused of paying too little regard for history and human agency. But this is misguided, for as the above quote shows, Lévi-Strauss, notwithstanding the importance he attached to the study of the unconscious mind, clearly felt that history and agency contribute crucially to the way in which *we* live our lives, for otherwise (and whether or not we call a society "hot" or "cold") he would not have said that Australian Aboriginal society is the result of a "long series of deliberate elaborations and systematic reforms" that would constitute a "planned sociology." The question, then, is why this aspect of his work is given so little attention.

Based on the period when he focused on the study of kinship, I will address what I have come to understand of Lévi-Strauss's thought on the role played by the choices we make consciously with respect to two enduring themes in what we have come to call Universal History with which western anthropological and political thought has been occupied: the origin of inequality, and the origin of agriculture. To that end I will focus on three of his contributions that well exemplify the direction his thought took at that time: chapters 15 and 16 of his 1947 publication *The Elementary Structures of Kinship*; his article "Do Dual Organizations Exist?" which was published in French in 1958 with the title "Les organisations dualistes existent-elles?" and, as far as I know, his last contribution on the subject of kinship, The Huxley Memorial Lecture of 1965, in which he provides an intellectual justification for his move from kinship to myth. What I believe I will show is that there is a trend in his thinking in which the role of consciousness in human history takes on more importance so that the publication of the last paper provides an explanation of how we operationalize the kind of agency that enables us to produce history as a planned sociology. And to the extent that we take into account how he represents consciousness in his final contribution on kinship, we are wrong to say, based on his later work, that he took little notice of processes such as agency and history. But first a parenthetical remark: because I am reporting on his thinking and not on my own, I will not dwell on the fact that he, mistakenly in my view, represents practices of peoples living today as though they transparently reflect the practices of our ancestors—a point, as the quote cited above indicates, that he contradicts.

I was introduced to the materials I am focusing on today by Rosman and Rubel in a class that they taught on exchange theory in the spring of 1967 or the fall of 1968—that is, in the year (or close to it) not only of the events at Columbia and around the world but the year in which the draft English translation of *The Elementary Structures of Kinship* was passed on to a few scholars, including my supervisor, Robert Murphy. As I recall, we started the course with the rather poor précis of this work by P. E. de Josselin de Jong, and midway through it that draft appeared and I must say that Rosman and Rubel did a masterful job in rejigging the course to take into account that everything we had thought the book was about was wrong. In addition to *Elementary Structures,* we read a number of other Lévi-Strauss works, including the pieces I am addressing. In that sense, one might see this chapter as substituting for the term paper on political organization and marriage patterns among the Natchez that I submitted for that course. This course changed the course of my life as an anthropologist, for I know that it was the insights this course gave me into kinship and politics that enabled me to have the serious discussions with the Dene on those subjects and thus a career in which political relations remains a focus.

To set the context, I wish to begin with a few words on the subject of Universal History, which, in the form discussed here, is organized around the idea that humans move through stages of progress from, to use the sociopolitical frame, Savagery to Barbarism and then to Civilization or, to use the socioeconomic frame, from hunting-gathering to pastoralism, agriculture and (to use Smith's version) commerce. While it is sometimes understood as a development on the medieval theme of "the great chain of being," it is more useful to think of it as a pole in a debate between biblically oriented thinking and thinking based on abstract thought experiments concerning the placement of the people of the New World in history that could have only arisen after what we call the Age of Discovery and thus not until the end of the fifteenth century. Key scholars in its development include, as Ronald Meek points out, Turgot and Adam Smith, who both first articulated the four-stage theory, as well as Immanuel Kant's 1784 essay "Universal History from a Cosmopolitan Point of View," and Jean-Jacques Rousseau's 1754 essay "Discourse on the Origin of Inequality," as well as the work of earlier scholars in this tradition such as Thomas Hobbes and John Locke.

The intellectual home for the study of Universal History in this period is political philosophy and political economy. However, particularly for the study of the so-called first stage, this shifts by 1870 to Geology and Anthropology, when the "speculations" of the political theorists are replaced by empirical "evidence" (i.e., artifacts) collected in a scientific manner. However, by and large, the archaeologists and anthropologists from the time of Morgan's *Ancient Society* (1877) to the present remain faithful to the idea that humanity develops through stages, as can be attested to by an examination of virtually any introductory text in which the four fields of anthropology are introduced.

The idea that humanity passes through stages invites us to consider what causes humanity to move from one stage to another. And thus to ask questions such as: What factors were involved when humans moved from the Paleolithic to the Neolithic, from nomadic forms of existence (hunting and pastoralism) to sedentary ones (agriculture and commerce)? What is the origin of agriculture? It is a question that is generally answered by reference to material conditions, either as a necessity due to increasing population or as an opportunity due to the invention of new technologies. In contrast, Lévi-Strauss relies on innovations in kinship relations that lead to new forms of sociopolitical organization as central to it.

The second perennial question that Lévi-Strauss addresses, again through the lens of kinship relations, pertains to the origins of inequality. It is a question that as traditionally posed presupposes that, in our original condition, humans were equal so that inequality arose some time later and as a consequence of something that we did. Again, as with respect to the origins of agriculture, our explanations of the origins of inequality focus on the material dimension and more specifically the consequence of the idea that land and/or technology can be owned individually rather than shared in common. In 1754, Rousseau, for example, used the following argument:

> The first man who, having fenced in a piece of land, said, "This is mine," and found people naïve enough to believe him, that man was the true founder of civil society. From how many crimes, wars, and murders, from how many horrors and misfortunes might not any one have saved mankind, by pulling up the stakes, or filling up the ditch, and crying to his fellows: Beware of listening to this impostor; you are undone if you once forget that the fruits of the earth belong to us all, and the earth itself to nobody. (Discourse on Inequality 2005)

A BRIEF SKETCH OF COUNTERARGUMENTS

Of course, as we know, the trope of universal history was and is hegemonic. But it certainly was and is not without criticism in western intellectual thought. One traditional strain has been to critique the notion that there can be a "universal" history, by suggesting that histories are particular to peoples. It is a tradition that originates in Herder and is carried forward by his students and students of his students such as Franz Boas, to form a branch of cultural anthropology in which it is held that each culture has its own way of doing things in the world so that the accumulation of knowledge produces histories. Clifford Geertz and the interpretivists are more recent exemplars of this view. The second strain, out of which social anthropology develops, argues that it is premature to study history as a universal phenomenon, as we still do not know enough about the rules by which we organize ourselves in the present. It is a strain that runs through Compte's assertion that while that phenomenon can be analyzed from both a synchronic and a diachronic perspective, the appropriate procedure to avoid slipping into metaphysics is to avoid addressing the diachronic until there is sufficient knowledge of the synchronic to avoid deductive reasoning. On the one hand, this way of thinking gives rise to Saussure's prioritizing the study of language as it is spoken in the present day over language history that in the hands of Roman Jakobson leads to structural linguistics. On the other, it leads (albeit through a different method) to Sociology and to the privileging of synchronic analysis and the sociological method in the social anthropology of Radcliffe-Brown. As Radcliffe-Brown says:

> The acceptability of a historical explanation depends on the fullness and reliability of the historical record. In the primitive societies that are studied by social anthropology there are no historical records. . . . Anthropologists, thinking of their study as a kind of historical study, fall back on conjecture and imagination, and invent "pseudo-historical" or "pseudo-causal" explanations. (1952:3)

THE CONTEXT OF LÉVI-STRAUSS'S CONTRIBUTION

Leaving its importance to the justification of colonialism to one side (something I do not do without reservation), the strength of the Universal History argument is that it seeks nomothetic rules (i.e., general explanations). And that is a central weakness of the counterargument. Notwithstanding Radcliffe-Brown's snide characterization of the universal history crowd as dealing in "pseudo-history" and "pseudo-causality," the truth is that, without a countertheory of history, the arguments from Herder and Radcliffe-Brown to Geertz remain critique in that they are critical responses to the argument and therefore only exist as counters to it. They are, to use Foucauldian terms, practices of liberation in that they only exist because the hegemonic discourse exists. What is necessary to defeat the argument is either to find another way to account for the processes of history or to shift the discussion of origins into a different terrain. As I see it, Lévi-Strauss struck a blow in both directions: the latter in his more familiar work on the unconscious mind and the former in his work on kinship. And, as it is the focus, where I think he was heading with respect to kinship is to the position that universal history can be understood to exist in multiple versions, for, although all humans are presented with the same set of matters to address (hunger, defense, reproduction), we address them differently, and in so doing we accumulate knowledge in different ways so that there is one version that leads to the planned sociology of the Australian Aborigines and another planned sociology of the state form of political organization or to the capitalist mode of production. It is an idea that I derive from my reflection on chapter 7 of the *Elementary Structures of Kinship* entitled "The Archaic Illusion." With that in mind, I turn first to the analysis of the rise of inequality that Lévi-Strauss presents in his discussion of generalized exchange.

UNIVERSAL HISTORY 1: GENERALIZED EXCHANGE AND THE ORIGINS OF INEQUALITY

Lévi-Strauss's explanation of the origins of inequality in this book was the subject of a rigorous debate with Edmond Leach and was also addressed from a Marxist perspective in Jonathan Friedman's *System, Structure, and Contradiction in the Evolution of "Asiatic" Social Formations,* which was greatly influenced by the courses he took with Rosman and Rubel (and, like me, also with Harvey Pitkin).

Of course, it is well beyond my ability to fairly summarize the argument that leads to his discussion of generalized exchange. But let me make this attempt. The argument in *Elementary Structures of Kinship* runs like this: At the time of consciousness, humans are presented with the problem of how to reproduce themselves. We solve the problem by turning mating (which is the indiscriminate way in which animals reproduce sexually) into marriage (i.e., a rule bound system) when we institute the incest taboo to regulate the process. The consequence of this shift is that humans move from a natural to a cultural world. In this world, society in its logically most basic form is composed of two intermarrying groups. The theme of this version of universal history, that is, the planned sociology of which he speaks, is the drive to incorporate more and more groups into a single system by means of intermarriage. This leads to systems with four, then eight, and then sixteen groups, each of which may live in a different location. However, he argues that the system has finite limits in that one cannot incorporate more than thirty-two groups into a single system through this method. That is, the system he calls "direct exchange," which is based on the principle that A gives to B and B gives to A, has a finite limit. To move beyond thirty-two groups, then, requires a different solution. And, he argues, that solution is to shift from a logic based on two groups (or in principle an even number of groups) that create marriage relations using direct exchange into a logic based on three groups (although he says that in practice the minimum number is five) or in principle an odd number of groups that exchange marriage partners indirectly. That is, A gives to B, B gives to C, and C gives to A. And as he argues, this solution eliminates the restriction as to the number of intermarrying groups within a system, for the system is open to including an infinite number of groups as long as they constitute an odd rather than an even number. That is, in principle (if infinity = N) A gives to B, B to C, C to D, D to E, E to N, N to A. This means that the system is sufficiently open to include all the people living in the world in a single society. It is thus, in principle, a universal solution to the problem of political organization.

Before going on, let me pause once again. As he shows, this system is supported by matrilateral cross-cousin marriage in that it creates long-term obligations that always move in the same direction (A to B to C to A), but it is not supported by patrilateral cross-cousin marriage in that this form creates short-term obligations in that returns are made in the succeeding generation (A to B to C to A and then C to B to A to C). I do not know the reason for this.

Back to the story: Thus, in principle the world is imagined as composed of an infinitive number of groups, all of which are equals, for each provides a marriage partner, no more, no less. In this regard, the system can be imagined as conforming to what Mauss called "Kula." So how does inequality arise? This answer is that this solution leads to an unanticipated difficulty. It is that, as the system incorporates more and more groups, the relationship with the group from whom one receives marriage partners becomes more and more tenuous. That is, if there are three groups, then the relationship is clear: I know I will receive a marriage partner from C because I have a direct relationship with B and thus I can monitor whether B has fulfilled the terms through which C will be obliged to provide me with one. However, when the system is large, this does not hold. That is, I give to B in good faith that I will receive a marriage partner from a group N with which I am not in direct contact. I also need to rely on a large number of intermediate groups with which I have no contact to follow the rules. This leads me to think about how to create obligations directly with group N. If the system was direct, I could do so by offering a marriage partner. But I cannot do that. Instead, Lévi-Strauss says, I turn to another system of exchange (he calls it a system of communication), which is that of material objects. That is, I will give a material object to ensure that I will receive a marriage partner. Now, in his model as with marriage partners (I know he says women, but he is wrong on that point for reasons I have discussed elsewhere [Asch 2005]), our relationship with the material world is also egalitarian. However, once we intertwine the two systems, we create the opportunity to place a material value on a marriage partner, and thus we introduce a way to assess their relative value. And that opens the door to inequality. Hence, like society itself, in this argument inequality arises as a consequence of the way in which to solve a different problem. Lévi-Strauss puts this more economically and certainly more eloquently at the end of chapter 16:

> Generalized exchange can provide a formula of organization of an exceptional clarity and richness, a formula which can be widened indefinitely and can express the needs of as complex a social group as may be imagined; its theoretical law can function uninterruptedly and without fail. The dangers which threaten it come from outside, from concrete characteristics, and not from the formal structure of the group. Marriage by purchase, by substituting itself, then provides a new formula which, while safeguarding the principles of the formal structure, furnishes the means of integrating those irrational factors which arise from chance and history, factors which the evolution of human society shows to follow—rather than precede—the logical structures. (268)

In sum, then, in this discussion Lévi-Strauss has demonstrated that a key element in Universal History, the rise of inequality, may be explained in sociopolitical rather than material terms, but it also opens up the possibility either that there is more than one way to explain the rise of inequality or that it may arise through different processes in different places. However, notwithstanding what he says earlier about "planned sociology," here Lévi-Strauss is clear that human consciousness plays no role in its appearance, for he concludes the chapter by saying that the "logical structures" of which he speaks "are elaborated by unconscious thought, access to which is often more easily gained through very primitive forms of organization."

UNIVERSAL HISTORY 2: INEQUALITY
AS ORIGINAL CONDITION

My next example is "Do Dual Organizations Exist?" which was first published in 1958, roughly a decade after the publication of *Elementary Structures of Kinship*. This article, which the Norwegian anthropologist Finn Sivert Neilson quite rightly calls "abstruse," appears to me as connected to Lévi-Strauss's engagement with the position of those like Louis Dumont and in a sense Jacques Derrida (as well as certain Marxists and feminists) who take the view that we begin with inequality. As I read it, in this article, Lévi-Strauss takes the view that neither position is correct, for we do not begin in equality as Rousseau would have it, nor do we begin in hierarchy as would Louis Dumont (whose book *Homo Hierarchicus* appears in 1966, some eight years later). Rather, Lévi-Strauss suggests, both exist from the beginning, and thus reconciling the two tendencies is one of the themes of Universal History. And to the extent that this interpretation is correct, this suggestion opens the door to the idea that there can be multiple versions of Universal History in that different societies would solve the same problem in different ways. As he says, the "common substratum" of the kind of societies he will be discussing regardless of their cultural histories might well be a case of "structural similarity between societies that have made related choices from the spectrum of institutional possibilities, whose range is probably not unlimited" (133).

Here, in brief, is how I come to this conclusion. In this article Lévi-Strauss distinguishes between two types of dualism: diametric and concentric. The former, which is egalitarian, leads to the kind of marriage exchanges he discusses in *Elementary Structures of Kinship*—that is, between two equal partners. The latter is hierarchical. Visually, the former is represented as a line bisecting a circle (i.e., the diameter of the circle), and the latter as two circles, one inside the other. Recalling the work of earlier anthropologists, and using Paul Radin's depiction of the Winnebago as his orienting example, Lévi-Strauss concludes that both representations exist within the same social system, for there is no contradiction visually between representing both diametric and concentric dualism simultaneously. He thus creates a molecule of society in which both dimensions exist. As he says:

> These forms, as described, do not necessarily relate to two different organizations. They may also correspond to two different ways of describing one organization too complex to be formalized by means of a single moiety, so that the members of each moiety would tend to conceptualize it one way rather than the other, depending on their position in the social structure. (1963:134–135)

And, in what I think may be a tip of the hand to the Marxist notion of false consciousness, he points to Radin's observation that the superior side of the society invariably represented Winnebago camps as exhibiting the features of diametric dualism and the inferior side as exhibiting the concentric features (1963:133). Then, as I understand it, he shows how moiety systems reconcile the coexistence of the contradictory strains by creating triadic forms. (In his online article "The Dual and the Real," Nielson provides an instructive discussion of this process, although not in the context of political relations. Then, reinforcing my view that Levi-Strauss's intention is to demonstrate that from the beginning societies contained tendencies to both the egalitarian and the unequal, he makes this observation in the penultimate paragraph:

> First Marcel Mauss, then Radcliffe-Brown and Malinowski, revolutionized anthropological theory by substituting a socio-psychological interpretation, based on the concept of reciprocity, for the historical

interpretation. But as schools grew up around these masters, asymmetrical phenomena faded into the background, since they were not easily integrated into the new perspective. The inequality of the moieties came to be treated as an irregularity of the system. And—much more serious—the striking anomalies that were discovered later were completely neglected. As has often happened in the history of science, an essential property of an object was first taken by researchers to be a special case; later on, scientists were afraid to jeopardize their conclusions by submitting them to more rigorous proof. (1963:161–162)

Then he ends by calling for someone who, like Einstein, would have the courage to examine this form of organization and the ability to create a theory that would account for the contradictory tendencies that it displays that are there from the beginning.

In short, in this article, Lévi-Strauss offers a theory of Universal History that departs radically from that espoused by Rousseau and Marx, in which the goal is either to lament or return to an original condition in which we were all equal. Instead, he argues that Universal History is concerned with the varying ways in which we seek to resolve the problematic that, from the beginning, both dimensions play a significant role in our ways of living, no matter how these are constituted culturally and thus implies that there may well be differing versions of it. However, there is no evidence here that Lévi-Strauss has taken the view that the conscious choices we make may determine the varying directions that Universal History may take.

UNIVERSAL HISTORY 3: KINSHIP AND
THE ORIGINS OF AGRICULTURE

In my final example of Lévi-Strauss's engagement with Universal History, I turn to his Huxley Memorial Lecture of 1965, presented to the Royal Anthropological Institute, "The Future of Kinship Studies." Here he returns to a more conventional view of key points in what I will now call Cultural Evolution, focusing as he does on the origins of agriculture. But he provides an explanation in which he reveals that human agency features centrally in the process of History at all of its stages and no matter which direction it may take.

In my reading, this lecture is crucial to understanding the trajectory of Lévi-Strauss's work. His discussion ranges from a critique of critiques of his work on empirical grounds, such as that of Alan Coult, a defense of argument by deduction (in which he sides with Leach), and a comparison between his approach to the analysis of kinship and that developed in British social anthropology, and an explanation for the shift in his research from a focus on kinship to mythology. Along the way he discusses a problem at the heart of that aspect of his project that is seeking a synthetic theory of kinship and marriage that can apply to all societies: what he calls the problem of systems based on Crow-Omaha kinship or what we generally call clan organization. That is, whereas he has been able to explain various social formations in what he has called "elementary structures" of kinship by demonstrating that we create society through marriage systems in which individuals have no choice from which category to choose a marriage partner, here, choice appears to be central. Therefore, how do we create rules that all must follow? His answer is that Crow-Omaha systems only appear to be open because, while they produce a large number of possible marriage arrangements, they are composed of small numbers of people. It is a proposition disproved by my former student, Mark Lathrop, who passed from an undergraduate degree in mathematics through an MA in anthropology to a PhD in genetics where he specialized in mathematical modeling. He is now head of the Center for the Study of Human Polymorphisms in Paris. What he demonstrated (though never published) is that the problem of Crow-Omaha systems is exactly the opposite: even small differences in the numbers of people in different clans soon lead to one clan becoming unpopulated, thus requiring the invention of a new clan (which is joined with the older one to create a phratry) to keep the number of clans at four (thereby allowing for choice).

However, what is paramount in this article for present purposes is that Lévi-Strauss connects the rise of agriculture with the introduction of clan organization, and through this he reveals his view as to the importance of consciousness. Here is how his argument goes. We understand that agriculture arose at a time of population growth (Lévi-Strauss 1965:16), and (this he does not mention, probably because it is commonly understood within the anthropological community) we often think that population growth was the trigger for inventing agriculture or that the increase in productivity associated with agriculture was the trigger for population growth (in more current theory the argument is that agriculture arose slowly and over a long period of time–an evolution, not a revolution). But that does not matter. The missing element in this argument is that population size is a statistic, not an explanation, in that what is key is not larger numbers but a method of organizing more people into a single society so that we achieve the size of community requisite for agriculture. For that, we need a new kind of organization, and clan organization is the primary solution.

Lévi-Strauss argues that the process through which clan organization arises is linked directly to the way in which marriage relations are organized. Furthermore, the distinction between elementary structures and Crow-Omaha systems is reflected in the different forms taken by myths associated with each type.

> What renders the distinction still more interesting is that the same myths link the birth of agriculture with population increase, dispersal of the primal group and diversification of languages and customs. It can thus be said that by making a clear opposition between "cross" in-laws and "parallel" in-laws, the first considered necessary and the second contingent, myths use what, for the sake of argument, I shall call a "palaeolithic" and a "neolithic" model, without loading these terms with historical content. (1965:16)

But is this shift, as might be suggested by the reference to myth, the product of an unconscious mind that somehow, like the hand of God, introduces a new form at the right time? To this, Lévi-Strauss says no. Rather, in his view, it is a conscious invention.

> As a first consequence, I would suggest that the capacity of the so-called primitives for theoretical thinking of a quite abstract nature deserves a great deal more respect than we usually give it when inquiring into the "efficient" causes of their systems of kinship and marriage. These causes may often reside in a correct forecast of the very results which it takes the more sophisticated kind of anthropologi-

cal theory to deduce. A second consequence is that models do not exist solely in the minds of anthropologists, but are to be found in the minds of the native themselves, and in conscious form far more often than superficial evidence would lead us to believe. (16)

And this is connected with the powerful critique of those who (as he once did) would deny the central role played by consciousness in the history of human affairs:

> Only by professing the crudest form of the naturalist philosophy in vogue in the late eighteenth century can one be brought to believe that scientific knowledge is the blind product of a series of trials and errors. Today we know that this is not even true on the level of animal learning. In my own past work, I may have been trying in some degree to evade the issue when I invoked rather hastily the unconscious processes of the human mind, as if the so-called primitive could not be granted the power to use his intellect otherwise than unknowingly. But the findings of physical anthropology are extending further and further back the span of man's existence on earth and I see no reason, just because we know almost nothing of this protracted past, not to admit that plenty of theoretical thinking of the highest order has been carried on all the time, not among all the representatives of the human species—that would not even be true of ourselves—but among a small minority of learned individuals. We may assume that they were concerned not with the same problems as we are, since they did not attempt to solve them, but with some others of a different nature, among which were those dealing with kinship and marriage. Elegant solutions such as the rules of bilateral, patrilateral or matrilateral cross-cousin marriage, so well adapted to small, stable groups, or that of bride-price, or of extended prohibited degrees better suited to larger or more fluid ones, far from being the recent outcome of unconscious processes, now appear to me as true discoveries, the legacy of an age-old wisdom for which more evidence can be found elsewhere.

And it is because myths became the vehicle through which the wise Elders conveyed the rules that they had developed to the population as a whole he now needs to turn to myths. And in conclusion, he pre-

dicts that "in so doing we will find ourselves more and more in agreement with native theories, either expressedly formulated or still hidden in symbolic representations, rituals, and mythologies" (1965:21).

CONCLUSION

In sum, to the extent that my interpretation of these articles makes
sense, it becomes clear that in the period in which his work focused
on kinship, Lévi-Strauss, notwithstanding the crucial role he assigned
to the unconscious, came to the view that consciousness plays a crucial role in our history and in particular that we are creatures who are
confronted with problems (such as the relationship between equality and inequality or a rising population) that we seek to solve by the
application of reason, but that we can never be sufficiently prescient
(as, for example, with generalized exchange) to anticipate all of the
consequences of the plans we make.

I do not gainsay reports of Lévi-Strauss's contributions that focus
on matters that are ahistorical, unconscious, and universal, for those
are precisely the concerns of structuralism as narrowly defined. What
concerns me is that we often limit ourselves to such contributions and
then go on to criticize his oeuvre for not attending to agency and history. But I hope that I have provided sufficient evidence here to indicate that his work also made important contributions to the study of
society and of history that entailed engagement with consciousness
and agency, contributions that are arguably among the most significant
of any scholar in the past century and are certainly among the most
significant in his own work. What I find puzzling, then, is that we have
ignored this dimension of his contributions to the understanding of
the human condition in our assessment of his place in the history of
western intellectual thought.

REFERENCES

Asch, Michael. 2005. Lévi-Strauss and the Political: The Elementary Struc-
    tures of Kinship and the Resolution of Relations between Indigenous
    Peoples and Settler States. In Journal of the Royal Anthropological Insti-
    tute 11(3):425–444.

Dumont, Louis. 1966. Homo Heirarchicus: Le systeme des castes et ses implications. Paris: Éditions Gallimard.

Friedman, Jonathon. 1979. System, Structure, and Contradiction in the Evolution of "Asiatic" Social Formations. A revision of the author's thesis, Columbia 1972. Copenhagen: National Museum of Denmark.

Lévi-Strauss, Claude. 1949. Les structures élémentaires de la parenté. Paris: Presses Universitaires de France.

———. 1958. Les organizations dualistes existent-elles? *In* Anthropologie Structurale. Pp. 147–180. Paris: Librairie Plon.

———. 1963. Do Dual Organizations Exist? *In* Structural Anthropology. Clair Jacobson and Brooke Gundfest Schoepf, trans. New York: Basic Books.

———. 1965. The Future of Kinship Studies: The Huxley Memorial Lecture 1965. Proceedings of the Royal Anthropological Institute of Great Britain and Ireland. Pp. 13–22.

———. 1969. The Elementary Structures of Kinship. James Harle Bell and John Richard von Sturmer, trans. Rodney Needham, ed. Translation is based mainly on the second French edition, published in 1967. Boston: Beacon Press.

Morgan, Louis Henry. 1877. Ancient Society. London: Macmillan.

Neilson, Finn Sivert. 1987–96. The Dual and the Real: Thoughts on an Essay by Claude Lévi-Strauss. http://www.fsnielsen.com/txt/mir/mirrors-ch2.htm, accessed July 19, 2012.

Radcliffe-Brown, A. R. 1952. Structure and Function in Primitive Societies. Glencoe IL: Free Press.

Rousseau, Jean-Jacques. 2005. "Discourse on the Origin of Inequality," www.digireads.com (Stilwell KS), accessed 26 March 2014.

9

Historical Massacres and Mythical Totalities

Reading Marshall Sahlins on Two American Frontiers

The human race is intoxicated with narrow victories, for life is a string of them like pearls that hit the floor when the rope breaks, and roll away in anarchy and perfection.

MARK HELPRIN, *Memoir from Antproof Case* (1995)

Historical events, as opposed to trends and processes, have always been difficult to capture in a "scientific" frame. Trends and processes can be explained, in principle, by feedback mechanisms such as self-regulating markets and balances of power. Indeed, simple homeostatic devices such as the fantail, even as they made possible the industrial revolution, served as the first modern models of political economy (Wootton 2007:42). Specific events, however, seem to slip the net of scientific explanation. Whether they are truly random or just impossible to predict from a human standpoint, events often defy our best efforts to organize and make sense of the world.

At the same time, the common assumption that history is profoundly altered, even determined, by specific events is difficult to deny, although a number of prominent social theorists have tried to do so. In American anthropology, for example, Alfred Kroeber and Leslie White both attempted to reconstruct the past while eliding the actions and experiences of individuals, focusing instead on the glacial transformations of civilizations and other social wholes. "History is a series of chance occurrences," claimed White in 1947. "No one can foretell when an archduke will be shot, or whose archduke it will be, or what will happen when he *is* struck down" (1987:112). History in this sense was sharply contrasted with what White called "evolution"—an orderly, law-governed, even predictable "sequence of forms."

Similarly, the *Annales* school of historiography, led by Lucien Febvre and Fernand Braudel, renounced the traditional narrative mode, with its emphasis on battles and kings, in favor of long time spans, anonymous processes, and enduring institutions. The events of narrative history, argued Braudel in 1949, are like the "brief, rapid, nervous fluctuations" on the surface of the sea—more obvious and less consequential than the powerful tides of the *longue durée* (1972:21). Just as White's anthropology turned to the sequence of forms, *Annales* history turned to the sequence of *structures*—"coherent and fairly fixed series of relationships between realities and social masses" (Braudel 1980 [1958]:31). Transitions from one form or structure to another could be analyzed, according to these theorists, without having to "tell a story" about specific events. Thus over the same decades (c. 1940–1980), social scientists and historians on both sides of the Atlantic witnessed what Paul Ricoeur (1984) called an "eclipse of narrative."

Apart, perhaps, from Ricoeur himself, the one leading theorist with a transatlantic perspective on these developments is the American anthropologist Marshall Sahlins. An erstwhile student of both Leslie White and Claude Lévi-Strauss, Sahlins has been uniquely positioned since the 1960s to appreciate and rethink the assumptions of cultural evolutionism, on the one hand, and French structuralism, on the other (cf. Sahlins 2000a:11–20). The two schools, though emerging from quite different traditions, can be seen now to share a number of distinctive theoretical attitudes, including a general distrust—"almost what amounts to a horror," as Braudel put it—of the event (1980 [1958]:28). Accordingly, for much of his career, Sahlins committed himself to the study of culture as "a scheme of relationships between symbolic categories," a scheme that exists in a "merely virtual" sense, outside "actual being" (Sahlins 2000b:286).

Remarkably, however, in the 1970s, Sahlins began to confront the event—not as a horror beyond the pale of rational understanding but as an invitation to expand such understanding, to bring more human experience within the grasp of reason. The breakthrough came with *Historical Metaphors and Mythical Realities*, which suggested that the social sciences, under the influence of structuralism in particular, had been unnecessarily restricted to the study of virtual entities—symbolic categories, forms, or structures and the systemic relationships among them. What Sahlins called "the fatal argument," originating in structural linguistics, had come to permeate social and cultural anthropology in general (1981:4): "From the perspective of a system of signs, the changes to which it submits will appear fortuitous. The only *system* consists in the way these historical materials are interrelated at any given time or state of the language." On this basis, the actual experiences of human beings in space and time had been deemed contingent and unsystematic, thus scientifically opaque and intractable. But such a concession to fortuity, suggested Sahlins, is simply too high a price to pay: "Some might think that what is lost is what anthropology is all about" (6).

Could anthropology say something about events as well as structures, human acts as well as cultural logics? Sahlins set out to show that it could, with special attention to the history of Polynesia (his area of expertise since his fieldwork in Fiji in the 1950s). The case presented in *Historical Metaphors*—the death of Captain Cook at the hands of the Hawaiians in 1779—is familiar enough, in part because of its central role in a protracted debate between Gananath Obeyesekere (1992) and Sahlins (1995) about "native" categories of thought. Yet the debate itself tended to distract from the major trend in Sahlins's work, which was moving beyond questions of cultural cognition to a theory of historical agency.

The scope of this enterprise became manifest only in recent years. With *Apologies to Thucydides* (2004), Sahlins revealed himself to be as much a philosopher as an anthropologist or historian. Indeed, the major influence looming over the book, aside from Thucydides himself, is Jean-Paul Sartre. Sahlins read Sartre, no doubt, while studying in Paris in the 1960s, but the philosopher was long overshadowed in Sahlins's work by the more immediate and towering presence of Lévi-Strauss (cf. Sahlins 2010). Since 1990, however, this work has taken a discernible "Sartrean turn"—not in opposition to structuralism but in constant dialogue with it. The result is the theory of historical events most fully developed in *Apologies*, a work that deserves closer scrutiny than it has yet received in the literature.

My aim in what follows is to explicate and extend Sahlins's theory, first by investigating what he means by key terms such as "event" and "agency." In this I am guided by two theorists whose works have added critical and enduring insights to the Sahlinsian tradition: Sherry Ortner (1989, 1994, 2006) and William Sewell Jr. (2005a, 2005b, 2005c). Their contributions are ever present in my argument, even if I sometimes diverge from their specific formulations.

Having explicated Sahlins's concepts, I apply them in two cases far removed from Polynesia. In some ways, the cases are similar: both unfolded in the United States in the mid-nineteenth century, and both involved the systematic murder of scores of American citizens by paramilitary forces. The incidents took place, however, on either side of a great war and on two distinct "frontiers"—southern Utah in the 1850s and central Louisiana in the 1870s.[1]

The first case, known as the Mountain Meadows massacre, was carried out by a well-trained company of Mormon militiamen in a remote desert valley in 1857 (Bagley 2002; Walker et al. 2008). The victims were overland travelers, including many women and children, from the white rural communities of northwestern Arkansas (Novak 2008). The second case, set in Grant Parish, Louisiana, in 1873, was locally known as the Colfax "riot," but it is more accurately described as a pitched battle followed by a massacre (Keith 2008; Lane 2008). The perpetrators were white supremacists, including many Confederate veterans, who formed an ad hoc militia to seize the Colfax courthouse from an occupying force of former slaves.

I consider these massacres to be quintessential examples of "events" in Sahlins's sense: "In the general category of human actions, historical events are a subclass only, consisting of *those actions that change the order of things*" (2000c:302, emphasis added). That the massacres were actions—more specifically, "team projects" planned, initiated, and orchestrated by recognized leaders—will be clear enough as we go along. That each changed the "order of things" is also demonstrable, but only if we carefully specify what this order amounted to in the cases at hand.

In Utah, the Mormon hierarchy was the de facto establishment, both culturally and politically, and the atrocity at Mountain Meadows cast a lingering moral shadow on the Church. Along with the practice of polygamy, the massacre came to epitomize Mormon "barbarism" in the eyes of the American public (Gordon 2002). With the end of the Civil War, however, and especially with the completion of the transcontinental railroad, Utah's theocracy was rapidly dismantled (Bigler 1998). Federal authority was decisively imposed through congressional legislation, and in 1874 the first grand jury to be called under the new laws indicted nine militiamen for the massacre, now seventeen years in the past (Bagley 2002:283). In this light, Mountain Meadows was not only a powerful symbol in the culture war over Mormonism but a strategic point of leverage for federal intervention and the "Americanization" of the intermountain West.

In Louisiana, the "order of things" was even more fragile. In 1867, Congress had imposed so-called Radical Reconstruction across the former Confederacy. Southern white reaction against "bayonet rule" initially took the form of vigilante terrorism carried out, most notoriously, by the Ku Klux Klan. By 1873, however, federal enforcement of the Civil Rights Act had busted the Klan and enabled former slaves to vote and hold political office. This was the situation on the eve of the Colfax massacre, which ushered in what James Hogue calls the paramilitary phase of reactionary violence: "The battle of Colfax became a blueprint for white supremacy across Louisiana because it pointed the way toward a successful strategy of paramilitary action narrowly aimed at seizing local political power" (2006:139–140). Over the next four years, Reconstruction was destroyed from the "bottom up," as Hogue puts it, and white rule was promptly consolidated in Louisiana and all the Southern states. In a sense, the trend here was the mirror image of Utah's at the same time: federal authority, rather than expanding, was being rolled back, allowing for the development of a distinct regional regime.

The inverted histories of the regimes in Utah and Louisiana will be essential to the account that follows. For now, the point is that the events in question were regionally motivated and orchestrated, with mainly regional consequences. The salient social order in each case must be specified accordingly.[2] At the same time, the fact that there *was* an encompassing system—"American culture," or at least the United

States as a political entity in the mid-nineteenth century—reminds us that distinct "patches" of culture are known to weave together and come undone in ways that are still rather mysterious. Thus any analysis of events in terms of *the* cultural system, *the* order of things, will eventually confront the problem of patchy, multiplex organization. In extending Sahlins's model to U.S. history and applying it especially to the frontiers of federal control, I hope to demonstrate both the power and the limitations of his approach.

Much of the power, I will argue, derives from deep and underappreciated currents of social theory, traceable to Durkheim, Weber, and Sartre, that Sahlins is able to draw together and synthesize. Yet the resulting theory does not go far enough. The very approach that Sahlins takes to historical events must be extended, I suggest, to the contentious process of capturing and fixing such events within various cultural frames.

SOCIETY AND BIOGRAPHY

The starting point for Sahlins's argument, Sartre's *Search for a Method* (1963), includes a rather surprising foray into U.S. history: "The American Civil War, despite the Puritan idealism of the Northerners, must be interpreted directly in economic terms; the people of that time were themselves aware of it." Viewed as one titanic struggle between an industrial North and an agrarian South, the Civil War lends itself to standard Marxian analysis. We explain such a case by "referring immediately," as Sartre puts it, "to economic contradictions and to conflicts of material interests." This example is cited, however, just to draw the comparison with a more complicated case (1963:42):

> The French Revolution, on the other hand, . . . is not *directly reducible* in 1792 to the age-old conflict of mercantile capitalisms. It must first be made to pass through a process of mediation, one which will bring into play the concrete men who were involved in it, the specific character it took on from its basic conditioning, the ideological instruments it employed, the real environment of the Revolution.

The war with Austria, the September massacres, the arrest and trial of "Citizen Capet": such episodes must be interpreted from *within*, according to Sartre, and not merely analyzed from an economic or other objective viewpoint. What he calls "mediation" is, in effect, the opposite of "reduction": it allows "the individual concrete—the particular life, the real and dated conflict, the person—to emerge from the background of the *general* contradictions of productive forces and relations of production" (1963:57).

Whatever we may think of Sartre's examples (especially his glib assessment of the Civil War), he draws a vital distinction: some histories are easily understood in the abstract, whereas others require close attention to particulars. Why this should be so, however, is never explicitly addressed in his account. What makes some historical phenomena "directly reducible," while others must undergo "a process of mediation"?

An answer was provided by the American historian J. H. Hexter (1971), who seems to have independently invented Sartre's distinction from the point of view of a baseball fan. Hexter's examples, like Sartre's, involve protracted struggles between committed adversaries; in place of wars and revolutions, however, we have pennant races and deciding games. An appropriately Hegelian synthesis is offered in turn by Sahlins (2004), whose mastery of French theory is equaled only by his passion for American baseball. Indeed, in bringing Sartre and Hexter together, Sahlins returns to the role he has perfected over four decades—the consummate transatlantic theorist.

Hexter's argument, by way of Sahlins, runs like this. Some championship teams, such as the New York Yankees in 1939, enjoy a consistent advantage over their opponents (Hexter 1971:35–36). For weeks at a time, the Yankees won many more games than they lost and thus gradually pulled away from their nearest rivals (Sahlins 2004:129):

> To understand this history of progressive domination, it suffices to demonstrate the Yankees' superiority as a team, over the whole season, in the critical baseball functions of hitting, fielding, and pitching. The historical subject is the collective, and accordingly the relevant historical factors are its properties as a collective.

Perhaps Sartre meant to suggest something similar about those other Yankees—the ones who won the Civil War. The superiority of the North as a war-making machine, measured in terms of military-industrial output more than individual leadership or personal heroics, made the difference in the conflict. Despite the many historical accounts focusing on specific battles, generals, maneuvers, and surrenders, the basic trajectory of the war, including its outcome, was determined by collective and systemic properties of the Union as opposed to the Confederacy. This at least would bring Sartre's argument in line with Hexter's.

Both theorists, however, were especially interested in cases that require an account of personal actions and experiences, precisely because the historical outcomes in such cases cannot be understood on the basis of collective and systemic properties alone. While Sartre turned to the French Revolution, Hexter drew another example from the history of baseball. At the end of the National League season in 1951, there was no juggernaut comparable to the '39 Yankees—no consistently dominant team, alone at the top of the standings (Hexter 1971:30–43). Instead, the Brooklyn Dodgers and the New York Giants had been engaged for more than a month in a steadily tightening pennant race. As it happened, the season ended in a tie and the race came down to the last play in the ninth inning of the third game of a best-of-three playoff series. That last play was, of course, "the shot heard round the world," the three-run homer hit by Bobby Thomson that sent the Giants to the World Series. The significance of this event (for historiography, if not for history itself!) is succinctly captured by Sahlins (2004:130):

> What happened, again, was a specific kind of historical change: the overthrow, at the last possible moment and thus in dramatic fashion, of a longstanding relationship between the two teams or, if you will, the competing collective subjects. Here was a reversal of the order of things, a structural change that qualifies Bobby Thomson's home run as a historic event, even as it qualifies him as a hero, a history-maker.

Like the French Revolution in 1792, the baseball season in 1951 was an extremely close-run thing, one of the "narrow victories" with which the human race, according to Helprin (1995:175), is "intoxicated." In such cases it is not enough to analyze the collective or systemic properties of the contending parties. The history of an "overthrow," of a dramatic shift in the order of things, must refer in some detail to "the concrete men who were involved in it" (Sartre 1963:42). It must refer, in other words, to "the intervention of difference-making persons" (Sahlins 2004:129).

But how do such persons emerge from the social group, representing and perhaps reshaping that group at crucial historical moments? Sahlins raises the question in *Historical Metaphors and Mythical Realities*, and on the final page hints at an answer (1981:72):

> The place of the actor in a social hierarchy . . . gives his or her action structural weight, makes it more or less consequential for others. The example of Hawaiian chiefs and the tabus also shows . . . that a privileged position in the cultural-as-constituted may amplify the consequences of an individual's action.

These remarks would be echoed in *Islands of History*, where Sahlins emphasizes "the differential capacity of powers-that-be to make general understandings of their personal innovations" (1985:152). Here is one reason, indeed, that "the course of true history never did run smoothly" (Sahlins 2000c:323):

> Nothing guarantees that the king is the best of men, or even much of one. And though his status may multiply his intelligence by supplying it with the power of society—thus making him a genius—it could also amplify every defect, pettiness of disposition, or weakness of spirit into a historical debacle. At decisive moments the collective fate is at the mercy of the individual psyche.

For society to be vulnerable in this way, the anointed individual must be regarded as synonymous, in some sense, with the group. Polynesian rulers in particular are described by Sahlins as "social-historical individuals"—"persons whose own acts unfold a collective history . . . because they personify the clan or the land and because their acts, universalized through the acquiescence of the historic group, then signify its dispositions" (2000c:322). In the extreme case, he concedes, "society is decided by biography and—Durkheim and White forgive us—culture by psychology" (2000c:343).

Yet Durkheim, at least, would be unlikely to take offense, as he clearly anticipated Sahlins's argument. Tribal chiefs, for example, were described by Durkheim as "the first individual personalities who have risen from the mass of society" (1984 [1893]:143). Their "organized strength," while drawn from society itself, enables them to "depart from collective customs" and "engender something new." An inspired orator, furthermore, is "no longer a simple individual speaking" but "a group incarnate and personified," and this is precisely the source of the "overabundance of forces that spill out around him" (Durkheim 2001 [1912]:158). Sahlins's concept of agency, it would seem, is none other than Durkheim's own.

THE LOGIC AND LOGISTICS OF INSTANTIATION

What Durkheim sketched in a few suggestive sentences, however, Sahlins expands into a full-fledged model of history-making events. The model is formally developed in terms of three dialectical "moments" (Sahlins 2000c:342):

> First a moment of *instantiation* wherein the larger cultural categories of the history are represented by particular persons, objects, or acts, in the manner that Fijian lands are embodied in their ruling chiefs. . . . The second moment is the denouement of the incarnated forces and relations, the incidents proper, being what the persons so empowered as main historical agents actually do and suffer. What they do and suffer, of course, is not simply the expression of the larger categories they are putting in play, since as persons they are subject to circumstances and interests that are not foreseen in the categories. The third moment, then, is the *totalization* of the consequences of what happened, or the return of the act to the system by the attribution of general meanings to particular incidents.

This is obviously meant to be a quite general scheme, applicable to all manner of historical events. Yet the prototypical case for Sahlins, as it was for Durkheim, is the personal deed of the paramount chief—that first *individual*, "risen from the mass of society," whose political authority ensures his historical agency.

Taking up such authority, especially in modern settings, tends to be a formal, systemic process: "Napoleon's singularity was historically empowered by his supreme position in collective entities—France, the army—that were hierarchically organized precisely to transmit and implement his will" (Sahlins 2004:157). The result is what Sahlins calls "systemic agency." The procedures by which such agency is bestowed vary a great deal, of course, from one cultural context to another. Yet coronations, ordinations, and the many other celebrations of official empowerment are all intended to express "the acquiescence of the historic group" (Sahlins 2000c:322). They are just the most visible of the social and political institutions that "authorize" and "relay" systemic agency (2004:155–56, 197–98). This much of Sahlins's argument is clearly consistent with Durkheim's (and, indeed, with the "common sense" of institutional authority).

Yet the formal bestowal of power is certainly not the only source of historical agency. Given a certain state of affairs—a crisis, a "tight spot," a "moment of truth"—even "ordinary people" are able to make history. Such is the *conjuncture*, in Sahlins's terms—a concatenation of historical circumstances in which a great deal depends on the actions of just a few individuals, whatever their office or social rank: "Bobby Thomson was circumstantially selected for his heroic role. . . . The situation put him in a position to make a significant difference, and the situation constituted the significance of the difference he made" (2004:157). Thomson's agency was thus *conjunctural* rather than systemic. It depended on what Sahlins calls "the felicity of his act under the circumstances" (2004:158).

Just as the notion of systemic agency can be linked to Durkheim, that of conjunctural agency can be traced back to Weber. Thus what Weber called "charismatic authority" tends to emerge unexpectedly, without official sanction, especially under conditions of crisis (Weber 1968:1111–1112):

> All *extra*ordinary needs, i.e., those which *transcend* the sphere of everyday economic routines, have always been satisfied . . . on a *charismatic* basis. . . . [T]he "natural" leaders in moments of distress—whether psychic, physical, economic, ethical, religious, or political—were neither appointed officeholders nor "professionals" . . . but rather bearers of specific gifts of body and mind that were considered "supernatural" (in the sense that not everybody could have access to them).

This dimension of Weber's argument has been obscured, no doubt, by the modern tendency to attribute charisma to any number of officeholders and professionals. His original remarks, however, clearly suggest that a leader's "gifts" could be demonstrated only by felicitous action, especially under trying and unforeseen circumstances.[3]

All of this suggests that Sahlins, in developing his theory of historical agency, has by no means broken with classical sociology but has in fact resurrected one of its venerable, though underappreciated, ideas. The idea amounts to this: an individual's capacity to make history derives from his or her *embodiment of the social group*. Such embodiment can take place, according to Sahlins, either through formal, institutional channels (in the case of systemic agency) or through the situational production of "heroism" (in the case of conjunctural agency). This formulation has the advantage of tacking between Durkheim and Weber, allowing us to draw on the insights of one master or the other as the empirical case requires.

What it does not attempt, however, is to *synthesize* the contributions of Durkheim and Weber by following the surprisingly convergent paths of their arguments (Tiryakian 1995). Common to both theorists is the assumption of an *audience*, whether formally assembled or spontaneously transfixed, as a basic ingredient of socially pivotal moments. Thus, while Durkheim traced social consciousness to the "collective effervescence" of religious rituals, Weber attributed charismatic leadership to the "collective excitement produced by extraordinary events" (1968:1121). Command of the group's attention, the linchpin of collective ritual, is also critical to historical events because they depend on "mutual focus" and "emotional entrainment" to be recognized *as* events (Collins 2004, Wagner-Pacifici 2010). Accordingly, a synthesis of Durkheim and Weber would place the history-making agent squarely in the presence of an effervescent audience, there to stoke, gather, and channel the energy of society at large.

Many important events, of course, do not have an audience in the literal sense. Yet even those that take place far from the public gaze come to be observed by second- and third-order "witnesses"—consumers of narratives and other representations (Peters 2001; Wagner-Pacifici 2005; Frosh and Pinchevski 2009). These indirect witnesses and their role in historical interpretation will be taken up below. For now it is worth noting that a rather large audience is physically present in all the major examples considered by Sahlins (2004). Whether the protagonist is Napoleon on the battlefield, Bobby Thomson at the plate, a Fijian chief at a village feast, or young Elián González being seized by federal agents, there are other people, often a great many, watching in synchrony with the action and each other. This is precisely the pattern that is identified by Collins (2004), following Durkheim, as the vital core of every ritual interaction.

Moreover, all of Sahlins's major cases are drawn from three domains that are metaphorically, if not literally, interconnected: warfare, team sports, and political theater. What these have in common is rivalry between well-defined social units, whether nations, teams, or political factions. Such rivalry seems to drive the process of instantiation. First, the sharpening of social boundaries and the enhancement of solidarity within those boundaries allows one group member to "stand in" for another. An injury to one, for example, is perceived as an assault on the group as a whole and may be avenged by injuring anyone of the enemy group (Kelly 2000). As this logic of social substitution becomes generalized, one individual can be imagined to encapsulate the collectivity, to embody and personify it, in the way Bobby Thomson came to embody the New York Giants (not to mention their fans and, indeed, the citizenry of Manhattan).

Yet our rendering can be even more precise. Instantiation is usually prompted by some kind of *standoff*—an episode of heightened opposition and stalled aggression between groups with equal or nearly equal competitive power. This is in accord with the definitive analysis provided by Robin Wagner-Pacifici (2000:7):

> Standoffs are situations of mutual and symmetrical threat, wherein the central parties face each other, literally and figuratively, across some key divide. Standoffs engage committed adversaries in a frozen and exposed moment of interaction. Everything is placed in high relief—actions and reactions, languages, gestures, behaviors.

The appearance of everything in "high relief," both frozen and exposed, is what makes a standoff so favorable to instantiation. The action has paused; the outcome is still to be decided. The adversaries remain committed and face each other across the same "key divide." What will happen next must be initiated by specific individuals—perhaps the recognized leaders of each group, perhaps their strategically situated followers. All eyes come to be fixed on the emerging heroes. "And as we thus focus in on the ultimate actors, we go into slow motion" (Sahlins 2004:134).

Frozen and exposed, the heroes are caught in the grip of the standoff, unable to act. Their paralysis is a manifestation of "confrontational tension," the central reality of potentially violent social encounters (Collins 2008:41–42). Yet this state is fragile and prone to abrupt, catastrophic collapse. In an instant, the tension can crumble and the heroes suddenly break through to the denouement. By their agency, whether systemic or conjunctural, history takes a turn. And soon enough, what has happened will be totalized, according to Sahlins (2000c:342)—returned to the cultural matrix and interpreted by its encompassing values.[4]

NO COUNTRY FOR NAPOLEONS

But what if totalization is incomplete? What if "particular incidents" can be assigned only partial and contested meanings? Mountain Meadows and Colfax are but two cases of historical standoffs that remain, in a sense, just that—standoffs between schools of historical interpretation.[5] More prominent examples, including the Haitian Revolution and the Battle of the Alamo, are cogently analyzed by Michel-Rolph Trouillot (1995). When it comes to contentious histories, it would seem, Sahlins's concept of totalization runs into problems. And the trouble often begins when historical narrators cannot agree on what *kind* of agency was, in fact, at work. All of this suggests we should take a closer look at the original distinction.

To tease apart the systemic and the conjunctural, Sahlins invokes radically different kinds of historical figures. Systemic agency is illustrated by the likes of Napoleon, Pericles, and the god-kings of Fiji. Their conjunctural counterparts include Bobby Thomson, his opponent on the mound (Ralph Branca), and the unwitting combination of Katherine Harris and Lazaro González—two otherwise obscure Floridians who may have gotten George W. Bush elected president (Sahlins 2004:133,

174–180). The rhetorical strategy here is familiar and effective—make the distinction as sharp as possible by highlighting "pure" or "ideal" examples. Yet we are left with the impression of two altogether different social universes, one grandiose, world-historical, and mythically tragic, the other humble, provincial, and sometimes farcically comic. The real social universe is more complicated, of course, weaving together elements we might prefer to keep separate.

Indeed, having grasped the distinction that Sahlins set out to make, we are challenged to put it to work in especially complex, even vexing, historical cases. What would be particularly useful for our purposes would be examples of systemic and conjunctural agents in the same social context, even operating side-by-side, or perhaps squaring off against each other. Cases of intermediate or ambiguous forms of agency would pose a further challenge—perhaps casting doubt on the original distinction. More optimistically, intermediate cases might suggest relationships between the systemic and conjunctural domains. If some agents, for example, are able to shift from one domain to the other, how do they do so, and to what effect? Such issues can be investigated only in richly ambiguous cases.

The massacres at Mountain Meadows and Colfax both involved systemic agents (such as U.S. presidents), conjunctural agents (such as heroic survivors), and a great many more participants who are difficult to classify one way or the other. Certainly each of the crimes had dozens of perpetrators—at least fifty at Mountain Meadows and perhaps twice that many at Colfax. Yet in each case one hardened zealot is known to have played a leading role.

In Utah, the key figure was John Doyle Lee (1812–1877). That Lee was deeply involved in planning and carrying out the Mountain Meadows massacre is hardly in doubt; the critical question, debated to this day, is whether he acted on orders of the Mormon hierarchy in Salt Lake City (for opposing views, see Bagley [2002] and Walker et al. [2008]). Appointed by Brigham Young to lead the colonization of southern Utah, Lee held the rank of major in the local militia and was one of two commanding officers at the site of the massacre (Walker et al. 2008:190).

Lee's counterpart in Louisiana was Christopher Columbus Nash (1838–1922). A veteran of combat at Bull Run, Antietam, Winchester, and Gettysburg, Nash would go on to recruit and deploy the para-military force that committed the murders at Colfax. While he may have been the tool of a broader network of white supremacists (Keith 2008:89), Nash was ostensibly acting as the newly elected sheriff of Grant Parish, under orders from the parish judge (Lane 2008:83).

The massacre in each case followed a long standoff. In the summer of 1857, Utah Mormons were on a war footing even before the unfortunate emigrants arrived in their midst. Rumors of an impending invasion by the U.S. Army had caused such alarm that overland travelers in general were vulnerable to Mormon abuse. Indeed, having met with scorn and suspicion since they passed through Salt Lake City, the riders on the Arkansas train were no doubt relieved to be departing the territory. They made their last camp in Utah beside a creek at Mountain Meadows. Just before dawn, however, on September 7, this large entourage—some 140 men, women, and children, along with hundreds of head of cattle—was fired upon from the creek bed by unseen assailants. Having lost a number of men in the first volley, the emigrants returned fire, dug defense pits, and managed to hold out for four days (September 7–11, 1857). By the time they were offered terms of surrender, the survivors were exhausted, dehydrated, and low on ammunition.

In the case of Colfax, the site of the standoff was a rural, one-story courthouse, about seventy-five feet long and twenty-five feet wide (Lane 2008:70). In the wake of a bitterly disputed election, the building was taken over on March 25, 1873, by Republican claimants to local offices. The few whites who had dared to support the occupation were soon scared off by threats of violence, leaving the courthouse in the hands of an all-black militia. While the former slaves dug trenches around the building, white vigilantes and paramilitaries gathered on the outskirts of Colfax. On April 13, Easter Sunday, the courthouse defenders received an ultimatum: give up their weapons and leave the building or they would be attacked.

Breaking a standoff seems to require the authorization of at least one group member to act on behalf of the collective—what Sahlins calls instantiation. The instantiated figure was Lee in the case of Mountain Meadows and Nash in the case of Colfax. Indeed, having accepted this role, each man enacted the same familiar ritual, approaching a representative of the opposing side under a flag of truce. What happened next, however, was entirely different in the two cases.

Lee lied to the beleaguered emigrants and tricked them into surrendering their weapons. The men were separated from the women and children, and the ambulatory from those who had to ride or be carried. The several groups were then escorted out of their campsite, heading to what they believed was safety. Nash, by contrast, gave fair warning of the impending assault and even made a concession to his adversaries: they had thirty minutes to evacuate any women and children from the courthouse. As a direct result, only men would be killed at Colfax, while the entire company, with the exception of seventeen children, would be slaughtered at Mountain Meadows.

Much more could be said, of course, about the massacres themselves. Indeed, if historical narration were the objective, we would shift now to the kind of "slow motion" account that Sahlins sees as the hallmark of eventful history. But I am more concerned here with the other two "moments" of Sahlins's scheme, before and after the event itself: instantiation and totalization. This requires a much closer look at Lee and Nash—their personal histories, structural positions, and strikingly different fates.

In the investigation of Mountain Meadows, federal authorities singled out Lee, just as they would single out Nash sixteen years later, and sought to charge him as the ringleader. Though Lee's role in the massacre and his fugitive status amounted to common knowledge in southern Utah, he managed to avoid arrest until 1874 (the year after the Colfax massacre). Now in his early sixties, Lee was tried twice, eventually convicted, and immediately executed by firing squad. Nash, on the other hand, was never brought to trial. He remained a prosperous and respected citizen of Colfax until his peaceful death at the age of eighty-three. This divergence of fortunes at the end of their lives stemmed, I suggest, from a key difference in the social circumstances under which Lee and Nash committed their crimes.

For most of his adult life, Lee was a trusted member of the Mormon elite. Indeed, he had been a Church insider since 1845, when he was first permitted to practice "celestial marriage" (polygamy) and was ritually "sealed" to Brigham Young as an adopted son (Brooks 1992 [1961]:65,

73). At Young's direction, Lee gave up his home in Salt Lake City and moved into the red rock desert, founding Fort Harmony, some twenty-five miles east of Mountain Meadows, in the early 1850s. Here he held the office of "Indian Farmer"—a lucrative federal position (assigned by the Indian superintendent, Brigham Young) with the principal objective of turning migratory bands of Southern Paiutes into settled agriculturalists. At the same time, Lee commanded one of the four battalions of the territorial militia based in southern Utah. In short, by 1857, Lee was a "made man"—officially empowered by the Mormon Church, the Utah Territory, and even the U.S. government to administer a frontier outpost, its armed forces, and the surrounding "Indian country."

Nash's position in 1873 was far more precarious. Raised in the backwoods of Sabine Parish near the border with Texas, he had never had it easy. He managed to survive the 1860s "despite his two stints as a prisoner of war and his participation in the bloodiest fighting of the nineteenth century" (Keith 2008:72). Returning to Louisiana, Nash settled in rural Colfax, the newly created seat of Grant Parish, and immediately entered the cutthroat world of local politics and law enforcement. Teaming up with another Confederate veteran—a hard case by the name of Alfred C. Shelby—Nash became Shelby's deputy sheriff in November 1870. Ten months later, Shelby and Nash were at the head of a raiding party that shot up the home of Delos White, the former sheriff and a so-called carpetbagger from New York City. Just before dawn, they torched White's house, then murdered him as he tried to escape. Nash himself was said to have fired the fatal shots at point-blank range (Lane 2008:51). Arrest warrants were promptly issued in New Orleans, and most of the suspects, including Nash, were rounded up by the Louisiana state militia. A few weeks later, however, the charges were dropped on a technicality. This allowed Nash to return home, burnish his reputation as a dashing and dangerous nightrider, and make his own run for sheriff. It was the disputed outcome of this election that set the stage for the Colfax massacre.

The point is that Lee and Nash, while carrying out rather similar crimes, exercised quite different kinds of agency. If Lee enjoyed a fair share of official power, Nash was still fighting for social recognition. In this respect, it might be said that Lee cut the more "Napoleonic" figure, Nash the more "Thomsonian" one. Yet this would have little to do with their "intrinsic" qualities (whatever those might be) and much more to do with the social matrix in which each man was embedded.

Lee's biography is inseparable from the early history of the Mormon Church. From the time of his conversion at the age of twenty-five, he had sought to serve the Church in any way he could and to be anointed by its leaders. His aims and efforts were merged with those of the Church, and the Church's success became in turn his success. Indeed, by 1857 Lee was an instantiation of the Mormon "nation"—not to the same degree that Brigham Young was, of course, but with Young's blessing and imprimatur.

Nash, by contrast, had pinned all his hopes on a famously lost cause, the Confederacy of the South, and arrived in Colfax with very little in the way of collective or institutional guidance. What there was for defeated and humiliated rebels like Nash was just the afterglow of the Confederacy—a loose network of veterans, all "searching for companionship among the devastation," who went on to form clubs and fraternal orders in which "they could drink, reminisce, and complain" (Lane 2008:3). There were no Napoleons in this network. Everyone was "conjunctural"—anonymous, unauthorized, seemingly powerless, but desperate for a systemic niche. Nash found his niche with the murder of Delos White. On this basis, he began to build a career—one that would provide him with a modicum of systemic agency, not unlike that which Lee had enjoyed before the 1870s.

From this comparison three general conclusions may be drawn. First, *historical agency is not an inherent, personal quality (or at least not that alone) but mainly a result of one's structural position.* "For granted that individuals may have historical effect," as Sahlins puts it, "they have to be in a position to do so, . . . and 'position' means a place in a set of relationships, whether institutional, conjunctural, or both" (2004:155). Lee's practices, for example, cannot be understood apart from the burgeoning organization of the Mormon Church, nor Nash's apart from the smoldering ruins of the Confederacy.

Yet this example brings into focus a second important conclusion, one that is somewhat at odds with the first: *social actors seem to have at their disposal—and find themselves constrained by—varying amounts of "structure."* Of course all human beings are embedded in complex social relations. But the assumption that these relations consistently form "big" structures, or very systematic ones, has been in doubt for a long time. In historical sociology, for example, the point was driven home by Michael Mann (1986:16):

> Human beings do not create unitary societies but a diversity of intersecting networks of social interaction. The most important of these networks form relatively stably. . . . But underneath, human beings are tunneling ahead to achieve their goals, forming new networks, extending old ones. . . . I term such processes *interstitial emergence.* They are the outcome of the translation of human goals into organizational means. Societies have never been sufficiently institutionalized to prevent interstitial emergence.

Even the Gramscian notion of hegemony implies not a total or enduring cultural order, as is sometimes suggested (Sahlins 2004:145), but only a dominant "formation" within the flow of history.[6] Thus "while one may talk of hegemonic formation(s) in the present, there are always also remnants of past ('residual') hegemonies and the beginnings of future ('emergent') ones" (Ortner 2006:6).

In the cases at hand, it might be argued that the Mormon Church in the 1850s was an emergent hegemony throughout the Intermountain West, while the Confederacy in the 1870s was a residual one throughout the Deep South. The structuring effects of these hegemonies would have been waxing and waning, respectively. But this immediately suggests that Lee and Nash, at the time of their crimes, were supplied with very different *quantities* of structure. Lee had, as it were, a growing "surplus" of structure, while Nash was running a "deficit." Little wonder, in this light, that Lee seems the more systemic agent—there was simply "more system" available to him. Nash, by comparison, was working with shards and splinters of the old regime, even as he tried to maneuver within the (now faltering) framework of the "present hegemony" (i.e., Reconstruction). To put this in Mann's 1986 terms—Nash was *tunneling ahead,* translating his goals into organizational means, and thus "outrunning the existing level of institutionalization." If he were successful, furthermore, Nash might be expected to alter both the surrounding "system" and his own historical agency.

This leads to a third conclusion, one that returns to the question of how history-changing agents might maneuver *between* the systemic and conjunctural domains. While Sahlins tends to treat "Napoleons" and "Thomsons" as discrete, even mutually exclusive types, the cases at hand suggest that *systemic agency and conjunctural agency often blur into each other—with important historical consequences.* Lee and Nash used whatever systemic credentials they could muster to leverage the tricky situations in which they found themselves. Neither had his historical effect by issuing authoritative, Napoleonic commands, or by simply rising, out of nowhere, to the heroic occasion. What each did, on the contrary, was to recognize and turn to his advantage the very ambiguities of his social position.

POSITION, PERFORMANCE, AND POSTERITY

Were these ambiguities, all the same, just a cloak for some institutional agenda? On whose behalf might these men have acted? Especially in the case of Lee, the prime question has always been whether he was operating on his own or following the dictates of a hierarchical system. The most incendiary charge, of course, is that Brigham Young secretly ordered the massacre at Mountain Meadows. If the charge is true, it would make Lee just a tool in the hands of a Mormon Napoleon. It could even be argued that the system as a whole—the Mormon Church—bears the stigma of the crime. This is not the place to pursue the matter, except to note that Lee, by virtue of his long-standing and publicly avowed loyalty to the Church, made an especially credible scapegoat on its behalf (Brooks 1992 [1961]:358–359; Bagley 2002:271–274). At the same time, Lee's removal from the Mormon capital to a semiautonomous colony in the desert makes it possible to this day to portray him as a merely conjunctural agent—indeed, a temperamental upstart—with no writ from the Church (Walker et al. 2008:61–67, 187–189).

The case of Nash in this regard is murky but intriguing. As a former Confederate officer, he knew what it was to be an insider—part of a formal, hierarchical system with the capacity to authorize social action. After the war, however, Nash stood for nothing so well established or publicly prominent as the Mormon Church. His "election" to the office of sheriff was almost certainly fraudulent, as most residents of Grant Parish were well aware (Lane 2008:66). There is the possibility that he represented an *underground* organization, namely, the Ku Klux Klan or its local equivalent. Indeed, LeeAnna Keith (2008:89) believes that "the Knights of the White Camellia and a group calling itself the 'Old Time Ku Klux Klan' played a major organizational role" in the attack on the Colfax courthouse (cf. Lane 2008:87). Yet any direct tie Nash might have had to such an organization remains, like the group itself, obscure.

In one important respect, at least, Nash's situation was the mirror image of Lee's. Both had known the pride and glory of serving under "great men"—the Napoleons of the Confederacy and the Mormon Church, respectively. The difference was that Robert E. Lee had been defeated, leaving loyalists like Nash to fend for themselves, whereas Brigham Young would survive his own battle with the United States, but only by sacrificing his devoted follower and adopted son, John D. Lee.

While the outcome for the agent, then, was certainly related to the vicissitudes of his institutional matrix, it was not a direct but an inverse relation. Lee was given up, it could be argued, precisely because his matrix was *recovering* from adversity. (To revert to a baseball metaphor—someone had to take the blame for last season's losses.) Nash, on the other hand, was able to escape justice because his institutional matrix had been shredded. (His team had disbanded, as it were, granting him "free agency" and the chance to play for some other outfit.) Such cases are counterintuitive if the agent and his matrix are assumed to rise and fall, flourish and suffer in synchrony.

Yet the premise of Sahlins's argument, derived from both Sartre (1963) and Ricoeur (1984), is that there is no such isomorphic relation between macro and micro, society and subject: "One could speak of multiple breaks, basically ontological, that make it impossible to resolve the social to the individual, thus to encompass or determine the one directly by the other, whether in one direction or reciprocally" (2004:151). If Lee had been just the Mormon Church in microcosm, he could not have been sacrificed to save it; if Nash had simply embodied the Confederacy, he could not have survived its demise. Each individual is socially *positioned*, not socially determined. And the full biographical implications of such positioning, its enabling and entangling effects over the life course, are what constitute historical agency in the first place.

Beyond positioning, however, is performance—the execution of intended acts in the face of contingency. Even the most advantageous position does not guarantee efficacious performance, and much of our fascination with historical events derives from mismatches between position and action. Systemic agents, fully authorized to act, may fail catastrophically; conjunctural agents, appearing "out of nowhere," may succeed beyond hope. Indeed, if position could explain everything, "the event" would not have posed such a problem for social theorists from Hegel and Durkheim to Sahlins himself. In short, if historical agency is made possible by social position, it can be realized only in historical performances that place such position at risk.

The point is amply demonstrated in the cases at hand. The strikingly different fortunes of Lee and Nash can be attributed in part to their tactical efforts to avoid arrest—what Sahlins would call the felicity of their acts at a critical conjuncture. Months after their respective crimes, when federal authorities finally arrived to investigate, both men narrowly escaped. Yet their escapes were performed in quite different styles and would attract the attention of quite different "audiences."

In the spring of 1859, a full year and a half after the Mountain Meadows massacre, a federal judge with a military escort headed south from Salt Lake City to investigate the crime and, if possible, arrest the culprits. Lee was forty-six at the time, a wealthy patriarch with eight wives and a molasses mill. His fort at Harmony, some twenty miles east of the massacre site, was a strategic oasis for overland migrants crossing the Mojave to the south. In the winter months, this arrangement netted Lee as much as $75 per day and kept his wives cooking most of the night to serve travelers in the morning (Brooks 1992 [1961]:245). Though his home was remote from any town, Lee was not a difficult man to find.

On April 2, federal warrants were issued for the arrest of the principal suspects at Mountain Meadows (Bagley 2002:218). With some two hundred troops en route to the southern settlements, Lee took to the rugged plateau overlooking Harmony (Brooks 1992 [1961]:246–247). He hid out there for several weeks, receiving news, provisions, and an occasional hot meal from one or another of his womenfolk. When the dragnet failed and the U.S. Army left the area, Lee returned to his household, rattled but unscathed. After this rather inglorious homecoming, "he was extremely nervous and would remain so for the next fifteen years" (Bagley 2002:226).

In the case of Colfax, the leading suspect seems to have been emboldened rather than daunted by the authorities on his trail. Six months after the massacre, Nash was thirty-five years old, without family or property, but free to move about the Red River valley, despite being indicted by a federal grand jury. In late October 1873, he pitched camp in a pasture about five miles from the massacre site, trying to elude the U.S. marshal and two dozen Metropolitan Police who had come up from New Orleans to arrest him. Acting on a tip, they raided his hideout with guns drawn, but Nash managed to flee on horseback (Lane 2008:150). What happened next, according to local whites, was indeed the stuff of legend (Keith 2008:132):

> Overtaken at Aloha, a romantically named river landing eight miles north of [Colfax], Nash plunged his horse into the Red River, escaping to the other side in a hail of gunfire. According to legend, the rebel leader paused to wave his slouch hat in defiance, spurred his horse, and made his getaway to Texas by an underground railroad of like-minded whites.

By early November, the posse had pulled out of the area, effectively abandoning the Red River parishes to vigilante gangs. Within months, a well-organized paramilitary network, the White League, had spread across central Louisiana (Hogue 2006:124–25).

Both Lee and Nash went on to live for years as free men. Faced with imminent defeat, each had managed to "stay in the game," and their performances, in this narrow sense, were equally effective. Yet their performances were not equally *felicitous*. While Lee went into hiding and was never discovered, Nash was exposed and hotly pursued. From this initial difference, other differences follow.

Lee's ordeal was mostly solitary, long, and dull. It never took on the drama of a standoff or the excitement of a chase. In this respect, it was like the history of the '39 Yankees, who "progressively distanced themselves from the competition" and then predictably prevailed, with "no pennant race . . . , no turning point, no contest" (Sahlins 2004:129). Such a triumph has little about it to sustain public attention or to invite what Hexter (1971) called "storytelling"—and so it was in the case of Lee's escape. There was no one moment, for example, when Lee could be said to have "escaped." He simply waited out his would-be captors until they left the area. Moreover, though the experience made him "nervous," Lee was apparently safe and well provisioned throughout his time "on the underground" (Kelly 1984:201). He was able to call on a large and experienced domestic "staff," not to mention the encompassing organization of the Mormon Church. Indeed, the entire episode serves to demonstrate Lee's crushing dependence on the Church and its "peculiar institution" of polygamy. Even in his wilderness redoubt, he was never wholly alone: it was, after all, *his* wilderness, part of his fiefdom in the desert, and ultimately an extension of his polygamous household.

All of this is inverted in the case of Nash. His hideout was a neighbor's pasture—a borrowed space, hardly remote or inaccessible, and promptly uncovered by the U.S. marshal. What should have been an easy arrest, however, turned into a classic getaway. Nash's dash to the Red River was brief, sensational, and decisive. His pursuers would have experienced what Collins (2008) calls "forward panic," a sudden release from the tension and anxiety built up during a standoff, followed by the "hot rush" of the chase. Such a chase, even more than a standoff, is likely to master the attention of participants and bystanders alike. Everyone recognizes the unfolding of a little drama whose outcome depends on the instantaneous actions and reactions of just a few principal players. These players, like Bobby Thomson at the plate, now become the white-hot center of the audience's consciousness. Under such circumstances, according to Sahlins (2004:132), "the appropriate historiographic form changes from 'analysis' to 'storytelling,' a difference of narrative mode marked by corollary differences in temporality and agency. Time is progressively magnified. The account that began in months will end in moments, ultimately one final moment of perhaps ten seconds." The moment is easy to identify. Just as Thomson took the pitch and swung for the left-field stands, Nash spurred his horse to the river's edge and plunged into the current, his eyes low and riveted on the opposite bank. Seconds later, it was over. Even if he never actually waved his hat in defiance, Nash's escape must have been breathtaking—to his enemies no less than his allies.

It was all the more so because Nash had no obvious accomplices or institutional support. If "an underground railroad of like-minded whites" did aid his passage to Texas (Keith 2008:132), this was probably an informal network of kith and kin rather than a Klan-like political or criminal organization. Even Nash's coconspirators in the massacre seem to have been bound together by diffuse personal ties and political loyalties as opposed to any established institution or formal ideology. These very ties and loyalties, however, would soon provide the political base for reactionary leaders intent on overthrowing Reconstruction and restoring white rule across the South. Such leaders needed "heroes" like Christopher Columbus Nash—individuals whose felicitous performances could inspire others to act or at least to follow along. In short, Nash's escape not only enhanced his own social position but helped to reconfigure the positions of others in a dynamic political field.

Nothing of the sort could be said of Lee's escape. It was a wholly defensive and largely passive performance, unlikely to inspire anyone's admiration or imagination. The patriarch did avoid arrest and was able to restore the *status quo ante*, at least for the next few years. But that, in a sense, was Lee's problem: his *incumbency*, we might call it, and the complacency that went with it, even as the Utah Territory, the Mormon Church, and the United States were all rapidly changing around him. Indeed, it was the dynamic, shifting nature of "the system" that would prove to be Lee's undoing, while that same dynamism would come, just in time, to Nash's rescue.

Thus, in their later years, Lee and Nash were turned into symbols, each standing in for a distinct segment of American society. Lee came to represent all that was wrong, from the national point of view, with Mormon Utah: theocracy, cronyism, polygamy, and a subterranean culture of violence whose most appalling manifestation was the Mountain Meadows massacre (Gordon 2002). Even fellow Mormons came to denounce Lee, and in October 1870 he was quietly expelled from the Church. Settling into exile in northern Arizona, Lee and his wives—the two who remained with him—dubbed their homestead "Lonely Dell."

In Louisiana, meanwhile, Nash became the hero of a broad-based and newly energized social movement. The events at Colfax were part of a wider insurrection—what Hogue (2006) calls a "counterrevolution"—intended to reestablish white supremacy across the South. In the wake of the massacre and especially after his spectacular escape, Nash emerged as a living icon of what had been lost with the fall of the Confederacy and what might be regained under a new, racially segregated regime. In short, while Lee was condemned and ostracized by the community to which he had devoted his life, Nash became a political emblem for a multitude of strangers ready to take up his cause.

In this light, the contrasting fates of Lee and Nash might be approached from a quite different angle. Instead of focusing on their own social positions or actions, we might turn to the key *narrators* who made these two murderers into national or regional symbols. Of course, any such "iconization" involves an untold number of personal perceptions, judgments, and micro-interactions. Yet such a process also has its leading agents and social circles, and the cases at hand offer two extraordinarily clear examples.

"Perhaps nothing did more to expose the lies surrounding Mountain Meadows than the revelations of Charles W. Wandell" (Bagley 2002:268). Wandell had been a loyal Mormon and longtime resident of southern Utah. Soon after the massacre, he passed through the killing fields, where scores of human skeletons had been scavenged by carnivores and exposed to the sun. After thirteen years of investigating the story, Wandell began to publish a series of open letters to Brigham Young about what happened at Mountain Meadows. The letters appeared under a pseudonym in the *Utah Reporter*, a dissident (i.e., non-Mormon) newspaper founded with the coming of the railroad in 1869. Without this paper and its intrepid correspondent, the massacre is likely to have been remembered quite differently, if at all. For his part, Lee might well have lived out his days in Harmony, surrounded by his wives and offspring.

Nash's fate was also powerfully affected by accounts in the press. Soon after the massacre, a number of white supremacist newspapers were founded across Louisiana. One of these, the *Caucasian*, was started by George W. Stafford, a former Confederate officer who had led one of the paramilitary companies at Colfax. Stafford's propaganda helped turn "Sherriff Nash" into a "chivalric superhero" (Lane 2008:217):

A front-page story in the paper recounted the supposed travails of a bankrupt Mississippi planter and his family who were repeatedly waylaid by savage Negroes as they traveled across Louisiana to their new home in Texas. Each time, the arrival of Sherriff Nash sent the Negroes fleeing in panic. The article concluded with a prayer asking God to "help and keep Sheriff Nash, who, we hear, is driven from his home and hunted like a wild beast, for protecting the helpless."

Were it not for the *Caucasian* and its impassioned publisher, Nash might well have stayed on the run until he was captured or killed. As it happened, however, he married into a prominent planter family and in 1888 became the mayor of Colfax.

None of this is to suggest that Lee and Nash were just so much clay to be molded and manipulated by the press—or, later on, by historians. "There are," as Sahlins insists, "structures *of* and *in* history. It's not all tricks the living play on the dead" (2004:128). Moreover, even tricks of this kind must be guided by a cultural sensibility and will have their intended effects only if they speak somehow to the yearnings or fears of audiences themselves burdened with the structures of history.

THE MEDIATION OF TOTALIZATION

Are we to conclude, then, that historical structures are self-regulating? That they can change, certainly, as a result of human action, but always in the end "have their way" by limiting the interpretation that can be applied to such action? If so, then the sequence of "moments" that Sahlins takes to constitute the event—instantiation, the happening itself, and its totalization—would appear to subsume historical agency within the kind of feedback mechanism that gave rise to the social sciences in the first place. What the agent does, in other words, amounts to a perturbation of the system, which returns to equilibrium—albeit in an altered state—through its own dynamic and not as a result of continuing purposive action. Thus the creative energies of the historical agent are harnessed to the more predictable processes of the cultural system.

Such a hybrid model of history, it should be noted, has a long and distinguished ancestry. Even without going back to Thucydides—whose narratives tend to shift between the doings of specific persons and those of city-states or peoples (Sahlins 2004:125)—the more immediate fore-runners are an interesting lot. The precedent set by Thomas Kuhn, for example, is clear enough (Sahlins 2004:9, 136–37). Long stretches of "normal science," according to Kuhn, are punctuated by rapid and heroic shifts in worldview (1970:144; 2000:17). Similarly rapid and comprehensive changes followed by social stabilization were traced by Anthony F. C. Wallace in his 1956 account of "revitalization movements."

But the classic model for this kind of argument (as Wallace, for one, clearly recognized) is Weber's theory of charisma and routinization. The dialectical process he outlined in the early twentieth century is by now familiar: after the brief phase of cultural creativity that surrounds an extraordinary religious or political figure, society reverts to an orderly, institutional existence, as if automatically (Weber 1968:1121–1122):

> When the tide that lifted a charismatically led group out of everyday life flows back into the channels of workaday routines, at least the "pure" form of charismatic domination will wane and turn into an "institution"; it is then either mechanized, as it were, or imperceptibly displaced by other structures, or fused with them in the most diverse forms, so that it becomes a mere component of a concrete historical structure. . . . In every case charisma is henceforth exposed to the conditions of everyday life and to the powers dominating it, especially to the economic interests.

Weber's reference to "mechanization" is revealing, inasmuch as economic interests operate like a feedback device to restore social and cultural equilibrium.

True to this Weberian logic but without explicitly acknowledging it, Sahlins tacks between historical events and the more-or-less mechanistic process of social reproduction. Indeed, the notion of totalization has much in common with Weber's concept of routinization: both processes transform the extraordinary into the ordinary, the intentional into the habitual, the named into the anonymous. Both involve an eclipse of narrative in favor of the cool glow of analysis. Yet this process for Sahlins is governed not by "workaday routines" or economic interests—not these, at least, in any narrow or conventional sense—but by thoroughly cultural values and sensibilities.

Totalization, in short, is *cultural* routinization. Routines of *thought* rather than economic practice guide the novelties of events into the manageable channels of daily life. Of course, some of these channels will have to be rerouted or even carved anew to accommodate changes in understanding; this is why Sahlins describes the event as "a relation between an incident and a structure" (2000c:301). Any event, by definition, reshapes structure, and a major event presumably transforms several distinct "orders of structure" at the same time (2000c:346, n. 11). Yet the system as a whole absorbs the change and, in some sense, fixes its significance.

This logic is evident, for example, in Sahlins's analysis of a political assassination in nineteenth-century Fiji. Having considered how the event might have gone differently, he goes on to conclude that "either outcome, factual or counterfactual, however contingent, would have been culturally coherent and structurally motivated" (2004:290). While "the happening" itself involved individuals with their own (culturally appropriate) reasons for what they did, it apparently "found its meanings" without any help from specific persons. Indeed, the sole determinant of "what followed" from the event, "the difference it made" in the long term, is what Sahlins calls simply "the culture." He then tries to head off the charge that he has ceded too much to the system (2004:291):

> Of course, the structural coherence of a contingent outcome gives the strong impression of cultural continuity, or even cultural determinism—as if the system were impervious to the event. But one need not be thus misled. The cultural contingency at issue was not the only one possible, and it was anything but prescribed. If the culture in this way reproduces itself, it reproduces itself in an altered state.

Yet this qualification does not address the real flaw in the argument, which is the absence of particular historical agents in the collective interpretation—the so-called totalization—of the event. The elision is especially puzzling in light of Sahlins's insistence that subjects and their dispositions must not be equated with the system as a whole (2004:151). Social positioning, so vital to Sahlins's analysis of "narrow victories," is curiously missing from his account of how such victories acquire cultural significance.

The tacit assumption guiding much of Sahlins's work is that "structure" is society-wide—shared, in some sense, by all members of a cultural community. His approach has been criticized on this count by Sewell, a very sympathetic reader, who was arguing as early as 1992 for "a far more multiple, contingent, and fractured conception of society— and of structure" (2005a:140). The direct challenge came in 2000 with the publication of "A Theory of the Event: Marshall Sahlins's 'Possible Theory of History'" (Sewell 2005b:204):

> Sahlins employs the term structure in the singular rather than the plural. This implies that a given society has one overarching system of meanings, a cultural system in the strong sense. According to this conception, all cultural meanings everywhere in a society are bound tightly into a network of mutual definition.

Sewell's own view, on the contrary, is that "Societies should be conceptualized as the sites of a multitude of overlapping and interlocking cultural structures . . . [that] exist at quite different levels or scales" (2005b:209). A similar point has been developed by Collins (2004:15): "'Collective conscience' can exist in little pockets rather than as one huge sky covering everybody in the society."[7]

One advantage of this kind of approach is the way it accommodates both change and continuity in the same historical moment (Sewell 2005b:211):

> A divorce or a remarriage that profoundly transforms the culture of a given family will simply reproduce the categories of the American matrimonial system. If structure is regarded as singular, this incident poses an agonizing problem. But if structures are regarded as multiple, the happening is simultaneously an event from the point of view of the local family culture and an implementation of structure from the broader viewpoint.

In this light, we see how a given historical outcome could be culturally "coherent"— consistent with a pervasive or broadly shared structure— without being "prescribed" or even "motivated" by culture at that very high level.

But the recognition of multiple and diverse structures has a more important consequence: it presses the question of how this particular ensemble of cultural forms has emerged, stabilized, and prevailed, resulting in a (more or less) well-defined "system." We still have "an urgent need," as Ortner put it, "to understand where 'the system' comes from—how it is produced and reproduced, and how it may have changed in the past or be changed in the future" (1994:390). The classic social science argument, going back to the eighteenth century (Wootton 2007), is that the system is *self*-organizing and *self*-stabilizing (though subject, of course, to perturbations that have changed it in the past and will change it in the future). Many social scientists are still in the grip of this kind of argument—the iron grip, it would seem, of the invisible hand.

Even an account explicitly intended to bring out the "eventfulness" of history is sometimes vulnerable to leaps of systemic faith. Thus in his analysis of the outbreak of the French Revolution, Sewell is quite clear about the historical contingencies involved: "In 1789, new arguments were tried out, new forms of organization were invented, and new ideas circulated in both old and new media," giving rise to a "clamorous and multi-sited public sphere" (2005c:251). Newspapers, pamphlets, political clubs, and other innovations allowed for remarkable cultural creativity—and contention. Presumably, the taking of the Bastille, for example, would have been reported, narrated, interpreted, and debated before anything like its "general" or "cultural" meaning could be discerned. Yet this meaning was somehow "revealed," according to Sewell (2005c:236), "in a moment of ecstatic discovery." Perhaps just a rhetorical flourish, this passage nonetheless illustrates that the acts involved in totalization—particular narrations, debates, and so on—are all too easily collapsed into sudden transformations at the systemic level.

To avoid this kind of collapse, we must subject the logic of totalization to the same critique that Sahlins borrowed from Sartre. Totalization, in other words, cannot be reduced to an anonymous mechanism but "must first be made to pass through a process of mediation, one which will bring into play the concrete men who were involved in it" (Sartre 1963:42).[8] Fortunately, just such a mediation of totalization has been undertaken in recent years by a number of social theorists, especially cultural sociologists. Some of these, such as Collins (2004, 2008) and Wagner-Pacifici (2000, 2005, 2010), have contributed directly to the argument above. Another school in the same tradition is led by Jeffrey Alexander and colleagues (2006), who describe their approach as "cultural pragmatics." For these theorists, what Sahlins calls totalization is treated as a series of social acts (Mast 2006:117):

> Structurally, events take shape from stark clashes of meaning structures within a broad cultural system of shared sign relations. At the same time, such clashes are both orchestrated and reactively mediated by purposeful, creative human agents who narrate the interconnections between occurrences.

In short, totalization is not an automatic, systemic process but the fragile outcome of "competitive narration" among the witnesses to an event, their critics, representatives, and historical interpreters.[9]

Ironically, this is just the approach that Sahlins takes in one exceptional instance: the Elián González affair, which he construes as a "melodrama" that was orchestrated, debated, and endlessly rehearsed by the news media, the Miami Cuban community, the U.S. and Cuban governments, and many other interested parties (2004:166–193). This is clearly an example of competitive narration. Yet Sahlins does not use the case to rethink or revise his concept of totalization (or, for that matter, his notion of the social "totality"). As a result, the discussion of Elián González stands apart from the more general theory that Sahlins presents.

Perhaps the multiplex, media-saturated setting of the González case renders irrelevant any Durkheimian concept of collective conscience and therefore any concept of totalization. After all, in a "highly differentiated, late capitalist" context, "gaining control over [an event's] meaning by persuading countless anonymous others to share one's interpretation... is an exceedingly contingent and combative process" (Mast 2006:118). The outcome of such a process is likely to be a loose patchwork, at best, of historical understandings rather than the "one huge sky" suggested by the term "collective conscience."

All of this reinforces the point that historical knowledge is produced by persons and factions situated within a specific social organization. Most of this production, however, goes on without fanfare and outside the historian's guild (Trouillot 1995:21). This encourages the tendency to view totalization as an anonymous, systemic process. Only if we *slow down* the narrative (and thus approach totalization in the way we would "events" themselves) is this impression of anonymity likely to dissolve. Now Sartre's "concrete men" might come into focus, along with the "ideological instruments" they probably employed. Even if we could not identify specific individuals involved in the process, certain categories of actors—journalists, artists, shamans, professors—would likely emerge as key participants. Among their ideological instruments would be the available media of communication and the social organization of the public sphere (Barth 2002). Indeed, by this path we would find ourselves on rather familiar terrain: the *sociology of knowledge* (or, if that term suggests an exclusively "modern" setting, an *anthropology of knowledge*, à la Fredrik Barth). The point is that we already have methods at our disposal for mediating (and demystifying) totalization. There is no need for an invisible hand when so many hidden histories await our investigation.

In most historical cases, furthermore, a patient investigation *would* reveal specific persons behind the process—the ones who actually told the story (wrote the novel, devised the myth, ran the seminar) that made the difference in how a foregoing event would be collectively imagined or remembered.[10] In this respect, the crafting of a successful historical narrative resembles another kind of innovation that Sahlins considers in an interesting aside (2004:158):

> Inventors especially may turn out to be the beneficiaries of what could be called the "*post-factum* event," as what they did, and accordingly their stature, grows over time in proportion to the social consequences of their invention. The Wright Brothers' experiments at Kitty Hawk or Alexander Graham Bell's first telephone conversation may have been little noted at the time, but they have been long and well remembered in proportion to the development of aviation and telephonic communication.

What is true of inventors surely applies to other creative agents as well: any one of their innovations, though unnoticed at the time, may become a postfactum event, worthy of our remembrance and, in a sense, our spectatorship. For the fundamental condition of all historical narration is an arena—a polo grounds of the mind—in which notable acts are "witnessed" by audiences ever more distant from the original setting (cf. Collins 2004:85; Wagner-Pacifici 2005:46). And because history is *made*, in the last analysis, not by heroism alone but by those who bear witness to it, the agency of narrators must be recognized alongside that of the players themselves.

ACKNOWLEDGMENTS

For moral support and intellectual guidance, I thank Shannon Novak and the late Bill Kelleher of the Department of Anthropology at Syracuse University. Will Bagley offered helpful suggestions in the case of Mountain Meadows and LeeAnna Keith in the case of Colfax. Special thanks to Marshall Sahlins for reading an early draft and treating my argument kindly.

NOTES

1. My characterization of the American South as a frontier is unusual but not unprecedented (Cash 1969 [1941]; Cashin 1991). Suffice it to say that I am interested in places beyond the effective reach of the modernizing state and its national culture (Rodseth and Olsen 2000; Rodseth and Parker 2005). The inland South in particular was a frontier in this sense until long after the Civil War.

2. Such specification is precisely what Sartre urged in his critique of Marxism: "The person lives and knows his condition more or less clearly through the groups he belongs to. The majority of these groups are local, definite, immediately given. ... The problem is to know whether Marxism will dissolve the residential group into its elements or whether it will recognize in it a relative autonomy and power of mediation" (1963:66).

3. In this light, Sahlins's distinction between systemic and conjunctural agency could be argued to parallel the Weberian one between bureaucratic and charismatic authority.

4. The term "totalization" is another borrowing from Sartre, but Sahlins's tendency to assume an existing totality seems to conflict with Sartre's usage. Thus Sartre warned against the "fetishism of totalization," the temptation to hypostasize and realize it in "*already made* totalities" (1963:68). On the intricacies of totalization in Sartre's theory of history, see Flynn (1997).

5. This is obvious in the case of Mountain Meadows, whose interpretation is still hotly debated by historians as well as segments of the general public. In the case of Colfax, so-called revisionist history seems for the moment (and from a national perspective) to have overcome traditional, white supremacist interpretations.

6. While this "coexistence of residual and novel forms" is acknowledged by Sahlins (2004:147), he still considers "Gramscian-inspired hegemonies" to involve "draconian notions of autonomous cultural behemoths with the powers of fashioning individual subjects in their own image" (2004:142).

7. This has been a minority viewpoint in American anthropology for a long time, but conventional wisdom only recently, if at all (Rodseth 1998; Borofsky et al. 2001).

8. Totalization in Sartre's sense would be a mediated process, by definition. As noted above, he warned against replacing "the movement of dialectical totalization" with "actual totalities" or "a unity already made" (1963:69).

9. At this point, the argument links up with the vast literature on collective memory and ethnic or national identity (e.g., Olick et al. 2011). For an analysis of Mountain Meadows as a case of historical "remembering," see Novak and Rodseth (2006).

10. The *reporting* of Watergate, to take an obvious example, came to be at least as historically significant as the break-in itself (Alexander 1988; Schudson 1992). See also the analysis of 9/11 by Wagner-Pacifici (2010).

REFERENCES

Alexander, Jeffrey C. 1988. Culture and Political Crisis: "Watergate" and Durkheimian Sociology. *In* Durkheimian Sociology: Cultural Studies. Jeffrey C. Alexander, ed. Pp. 187–224. Cambridge: Cambridge University Press.

Alexander, Jeffrey C., Bernhard Giesen, and Jason L. Mast, eds. 2006. Social Performance: Symbolic Action, Cultural Pragmatics, and Ritual. Cambridge: Cambridge University Press.

Bagley, Will. 2002. Blood of the Prophets: Brigham Young and the Massacre at Mountain Meadows. Norman: University of Oklahoma Press.

Barth, Fredrik. 2002. An Anthropology of Knowledge. Current Anthropology 43:1–11.

Bigler, David L. 1998. Forgotten Kingdom: The Mormon Theocracy in the American West, 1847–1896. Spokane WA: Arthur H. Clark.

Borofsky, Robert, Fredrik Barth, Richard A. Shweder, Lars Rodseth, and Nomi Maya Stolzenberg. 2001. WHEN: A Conversation about Culture. American Anthropologist 103:432–46.

Braudel, Fernand. 1972 [1949]. The Mediterranean and the Mediterranean World in the Age of Philip II. Vol. 1. Siân Reynolds, trans. Berkeley: University of California Press.

———. 1980 (1958). History and the Social Sciences: The Longue Durée. *In* On History. Sarah Matthews, trans. Pp. 25–54. Chicago: University of Chicago Press.

Brooks, Juanita. 1992 [1961]. John Doyle Lee: Zealot, Pioneer Builder, Scapegoat. Logan: Utah State University Press.

Cash, W. J. 1969 [1941]. The Mind of the South. New York: Alfred A. Knopf.

Cashin, Joan E. 1991. A Family Venture: Men and Women on the Southern Frontier. Baltimore: Johns Hopkins University Press.

Collins, Randall. 2004. Interaction Ritual Chains. Princeton NJ: Princeton University Press.

———. 2008. Violence: A Microsociological Theory. Princeton NJ: Princeton University Press.

Durkheim, Émile. 1984 (1893). The Division of Labor in Society. W. D. Halls, trans. New York: Free Press.

———. 2001 (1912). The Elementary Forms of Religious Life. Carol Cosman, trans. Oxford: Oxford University Press.

Flynn, Thomas R. 1997. Sartre, Foucault, and Historical Reason. Vol. 1: Toward an Existential Theory of History. Chicago: University of Chicago Press.

Frosh, Paul, and Amit Pinchevski, eds. 2009. Media Witnessing: Testimony in the Age of Mass Communication. New York: Palgrave Macmillan.

Gordon, Sarah Barringer. 2002. The Mormon Question: Polygamy and Constitutional Conflict in Nineteenth-Century America. Chapel Hill: University of North Carolina Press.

Helprin, Mark. 1995. Memoir from Antproof Case. New York: Harcourt Brace.

Hexter, J. H. 1971. The Rhetoric of History. *In* Doing History. Pp. 15–76. Bloomington: Indiana University Press.

Hogue, James K. 2006. Uncivil War: Five New Orleans Street Battles and the Rise and Fall of Radical Reconstruction. Baton Rouge: Louisiana State University Press.

Keith, LeeAnna. 2008. The Colfax Massacre: The Untold Story of Black Power, White Terror, and the Death of Reconstruction. Oxford: Oxford University Press.

Kelly, Charles, ed. 1984. Journals of John D. Lee, 1846–47 and 1859. Salt Lake City: University of Utah Press.

Kelly, Raymond C. 2000. Warless Societies and the Origin of War. Ann Arbor: University of Michigan Press.

Kuhn, Thomas S. 1970. The Structure of Scientific Revolutions. 2nd rev. ed. Chicago: University of Chicago Press.

———. 2000. The Road since Structure: Philosophical Essays, 1970–1993, with an Autobiographical Interview. James Conant and John Haugeland, eds. Chicago: University of Chicago Press.

Lane, Charles. 2008. The Day Freedom Died: The Colfax Massacre, the Supreme Court, and the Betrayal of Reconstruction. New York: Henry Holt.

Mann, Michael. 1986. The Sources of Social Power. Vol. 1: A History of Power from the Beginning to AD 1760. Cambridge: Cambridge University Press.

Mast, Jason L. 2006. The Cultural Pragmatics of Event-ness: The Clinton/Lewinsky Affair. In Social Performance: Symbolic Action, Cultural Pragmatics, and Ritual. Jeffrey C. Alexander, Bernhard Giesen, and Jason L. Mast, eds. Pp. 115–145. Cambridge: Cambridge University Press.

Novak, Shannon A. 2008. House of Mourning: A Biocultural History of the Mountain Meadows Massacre. Salt Lake City: University of Utah Press.

Novak, Shannon A., and Lars Rodseth. 2006. Remembering Mountain Meadows: Collective Violence and the Manipulation of Social Boundaries. Journal of Anthropological Research 62:1–25.

Obeyesekere, Gananath. 1992. The Apotheosis of Captain Cook: European Mythmaking in the Pacific. Princeton NJ: Princeton University Press.

Olick, Jeffrey K., Vered Vinitzky-Seroussi, and Daniel Levy, eds. 2011. The Collective Memory Reader. Oxford: Oxford University Press.

Ortner, Sherry B. 1989. High Religion: A Cultural and Political History of Sherpa Buddhism. Princeton NJ: Princeton University Press.

———. 1994 [1984]. Theory in Anthropology since the Sixties. In Culture/Power/History: A Reader in Contemporary Social Theory. Nicholas B. Dirks, Geoff Eley, and Sherry B. Ortner, eds. Pp. 372–411. Princeton NJ: Princeton University Press.

———. 2006. Anthropology and Social Theory: Culture, Power, and the Acting Subject. Durham NC: Duke University Press.

Peters, John Durham. 2001. Witnessing. Media, Culture, and Society 23:715–731.

Ricoeur, Paul. 1984. Time and Narrative. Vol. 1. Chicago: University of Chicago Press.

Rodseth, Lars. 1998. Distributive Models of Culture: A Sapirian Alternative to Essentialism. American Anthropologist 100:55–69.

Rodseth, Lars, and Jennifer Olsen. 2000. Mystics against the Market: American Religions and the Autocritique of Capitalism. Critique of Anthropology 20:265–288.

Rodseth, Lars, and Bradley J. Parker. 2005. Introduction: Theoretical Considerations in the Study of Frontiers. *In* Untaming the Frontier in Anthropology, Archaeology, and History. Bradley J. Parker and Lars Rodseth, eds. Pp. 3–21. Tucson: University of Arizona Press.

Sahlins, Marshall. 1981. Historical Metaphors and Mythical Realities: Structure in the Early History of the Sandwich Islands Kingdom. Ann Arbor: University of Michigan Press.

————. 1985. Islands of History. Chicago: University of Chicago Press.

————. 1995. How "Natives" Think: About Captain Cook, for Example. Chicago: University of Chicago Press.

————. 2000a. Introduction. In Culture in Practice. Pp. 9–41. New York: Zone Books.

————. 2000b (1982). Individual Experience and Cultural Order. *In* Culture in Practice: Selected Essays. Pp. 277–291. New York: Zone Books.

————. 2000c (1991). The Return of the Event, Again: With Reflections on the Beginnings of the Great Fijian War of 1843–1855 between the Kingdoms of Bau and Rewa. *In* Culture in Practice. Pp. 293–351. New York: Zone Books.

————. 2004. Apologies to Thucydides: Understanding History as Culture and Vice Versa. Chicago: University of Chicago Press.

————. 2010. Infrastructuralism. Critical Inquiry 36:371–85.

Sartre, Jean-Paul. 1963. Search for a Method. Hazel E. Barnes, trans. New York: Vintage Books.

Schudson, Michael. 1992. Watergate in American Memory: How We Remember, Forget, and Reconstruct the Past. New York: Basic Books.

Sewell, William H., Jr. 2005a [1992]. A Theory of Structure: Duality, Agency, and Transformation. *In* Logics of History. Pp. 124–151. Chicago: University of Chicago Press.

————. 2005b (2000). A Theory of the Event: Marshall Sahlins's "Possible Theory of History." *In* Logics of History. Pp. 197–224. Chicago: University of Chicago Press.

————. 2005c (1996). Historical Events as Transformations of Structures: Inventing Revolution at the Bastille. *In* Logics of History. Pp. 225–70. Chicago: University of Chicago Press.

Tiryakian, Edward A. 1995. Collective Effervescence, Social Change, and Charisma: Durkheim, Weber, and 1989. International Sociology 10:269–281.

Trouillot, Michel-Rolph. 1995. Silencing the Past: Power and the Production of History. Boston: Beacon Press.

Wagner-Pacifici, Robin. 2000. Theorizing the Standoff: Contingency in Action. Cambridge: Cambridge University Press.

———. 2005. The Art of Surrender: Decomposing Sovereignty at Conflict's End. Chicago: University of Chicago Press.

———. 2010. Theorizing the Restlessness of Events. American Journal of Sociology 115:1351–1386.

Walker, Ronald W., Richard E. Turley Jr., and Glen M. Leonard. 2008. Massacre at Mountain Meadows: An American Tragedy. Oxford: Oxford University Press.

Wallace, Anthony F. C. 1956. Revitalization Movements. American Anthropologist 58:264–281.

Weber, Max. 1968. Economy and Society. Guenther Roth and Claus Wittich, eds. Berkeley: University of California Press.

White, Leslie A. 1987 (1947). Evolutionism and Anti-evolutionism in American Ethnological Theory. In Leslie A. White: Ethnological Essays. Beth Dillingham and Robert L. Carneiro, eds. Pp. 97–122. Albuquerque: University of New Mexico Press.

Wootton, David. 2007. From Fortune to Feedback: Contingency and the Birth of Modern Political Science. In Political Contingency: Studying the Unexpected, the Accidental, and the Unforeseen. Ian Shapiro and Sonu Bedi, eds. Pp. 21–53. New York: New York University Press.

10

Anthropologists as Perpetrators and Perpetuators of Oral Tradition

The Lectures of Kenelm O. L. Burridge and Robin Ridington, Storytellers

Folk-culture: a culture characteristic of a small, tightly-knit society, in which kinship is all-important.

CHARLES WINICK, *Dictionary of Anthropology* (1984)

The discipline of anthropology is abundant with narratives by and about anthropologists, their unique research projects, their academic philosophies, and their theoretical approaches or contributions. I present here an unpublished 1988 student assignment as a conduit for my ideas on the value of oral tradition in the anthropology classroom, the construction of anthropological kinship networks, and the ways in which both anthropology professors and their students have persisted in telling and retelling the histories of anthropology over time. The 1988 paper incorporates some of my audio recorded lectures of Professors Kenelm O. L. Burridge and Robin Ridington at the University of British Columbia during the late 1980s; I focus on Drs. Burridge and Ridington in that paper, but I also pay homage to the storytelling techniques of some of my other professors as well.

The 1988 essay is a highly personal one. It is a narrative account of my own experience of learning and becoming part of a culture which is based, like any other, on kinship ties, shared mythology, and a common purpose. In the essay, I imagined anthropologists as a culture group and demonstrated how the culture of anthropology is passed on from generation to generation through oral tradition. As well, I described how my teachers slowly but surely incorporated me into their anthropological kinship system. Both professors Burridge and Ridington are retired from the Department of Anthropology and Sociology (now separate departments) at the University of British Columbia in Vancouver, Canada. Therefore, there is some urgency to the task of documenting their contributions to anthropological oral tradition.

Many Canadian anthropologists have also retired since 1988, including Elvi Whittaker, Helga Jacobson, Michael Kew, C. Roderick Wilson, and Anthony Fisher. Michael Asch retired in 1998 from the University of Alberta and now teaches at the University of Victoria. Some of our teachers and colleagues have passed away since 1988, including Kathleen Gough, David Aberle, Roger Keesing, Sally Weaver, Richard Salisbury, Fraser Taylor, and Michael Ames, director of the Museum of Anthropology at UBC for many years. These events have caused me to reflect upon the many anthropologists who have inspired and encouraged me in my own studies and research: through my undergraduate years at Langara College and UBC in Vancouver, a master's degree at the University of Western Ontario in London, Ontario, and a PhD program at the University of Alberta in Edmonton, as well as through my ongoing fieldwork, grant applications, letters of reference requests, and all those urgent telephone calls, faxes, and e-mails from student to "prof."

Between 1985 and 1991, I was an anthropology undergraduate at the University of British Columbia. I wrote the following essay for a class that Robin Ridington was teaching in 1988, Comparative Literature 503: Studies in Myth, Theme, and Tradition. Ridington took early retirement in 1995 at the age of fifty-five. Recently, I found this paper in one of those boxes we all carry around with us because we might need something in them someday. I offer it today, not only as a tribute to the storytelling and teaching skills of Kenelm O. L. Burridge and Robin Ridington, but to those of my entire anthropological kinship network.

Although sections of this paper now strike me as highly unsophisticated, I have chosen to leave it virtually in its original form. I have retained the spelling "Dunne-za" here, for example, although they now use the spelling "Dane-zaa." This is, after all, the work of an undergraduate student in the process of learning how to become a professional anthropologist, and altering the paper now would, I think, destroy its spontaneity and integrity. I hope it will be read in that spirit, and that it will contribute in some small way to the history of Canadian anthropology. I hope, too, that it might inspire readers to remember and celebrate their own professors and mentors.

According to the *Dictionary of Anthropology*, culture is "all that which is nonbiological and socially transmitted in a society, including artistic, social, ideological, and religious patterns of behaviour, and the techniques for mastering the environment." It is also defined, after Gustav Klemm in the mid-nineteenth century, as being "manifest in the transmission of past experience to the new generation." Language, claims Charles Winick, "is the most important means of social transmission" (1984:145).

FIELD METHODS

Aside from limited library research, I use as my database the audio documents (ethnographic fieldwork?), which I recorded as an undergraduate student in the Department of Anthropology and Sociology at the University of British Columbia. This includes many of the lectures given by Dr. Kenelm O. L. Burridge in Anthropology 300 (Social Organization) in 1985–86 and almost every lecture given in Anthropology 495/540 (Comparative Institutions, Advanced Anthropology) in 1987. It also includes almost every lecture given by Dr. Robin Ridington in two classes: Anthropology 401 (Indians of North America) in 1985–86, and Comparative Literature 503 (Studies in Myth, Theme, and Tradition) in 1988. The recorded lectures of these two professors represent hundreds of hours of anthropological oral tradition.[1]

DESCRIPTIONS

Kenelm O. L. Burridge is usually described as a British social anthropologist. He does not explain himself this way, however, and has told me that he has always thought of himself as simply an anthropologist. Dr. Burridge was born in Malta, but received most of his education in England. He attended Oxford and earned his PhD at Australian National University in 1954. He is most recognized for his fieldwork with Melanesians, Malaysians, and Australian Aborigines and for his

Fig. 7. Kenelm Burridge attends a retirement party arranged for him by the Anthropology and Sociology Undergraduate Society in 1988. He is wearing a sweatshirt designed for him by his students. Photo by Lindy-Lou Flynn, UBC.

expertise on social organization, millenarian movements, and the history of anthropological thought.

Robin Ridington is often seen as a cultural ecologist and ethnographer from the American school of anthropology. He, however, describes himself as a Canadian ethnographer and narrative anthropologist. He is best known for his fieldwork since 1964 with the Beaver (or Dunne-za) Indians of northeastern British Columbia and for his expertise in symbolic anthropology and on the worldview, power, and knowledge of Subarctic hunting and gathering peoples. Dr. Ridington spent the first twenty-seven years of his life in the eastern United States (for the

Fig. 8. Robin Ridington celebrates another of his thirty-ninth birthdays wearing his hot pink Harvard robe. His Anthropology 401 students provided the cake. Photo by Lindy-Lou Flynn, 1985, UBC.

most part in Maryland). He began teaching at the University of British Columbia in 1967 and received his PhD from Harvard in 1968.

Burridge and Ridington have been colleagues at the University of British Columbia for approximately twenty years, and although their approaches to anthropology differ considerably, they respect one another professionally as anthropologists and as friends. I, in turn, respect them both. Having announced this, I will attempt to describe why each one of them is a perpetrator and perpetuator of the oral traditions of the culture of anthropology.

THE LANGUAGE OF ANTHROPOLOGY

If language is the most important means of cultural transmission, then it follows that language must, for each culture, contain metaphors and meanings that are agreed upon, shared, and mutually understood by members of that culture. Ridington writes about how hunting and gathering peoples use a mythic language that communicates knowledge and is mutually understood. I have taken out the words "hunting and gathering adaptation" in his first sentence below and replaced them with "anthropological adaptation" in order to demonstrate to the reader how the same can be said if we are imagining anthropologists as a culture group:

> The anthropological adaptation typically generates some form of kin-based community in which most social relations take place between people who are well known to each other. It also generates a community of shared knowledge about the . . . shared environment. Knowledge in such a community is communicated through oral tradition and is often coded and organized through the metaphors of a mythic language. Day-to-day communication makes sense to the people because it is referenced to a large body of unstated but mutually understood information. People within such a tradition understand a common set of metaphors without the need of formal explanation. An outside observer, though, is likely to miss the metaphors implicit in such communication because many references are not part of his or her world of information. (Ridington 1988a:13)

Ridington goes on to explain how sociologist Basil Bernstein describes communication based on assumed mutual understandings as a "restricted" rather than an "elaborated" code of discourse, an elaborated form requiring the speaker to introduce information to an audience with a summary of the context to which it refers, taking nothing for granted from the audience. In the restricted form of discourse, claims Bernstein, the context is taken for granted (Ridington 1988a:14).

Just as a child in any culture learns the language—the mutually understood knowledge of that culture—so do anthropology students learn the language of anthropology. We are taught to think in the ways particular to anthropology. We are taught to conceptualize, categorize, and synthesize information within a framework that is typically anthropological. Certain codes are given to us and then often repeated until we, as students, understand the codes, think in codes, and communicate information to one another in codes. Eventually the codes—and the framework surrounding them—become so much a part of us that we no longer even notice them. We *think* like anthropologists. The codes have become our mutually understood language. When we speak to other anthropologists, we use a form of restricted discourse because it is no longer necessary to elaborate. Everything we say to one another comes from the shared knowledge and shared metaphors and meanings which we have been taught, by our professors, as students in the discipline of anthropology. "Day-to-day communication makes sense [to us] because it is referenced to a large body of unstated but mutually understood information" (Ridington 1988a:13). We have become part of a different culture.

THE FRAMEWORK AND THE CODES

Anthropologists teach students to think within a certain framework. When Burridge, for example, introduces his students to the ethnography of Australian Aborigines, he begins, as do most anthropology professors teaching ethnography, with descriptions of the environment (cultural ecology) in which the people being described are living. The first sentence of these descriptions usually identifies the culture area (code words for specifically identified areas which anthropologists have defined, such as Australia, Desert Southwest, Subarctic, and so on). Every anthropologist knows the meanings implicit in the mention of every culture area. Desert Southwest, for example, is a metaphor for Hopi, Zuni, Navajo, Apache, kivas, pueblos, kachinas, corn, deserts, and Frank Hamilton Cushing.

Next comes a description of the ways in which the people feed and clothe themselves (subsistence); the ways they organize themselves socially and politically (social organization, political organization, kinship); and how they think in relation to their environment, objects animate and inanimate, and supernatural phenomena (philosophy, worldview, and religion). In addition, there is usually an analysis of how the culture group under discussion has changed over time—pre- and post-contact and possible reasons for these changes (adaptation, diffusion, culture change).

Ridington (1985–86), when describing North American Native societies, uses the same modus operandi as does Burridge (1985–86) when he lectures on Malaysia, Micronesia, Melanesia, or Australia. Ridington and Burridge present these cultures to us within an anthropological framework: culture area, prehistory, cultural ecology, subsistence, social and political organization, kinship and marriage patterns, worldview and religion, and so on. After years of this training, it becomes impossible for an anthropology student (or anthropologist) to think of *any* culture without setting that culture into this carefully learned framework. After setting out the framework, each category (for example, kinship) is further described in the language of anthropology. Students are taught the codes implicit within the framework. Kinship is discussed using code words such as patrilineal, matrilineal, cross-cousin marriage, exogamy, endogamy, and bride wealth. Religion and worldview carry with them the anthropological codes of shamanism, vision quest, mana, creation myths, and so on. Within the framework, there are categories and subcategories, each one explained and coded into the particular way of thinking and speaking of anthropologists.

In theory, too, there is a framework. Burridge describes cultures as being within a framework that anthropologists have chosen to call structuralism. When describing Australians or other groups of people, Burridge fits them into a structural framework. Ridington, on the other hand, sees cultures as acting in response to their environment. When teaching, he fits culture groups into a theory of anthropology known as cultural ecology.

With Burridge, students are taught to think as structuralists do. We spend time looking for opposites and examining status and prestige. We are taught how to look for the underlying structures in social institutions such as exchange systems, feasts, sorcery, and men's clubhouses. We learn codes by which to examine social groups from a structural perspective. Dr. Burridge tells us about structuralists such as Claude Lévi-Strauss and his own teacher, E. E. Evans-Pritchard.

With Ridington, we begin to see how environmental factors and materialism affect human groups. We are taught code words and ideas such as "natural limitations" and "natural opportunities." Knowledge of theoretical culture heroes is passed on to us, and a name such as Julian Steward becomes a metaphor for concepts such as cultural ecology, culture core, and levels of sociocultural integration. Through the oral tradition of the university classroom, we are given the knowledge of anthropology.

And, in Julian Steward's model—his way of describing it is to say that over here there's physical environment . . . and under physical environment, he said, there are a certain number of features of culture that are determined by the physical environment. And he calls those cultural core. So he says that for hunting and gathering people, there are certain outside limitations having to do with the distribution of game, for instance, and he argued that for the Shoshonians, the fact that most of the time people were gathering in very small groups, the fact that the optimum unit of production is a single woman gathering pine nuts by herself (that's the most efficient or optimum unit of production)—he argued from that fact of the physical environment having to do with the distribution of pine nuts that a form of social organization resulted—a set of core features of social organization that he called the family band. So his argument was that there is a determination between physical environment and social organization through the intermediary of what means of production are the most efficient. (Ridington Lectures:1985–86)

We can see here how Ridington passes on the theory of cultural ecology to his students, but, later on in his lecture, adding his own ideas, he warned us to accept Julian Steward's arguments, but not all of his examples. Oral tradition, then, is passed on from one anthropologist to another, but it does not remain static. Each anthropologist adds something to the wealth of knowledge. Each passes on a story within his own story. Each interprets in his own way and passes on that interpretation. Vigilant teachers, such as Ridington and Burridge, are careful to pass on the original concept intact and are careful to inform the student when they are about to digress from, or add to, the original story. The student, so armed with an original story and a diversion from it, is free to choose what s/he wishes to retain. Therefore, students might later discuss how Ridington described Julian Steward's theory pertaining to primary efficiency and family bands, but that Ridington had warned them not to use all of Steward's examples because recently acquired knowledge, such as that of June Helm, has shown Steward to be incorrect about them. We now have Steward's original ideas and those that came afterward. In this way, Ridington provides us with a history of anthropological thought.

In a case where no further knowledge has been added to a theory or a concept, but where Ridington simply wishes to add his own opinion, I have heard him remark that it is his personal opinion. When this happens, anthropological ideas are, perhaps, more perpetrated than perpetuated, as it is a new idea that a professor is passing on to the next generation of students. If his students someday pass on his ideas, they become perpetuated and part of the oral tradition of anthropology. When passing on new ideas or arguing old ones, then, the anthropology professor not only adds to a wealth of knowledge but makes it possible for the student to be brave enough to take the intellectual risks necessary in becoming an imaginative scholar. We emulate our teachers. If we hear them taking risks, we will do so ourselves. We are taught not only the mythology of anthropology but also how to analyze, criticize, and reinterpret it. We are learning not only the history of anthropology but also how to think like anthropologists.

THE STORIES

Lectures from anthropology professors such as Ridington and Burridge provide a wealth of stories. We, as students, hear stories about the history of our discipline. We hear stories about our own anthropological culture heroes. We hear stories about the theoretical discoveries and ethnographic fieldwork of our predecessors and our contemporaries. We hear stories about other anthropologists and about other anthropology students. The stories are ever-present and never-ending.

Burridge gave us wonderful stories about the writings, fieldwork, and personal lives of many of the greats in British social anthropology. In addition, he told us tales about American fieldworkers such as Margaret Mead ("She had charisma") and about early Canadian missionaries such as Lafitau and Sagard, their intentions, and their errors. We heard analyses of the work of Marx and Engels and of French philosophers such as Durkheim and Mauss. We were regaled with the adventures of Bronislaw Malinowski's fieldwork in the Trobriand Islands, and we took trips of the mind with Dr. B. so that we could see W. H. R. Rivers asking about color blindness and discovering, instead, the importance of mother's brother in kinship systems. We heard it all. From Frazer's toga parties held under imitation golden boughs, to Rivers and his terror at the sight of Indigenous men in penis sheaths, Kenelm Burridge left us students with a glimpse into a world of anthropology which most students will never hear. In addition to heroes and personal glimpses, he gave us his personal philosophies and insights into anthropology which will stay with us always.

> The other end of forgery is, of course, good fieldwork. If the forger can write as good fieldwork . . . if a chap who's never been there can write as well about Indians as the chap who's spent all his life there— then *what* are we doing?

> The whole enjoyment and education in anthropology is to move your mind through time or across space—from one culture to another—in an effort to understand one culture in terms of another, or another culture in terms of the first, and so on.

> Is an axe like a bulldozer in some cultures, or is an axe just an axe?

> Reality is something that is constructed. We don't actually *see* reality, but only its appearance. We *construct* reality. What are the facts? Are there any facts? Or are there just constructions?

> At the time I was a student . . . the students were always asking, you know, what is a society? Where does a society start? Where are the borders? And we were always getting weasel answers because, in fact, nobody *knew* the answer. Where is the border? So that's why lots of anthropologists went to an island! *There's* the border! That's why Firth went to Tikopia. A nice little island, Tikopia—must be homogeneous, there's nothing to interfere with it, not for five or six hundred miles around . . . and then there's the sea. And a lot of us went to islands, Trobriands, too, see . . . I specifically did *not* go to an island because I didn't want borders. . . . Now, Evans-Pritchard was the first to say . . ."To hell with all these little [groups] of people. I'll take on a population of several million—the Nuer." It was the first time an anthropologist did work in a large population.

Like Burridge, Ridington perpetrated and perpetuated the stories of anthropological history. He told us about his teachers at Harvard in the 1960s, such as Cora Dubois, and about the school of psychological anthropology that was in vogue at that time. He reflected upon how he, as a graduate student, had come across the Omaha Sacred Pole lying exposed and forgotten in the Peabody Museum and how, years later, he had (in the very year in which he was lecturing to us—1985) visited the Omaha people and written a paper about that pole. He told us about the Omaha Mark of Honor and how he had met two elderly Omaha women who still carried it. He told us about Alice Fletcher and Francis La Flesche, and he introduced us to the Twenty-seventh Annual Report of the Bureau of American Ethnology.

In 1988, in another class, he continued the Omaha story. It had now become a story of how an anthropologist had become a part of the story, in that the Omaha people had asked for his assistance in having their Sacred Pole returned to them, and Ridington, in response, had answered them by sending a letter supporting this request to the Peabody Museum at Harvard (all taken from Ridington Lectures:1988b). We learned about museum repatriation and anthropological advocacy.

In addition to stories about his own fieldwork and the stories we heard about the cultures of Native Indian groups throughout North America, such as the Natchez, Creeks, Muskogeans, and Cherokee, Ridington continually passed on to us the stories of our own anthropological heroes.

> And again, I think Stevenson is one of the great unappreciated treasures of American Indian ethnography. It's just a wonderful book [referring to the Bureau of American Ethnology Report written by Matilde Coxe Stevenson]—whatever her reasons for being there might have been, and however she might have gotten the information, it's a wonderful book. And that, together with Cushing, who also, for whatever his reasons were, he also wrote wonderful descriptions. Together, we have a portrait of Pueblo societies as they existed in the 1880s that is as vivid and detailed and intelligent . . . in its understanding and commentary as anything that any anthropologist has ever produced. And in my opinion . . . I would trade in . . . Franz Boas for Matilde Coxe Stevenson any day. [Remember what I wrote earlier about professors and their own opinions?] And although she . . . is always considered to be—"Oh, well she's an amateur, and she was

just the wife of this old guy, and wasn't a real anthropologist; she didn't have a PhD, she didn't write theory," but boy, was she a hot-shot ethnographer. And she wasn't bad at interpretation, either. So there! (Ridington Lectures 1985–86)

One of Ridington's finest qualities as a teacher, I think, is that he is always willing to allow other teachers to share with him in the pleasure of passing on the oral traditions of anthropology to his students. We heard on tape, and then in person, the dynamic presentations of Ines Talaman-tez, an Apache anthropologist and poet who teaches Native American religious studies at the University of California, Santa Barbara. We were visited by many more of Robin's friends and special guest lecturers, who passed on stories of their own. And we were gifted with the beautiful and compelling audio documentary work of Robin's friend and colleague Howard Broomfield, who, like Matilde Coxe Stevenson, may not have been a "real" anthropologist with a PhD, but boy, was he a hot-shot eth-nographer. And he wasn't bad at interpretation, either. With Robin Rid-ington, students always get a dozen or so teachers for the price of one.

STORIES ABOUT "OTHERS"

One summer afternoon in 1987, while working for Robin Ridington in his office (as his research assistant), I came across an old black-and-white photograph taken on the Halfway River Beaver Indian Reserve in 1966 when Robin was a young man. In it, he sits, microphone strung up and dangling from a bent pole, reel-to-reel tape recorder set on an old washtub in front of him. Beside him are three Dunne-za men. While they sing and play hand drums, the ethnographer remains silent. He is Listening. And, simultaneously, he is recording the songs and stories of the Dunne-za so that they may be held forever and retold for all time. That picture left an impression on me that I will always remember. It is, for me, a photograph that captures exactly the beauty and purpose of cultural anthropology. It is the ethnographer documenting for poster-ity the musical and oral traditions of a culture. It allows for "the events of oral tradition to come to life again and again in the actuality of their telling and retelling" (Ridington 1988a:4). It is an act of respect for past and future. Ultimately, it is an act of Love.

Fig. 9. Robin Ridington recording Dunne-za singers at Jimmy Field, Aballi Field, and Sammy Fox at the Halfway River reserve in 1966. Charlie Yahey listens behind. Photo by Antonia Mills.

Anthropology is unique in that we not only perpetrate and perpetuate the stories implicit in our own discipline but we pass on the stories that we document about the cultures that we study. Kenelm Burridge passes on stories to us about cultures with whom he has lived, such as the Australian Aborigines. From Burridge, we hear tales of four-section marriage systems and the Australian Dreamtime. We travel with Dr. B. over the expanses of the Australian desert into another place and another time. We hear the oral traditions of the Australian people and the stories of Dr. Burridge's experiences with Australians. We are transported, as if by magic, to another world. Through Burridge's stories, we ourselves spend dream time with another culture.

Robin Ridington, who has worked with the Beaver Indians (or Dunne-za) since 1964, passes on story after story told to him by Dunne-za people. At times, Ridington's classroom lectures become storytelling extravaganzas, one story following and overlapping another, like notes in a musical score, leaving the student mesmerized and feeling as if he or she has just spent days in the field listening to storytellers such as Johnny Chipesia, Augustine Jumbie, and Charlie Yahey, some of

Ridington's Dunne-za teachers. Ridington's lectures, then, sometimes seem to involve a storyteller (the anthropologist) telling stories about storytellers (the Native people with whom he works) telling stories.

In the lectures that I recorded, Ridington told hundreds of stories. We heard how Johnny Chipesia (also known as Johnny Bullshit) lost the chance of obtaining snake power because he couldn't keep a secret. We heard about a boy named Swan who was transformed into Saya, the Dunne-za culture hero. We heard about Dunne-za prophet dances and the trail to heaven (*yagatunne*), and we heard stories about how Jumbie couldn't stand flash pictures because his medicine was thunderbird. Ridington's lectures were sometimes not lectures at all. They were encounters with the fabulous. They were adventures and meetings with giant animals (*onli nachi*) who made the grease under the earth; with an old man named Japasa who knew foxes and was visited by them before his death; with frogs who play-gambled on the bottom of ponds; and with beautiful white swans who fly from life to death and back to life. Robin Ridington does not simply *recite* for his students the stories of the Dunne-za people. He breathes life into them.

THE STORYTELLERS

Robin Ridington and Kenelm Burridge have had a profound impact on the lives of many people. The stories they tell have changed the way their students think about themselves and about "Others." The stories they tell have helped bridge the gap between Native peoples and those who are not Native. The stories they tell have become part of anthropological history.

But for one of these perpetrators and perpetuators of oral tradition, the storytelling has come to an end, at least in the academic setting. On December 3, 1987, I recorded the last lecture that Kenelm Oswald Lancelot Burridge would ever give an undergraduate class in his capacity as a professor in the employ of the University of British Columbia. Dr. Burridge was about to retire, or, perhaps a more accurate analysis would be to say that he was about to *be* retired. Dr. Burridge had reached the age of sixty-five.[2]

During that last lecture, I sat, as I always had, right beside my teacher, my microphone discretely half-hidden under a book, my tape recorder on. When Dr. Burridge entered the room, the class was uncharacteristically silent. He took his seat at the head of the seminar table, and he smiled at me. Quietly, I waited for the closing chapter in my audio notebook. The stories began. Several times during that last seminar, Dr. Burridge's eyes filled with tears. Several times, so did the eyes of some of his students.

During that final lecture, Kenelm O. L. Burridge delighted us with ninety minutes worth of stories. He told us about how an East Indian ethnographer he had once met in Australia had excitedly played for him the wonderful authentic Aborigine songs he had just collected, which, to Dr. Burridge's amusement, turned out to be recently learned American cowboy songs such as "She'll Be Comin' Round the Mountain When She Comes." He told us about how the anthropologist who went to Africa intent upon writing a "colossal" ethnography ended up, instead, filling his field notebooks with "intimate" drawings of the chief's daughter, with whom he had spent considerable amounts of nocturnal time in an effort to combat the boredom and frustrations of life in the jungle (the harsh reality of fieldwork). Dr. Burridge summed up the situation: "Great ambition just comes down to good old sex." Story after story spilled out of Dr. B. Finally, I asked him who was the most dynamic and interesting woman anthropologist he had ever met. Without hesitation he replied, "Mary Douglas," and then told us yet another story—about *her* and, incidentally, about Mother Teresa, whom, of course, Dr. Burridge had met! (Dr. Burridge has met everyone, it seems.)

When it was time to go, our teacher invited us to come by to see him any time "just to have a chat," and we said "for he's a jolly good fellow" and "thanks for the wonderful anthropology course." We all laughed a lot, sort of nervously, I'd say, and we tried to keep things light, but we didn't do too good a job. We wanted to give Dr. B. a hug and tell him we didn't want him to leave us. We wanted to tell him that we loved him and that we'd never forget him as long as we lived. We wanted to tell him that we had learned things about anthropology from him that no one else had ever told us. But we didn't tell him any of these things. We took him out for a beer instead, and we told him good-bye.

Later, alone in my apartment that night, I played the tape I had made that afternoon. I thought of Dr. Burridge telling our Social Organization class in 1985 about the Australian Aborigines and of how their government is one of gerontocracy—rule by knowledgeable elders. I thought of him explaining to us that for the Australians, wealth was not anything that could be seen or bought. Wealth, for the Aborigine, said Dr. B., was in a knowledge of "the Law." And what was the Law? It was, he said, the stories and myths of the People. It was, he said, the oral tradition of their culture. It was, he said, a knowledge of their mythical ancestors.

I remember thinking, as that final tape spun around and around that night, how ironic it was that Dr. Burridge, who had spent so many years studying a culture that so respected its elders and their teachings, was being asked so disrespectfully by his own society to refrain from teaching now that *he* was an elder. I remember thinking, too, about Robin Ridington's words in a paper I had just read entitled "The Anthropology of Experience":

> If we close ourselves to the intuitions, feelings, and introspections of the Old People we will be unable to receive the wisdom that is there to bestow upon us. If we relegate them to the bygone times of past history we will not recognize them as our guides when they appear alive before us. Stories are the eyes through which we are given visions of one another. We have all been gifted with a knowledge of beginning and end. We tell the stories of our lives to those who share life with us. They are experiences that happen to everyone always. (1976:3)

IN CONCLUSION—1988

As evidenced by this essay, the anthropology student has herself become a perpetrator and perpetuator or oral tradition. Robin Ridington has taught me to use the tape recorder in a way particular to anthropologists, and I have documented countless hours of conversations and lectures from Native people with whom I work, as well as from anthropologists. It would seem, then, that I, too, am becoming an ethnographer. Robin Ridington and the Dunne-za have become a part of my own anthropological history, as have Kenelm Burridge and the Australian Aborigines. I tell the stories that these anthropologists have told me to just about anyone who will listen. It is my hope, however, that some-day I will pass on the culture of anthropology to students of my own. I have dreamed about becoming an anthropologist and a teacher ever since my first anthropology teacher, Fraser Taylor, told me about his experiences with the Blackfoot and the Hopi and the Laplanders and the Cheyenne and the—But that's another story!

This essay has focused on the lectures of two anthropologists, Kenelm O. L. Burridge and Robin Ridington. I would be remiss, however, if I did not point out that I have been given a wealth of stories from my other anthropology teachers as well.

Fraser Taylor (Vancouver Community College, Langara campus) inspired me to want to become an anthropologist. His words "Always consider worldview" still echo through my thoughts whenever I am attempting to understand "Others."

Marie Françoise Guédon (University of British Columbia) taught me that culture is a process, not a product, and she told many stories about her work with the Inuit. In addition, she passed on to me the thoughts of anthropological greats such as Stanley Diamond, Edward Sapir, Frank Speck, Adrian Tanner, and her own teacher, A. Irving Hallowell.

Helga Jacobson (University of British Columbia) told stories about female anthropologists and women in the societies studied by anthropologists. Through her stories, she taught me to go back to old ethnographies (mostly written by men) in an attempt to find out why and how the women's perspective had been left out of many of them.

Jay Powell (University of British Columbia), although never my "official" anthropology professor, impressed upon me the importance and value of Native languages and told me stories of his own experiences with Native cultures, mostly on the Northwest Coast.

Elvi Whittaker (University of British Columbia) told stories about the history of anthropological thought and of our anthropological kin, from Herodotus to Clifford Geertz. As well, she taught me that when analyzing a culture, I should always ask: "What are the silent questions? What is the silent agenda?" I have memorized her words: "Anthropology is the past, the present, and the connection. Anthropology is expanding the possible." Dr. Whittaker earned two degrees at UBC and then a doctorate in anthropology from the University of California, Berkeley, in 1973. Her PhD supervisor was the imaginative and innovative scholar Gerald D. Berreman.

UPDATE, 2012

Since this 1988 paper was written, many other anthropology professors have passed on stories to me. At the University of Western Ontario, my MA supervisor, Regna Darnell, a former student of Dell Hymes, taught me a great deal about language and culture. The dynamic Dr. Darnell, pipe in hand, told us graduate students countless stories about Woodland and Plains Cree peoples and about the history of anthropology— from American Anthropological Association to Zdenek Salzmann. Also at Western, Jim Freedman, once a student of Lévi-Strauss, passed on vibrant stories about "L-S" and other theoreticians such as Michel Foucault and Edward Said. In our grad seminars, Dan Jorgensen, a former student of Kenelm O. L. Burridge, passed on fieldwork stories about Papua, New Guinea, and introduced us students to theoreticians such as Marshall Sahlins and Pierre Bourdieu.

In 1991–92 at Western, I was the teaching assistant for Lee Guemple. As such, I heard him regale his undergraduate classes with stories about anthropological theoreticians, ethnographers, and ethnologists. Guemple, one of the founders of CES (Canadian Ethnology Society), now CASCA (Canadian Anthropology Society/societé canadienne d'anthropologie), retired in 1996. In 1992–93, also at Western, I was the teaching assistant for Bryan D. Cummins and benefited greatly from his many stories on the James Bay Cree and current First Nations issues such as land claims. He spent many years at McMaster in Hamilton, Ontario, studying under the guidance of Harvey Feit, his PhD supervisor, and he now teaches there.

At the University of Alberta, I have heard stories about the Lubicon Cree of northern Alberta, African peoples in Kenya, the Waorani of Ecuador, and theories of culture change and applied anthropology from Rod Wilson and more about socio-linguistics, oral history, and Plateau and Northwest Coast peoples from my own PhD advisor, Andie Diane Palmer. Michael Asch, until his retirement, was always nearby with stories on the Dene, on political and economic anthropology, and on ethno-musicology. His own anthropological ancestry is remarkable. His PhD supervisor was Robert Murphy, and Dr. Asch, while at Columbia University in New York, was a teaching assistant for Margaret Mead. Also at the University of Alberta, David Anderson taught me about Aboriginal peoples in Russia and Native peoples in a global context; he is now teaching at the University of Aberdeen.

I am grateful to all of these perpetrators and perpetuators of anthropological oral tradition, and many others—for their knowledge, and because they have made me a part of their anthropological family.

CONCLUSION, 2012

Since 1988, I have documented the one hundredth pilgrimage to Lac Ste. Anne (Manitou Sakahigan or Spirit Lake in Cree) in Alberta; "Urban Aboriginal People" in Vancouver; the powwow circuit, mostly in western Canada; Iroquoian and Algonquian peoples in southwestern Ontario; and survivors of "Indian residential schools" across Canada, including ceremonial leaders and cultural teachers involved in the current Aboriginal healing and empowerment movement of decolonization. Over the years, I have recorded hundreds of hours of stories and songs, and joyously my life has been suffused and inspired by a wealth of oral tradition. Thanks to the Native people with whom I work, and to my professors (almost every one of them an ethnographer), it seems that I too have become an anthropologist. And yes, I now have students of my own. Perhaps not too surprisingly, they tell me I'm a storyteller.

NOTES

1. Recently, with the kind assistance of Dr. John Barker (another of Dr. Burridge's students and now chair of the Department of Anthropology at the University of British Columbia), I donated all of my recordings of Kenelm Oswald Lancelot Burridge to the Special Collections Library at UBC where they have digitized my original cassettes. It is my intention to make a similar contribution to UBC of the tapes I made of Dr. Robin Ridington.
2. Until only a few years ago, the mandatory retirement age for most Canadian employees was sixty-five.

REFERENCES

Bernstein, Basil. 1966. Elaborated and Restricted Codes: An Outline. *In* Explorations in Sociolinguistics. Stanley Lieberson, ed. The Hague: Mouton.

Burridge, Kenelm O. L. 1985/1986. Lectures in Anthropology 300: Social Organization. Vancouver: University of British Columbia. All lectures recorded by Lindy-Lou Flynn.

———. 1987. Lectures in Anthropology 495/540: Comparative Institutions/Advanced Anthropology. Vancouver: University of British Columbia. All lectures recorded by Lindy-Lou Flynn.

Ridington, Robin. 1976. The Anthropology of Experience. Reflections: A Journal of Interpretive Sociology 2:1–19.

———. 1985–1986. Lectures in Anthropology 401: Indians of North America. Vancouver: University of British Columbia. All lectures recorded by Lindy-Lou Flynn.

———. 1988a. Oral Tradition: Culture and Creation. Instructional essay prepared for Comparative Literature 503: Studies in Myth, Theme, and Tradition. Vancouver: University of British Columbia.

———. 1988b. Lectures in Comparative Literature 503: Studies in Myth, Theme, and Tradition. Vancouver: University of British Columbia. All lectures recorded by Lindy-Lou Flynn.

Winick, Charles. 1984. Dictionary of Anthropology. Totowa NJ: Rowman & Allanheld.

Book Reviews

The French Colonial Mind Volume 1: Mental Maps of Empire and Colonial Encounters. Edited by Martin Thomas (University of Nebraska Press, 2011). xlvii + 370 pp. Acknowledgments, Introduction, Part 1, Part 2, Part 3, Contributors, Index.

The French Colonial Mind Volume 2: Violence, Military Encounters, and Colonialism. Edited by Martin Thomas (University of Nebraska Press, 2011). liii + 382 pp. Preface and Acknowledgments, Introduction, Part 1, Part 2, Contributors, Index.

History of Anthropology (HOA) is not the central feature of the volume series The French Colonial Mind. Yet HOA is evident throughout the diverse chapters, providing a topical intersection of both anthropology and the French colonial mind. Altogether, anthropological personalities, concepts, theories, and methods are invoked throughout much of the volumes' content. Two chapters are especially significant contributions to the History of Anthropology as accounts of anthropology's entanglements with the politics of French colonialism: Ruth Ginio's "Colonial Minds and African Witchcraft: Interpretations of Murder as Seen in Cases from French West Africa in the Interwar Era" (1:49–71) and Joe Lunn's "French Race Theory, the Parisian Society of Anthropology, and the Debate over la Force Noire, 1909–1912" (2:221–247).

Ginio's chapter focuses on the two divergent practices of anthropology employed by Lucien Lévy-Bruhl and Marcel Prouteaux. She shows how each of their approaches to the cultural phenomenon of witchcraft produced different forms of knowledge and how these, in turn, became entwined with the politics of the legal and administrative challenges of the French West African courts of the 1920s and 1930s.

This intersection of anthropological work and colonial administration demonstrates the complex positions that individual anthropologists sustained in lieu of colonial and imperial interests. In this case, Ginio distinguishes between Lévy-Bruhl's knowledge of witchcraft as "academic" and Prouteaux's as "administrative."

These two anthropologies are deemed subservient to different purposes and are instantiated through widely disparate political positions regarding witchcraft and the correlating construction of the so-called primitive. Ginio relates these two perspectives as representative of the two dominant perceptions of witchcraft in the French colonial imaginary including their impact on colonial legal decisions vis-à-vis witchcraft-related "crimes." Ginio demonstrates how these contrasting perceptions of witchcraft endured throughout the interwar period, but only the one represented by Prouteaux prevailed in the colonial legal field, primarily because Lévy-Bruhl's "objective was to analyze the African mind and not to help colonial administrators solve murder mysteries.... For the colonial administration in FWA, this was the main disadvantage of the knowledge he produced" (54). Altogether Ginio succinctly asks and answers how "perceptions of African witchcraft reflected in such ethnographic studies affect how the colonial officials who investigated witchcraft-related cases dealt with problems they encountered in the courtroom" (59).

Lunn's essay is a revealing assessment of the dialogue and debate regarding la Force Noir: the proposed (and eventual) creation of West African conscripted soldiers to serve France's military needs. Lunn's analysis focuses on the relationships between prewar military advocates and their use of social science theory to gain approval for and implement the controversial la Force Noir (221). Moreover, Lunn emphasizes the significance of the Société d'anthropologie de Paris within the political sphere, especially to the architects and visionaries of la Force Noire as they solicited the society for validation and support. Noting the specific political positions of individual members of the society, Lunn handily demonstrates the messy political collusions of colonialism and the French intellectual community. More specifically, Lunn articulates the close relationships between "the ascendancy of biological determinism as a prevailing paradigm within the European scientific community and the onset of colonialism" as crucial to the racial categorizations that underscored the exploitive motives of la Force Noir as "corroboration for this view was provided by the 'findings' of physical anthropologists, who, in their attempts to classify the heredity characteristics of various peoples, stressed the innate 'primitiveness' of Africans, which was reflected in their less developed mental faculties and in a series of other 'animal-like' physical attributes" (229–230).

Many of the chapters introduce other interesting correlations between anthropology, history and French colonialism. William Gallois's "Dahra and the History of Violence in Early Colonial Algeria" (2:3–25), implicitly brings anthropological and political theory together in confronting the correlation between the brutal culture of violence and the humanistic qualities of liberal imperialism that mobilizes colonial violence. Utilizing Michael Taussig's notion of "Space of Death," Gallois's contribution is a superb treatise on the violence of liberal imperialism. Writing on the moral justification for the use of violence upon Algerians, Gallois writes: "This came in part from a willful misinterpretation of the modes of behavior of local cultures, but it also expressed a strategy on the part of the French to locate an ethical justification for killing as a form of intercultural dialogue" (7).

In "Conquest and Cohabitation: French Men's Relations with West African Women in the 1890s and 1900s" (2:177–201), Owen White tackles, with eloquent sensitivity, the "relationships between French men and 'colonized' women in a particular region in a particular time" (178). Exploring West African governor general Francois-Joseph Clozel's "extra-administrative requisitions," White also tells us of colonial administrator and ethnographer Maurice Delafosse's disapproval of such behavior in a welcome discussion on the politics of sexual relations and colonial administration.

Tony Chafer's "Friend or Foe? Competing Visions of Empire in French West Africa in the Run-up to Independence" (1:298–323) includes a discussion of "two competing notions [that] underlie French colonial policy: assimilation and association." Chafer's argument implicates cultural universalism, as the "roots of assimilation" and cultural particularism (emphasizing association) as distinct but not mutually exclusive "approaches to ruling colonial populations" (278) before the "intellectual landscape became more complex with the emergence in the 1930s of 'Colonial Humanism.'" Moreover, Chafer states in his contributing chapter on the dizzying politics of "decolonization" in Africa:

> The disputes within France's colonial elites revolved around the importance that should be attached to assimilation versus association, universalism versus particularism, and of a rational, scientific approach versus an ethnographic approach to empire. (279)

Todd Sheperd's "Thinking between Metropole and Colony: The French Republic, 'Exceptional Promotion,' and the 'Integration' of Algerians, 1955–1962" (1:298–323) draws further attention to the kinds of roles that anthropological knowledge and concepts are given in terms of public perception and policy. In this case, Sheperd notes, regarding the French politicians' use of social science, especially that of Jacques Soustelle:

> Soustelle announced the method he would always claim to rely on, the production of anthropological and sociological "scientific expertise," in order to devise remedies appropriate to the Algerian situation. Soustelle and the members of his cabinet (Germaine Tillion, Vincent-Mansur Monteil, and Jean Servier) were all trained ethnologists, and their schemas relied on models and evidence drawn from anthropological fieldwork; they also came out of a French anthropological tradition that believed in possibilities of revolutionary change. (310)

These are but a few examples of HOA in this impressive series, and there is much more to *The French Colonial Mind* in terms of HOA that may only be appreciated via a close reading of the series. Many of the subjects touched upon through the theme, concept, and analytic of *The French Colonial Mind* include, but are not limited to, anthropology, archaeology, craniology, ethnology, ethnography, fieldwork, historiography, legal anthropology-customary law, museum studies, physical anthropology, Institut ethnographique international de Paris, Institut français d'anthropologie, Société d'anthropologie de Paris, Durkheim, Evans-Pritchard, Lévi-Strauss, Lévy-Bruhl, Mauss, Marcel Prouteaux, and Paul Broca (to name a few).

Despite the impressive scope of subjects and theoretical explorations, it is unfortunate that the series does not include any materials dealing with French settler colonialism in Canada. (Perhaps volume 3 might be dedicated to such a worthwhile endeavor?) It is anticipated that *The French Colonial Mind* will be of immense interest to the readers of HOAA and beyond.

Joshua Smith, University of Western Ontario

Telling It to the Judge: Taking Native History to Court. By Arthur J. Ray (McGill-Queen's University Press, 2011). xli + 251 pg. Acknowledgments. Foreword by Jean Teillet. Introduction by Peter W. Hutchins.

Arthur J. Ray's *Telling It to the Judge* is a welcome contribution to the understanding of the politics of scientific testimony in Aboriginal rights litigation in Canada. The title refers to Ray's overall thesis of how he came to see his primary role in the many cases he participated in as educating the "judge-students." Ray, a professor of history, refers to his field specifically as "historical geography." However, *Telling It to the Judge* maintains enormous cross-disciplinary traction as an auto-ethnography, written from Ray's reflexive perspective as a participant observer in Aboriginal rights litigation.

The prologue (xxxviii–xxxix) provides a brief backdrop to the legal-intellectual atmosphere Ray entered in the mid-1980s as a novice "historical expert" in what would be his first case, known as *Regina v. Horseman*. Noting the earlier developments in the United States of the 1946 Indian Claims Commission Act (USICC), Ray recalls the emergence of ethnohistory as the result of numerous anthropologists' involvement as "expert witnesses" and the methods used to document their evidence.

Chapter 1, "Taking Fur Trade History to Court," recalls Ray's foray into the court culture:

> Since *Horseman*, court proceedings have become increasingly adversarial and often feature protracted battles of phalanxes of opposing historical experts bearing myriad documents and espousing conflicting historical interpretations and theories about the nature of pre- and post-contact Aboriginal cultures. (11–12)

This passage marks the beginning of an eye-opening account for those with little experience or knowledge of how Aboriginal rights litigation in Canada works, that is, the ongoing debacle of the court's approach to understanding Canada's (and Canadians') relationships vis-à-vis indigenous peoples. As Ray states:

> When viewed from the perspective of an ethnohistorical/historical expert, the decisions of the majorities in appeal courts in *Horseman* serve to highlight an inherent problem of Aboriginal and Treaty rights litigation. Once a case begins to wind its way through the legal process, it takes on a life of its own. (15)

Chapter 2, "Roles and Reversals of the Historical Researcher," is the author's experience and role in the trial of the Gitxsan-Wet'suet'en title claim taken before the Supreme Court of British Columbia (known as *Delgamuukw v. Regina*). Notably in this chapter, Ray addresses "the court's attitude to oral histories" and the chief's requests that "the court cast aside evolutionary perspectives that had portrayed their people's culture as being inferior to that of Euro-Canadians" in considering evidence such as oral histories. Remembering the hostile atmosphere of this case, Ray addresses this experience as "When Cross-Examination Becomes Inquisition" (30–33). Altogether, this chapter speaks to the colonial aspects of the courts in their perspectives and treatments of "scientific testimony" and the court's peculiar attempts to give weight and measure to varying qualities of academic-expert testimonies. This, in turn, speaks to the absurdity of the whole process in terms of justice as a legal exercise in ethnocentric interpretations from legal experts and scientists alike, not to mention the very people who are held hostage by such an ill-equipped and inappropriate means to presumably execute justice.

For example, the ongoing credibility given by the courts, as Ray mentions, to "Julian Steward's evolutionary cultural ecology framework . . . were based partly on research he had undertaken for the U.S. Justice of Department to counter claims from tribes from the American Southwest (Paiute and Shoshone) and California." This becomes a recurrent theme in Ray's experiences as a key witness in many Aboriginal rights cases.

Chapter 3, "Defending Traditional Fisheries and Harvesting Rights," is an account of Ray's experience in his first Ontario case, *Regina v.*

Spade, Regina v. Wassaykessic, beginning in 1992. In chapter 4, "Interpretation of a Treaty: Share or Surrender?" Ray reflects on his work in the case *Victor Buffalo v. Regina.* The Samson Cree Indian Band and Nation of Hobbema, Alberta, and the Ermineskin Band and First Nation sued Canada for violating Treaty 6. This is an intriguing account of the court's inability to assess treaty relations due to the limitations of the court's ability (or lack of will) to think through the treaty process based on a view of mutual understandings that included what it might mean in accordance with indigenous practices of treaty making. These were overshadowed by the narrow questions asked and answered from deeply ethnocentric viewpoints, thus negating the possibility of a profound mutual resolution. Instead, it was the "paper-talk" that Ray describes in this chapter as evolutionary perspectives held sway through the reports of archaeologist Alexander von Gernet and political scientist Thomas Flanagan, who sought to discredit the plaintiff's claims.

Ray's involvement in *Powley,* a case that tested a Métis community's hunting rights in Ontario, is the subject of chapter 5, "Witnessing on Behalf of a Forgotten People," for the author, "raised yet again the question of how broadly or narrowly Aboriginal livelihood rights should be construed" (91). Chapter 6 builds on Ray's experience in *Powley* and begins to unpack some of the ways the courts moved forward from *Powley* in their struggle to define communities, such as how the "provincial governments have sought to limit the spatial extent of Métis rights by equating communities with physical settlements; Métis litigants, on the other hand, have emphasized the socioeconomic interpretation to promote a more expansive determination of their rights" (106). Ray discusses the *Belhumeur* trial in Fort Qu'Appelle, where his "findings included a discussion of the problems of terminology, the cultural-evolutionary aspects of scholarship about Métis history, and my conclusions about how the nature of nineteenth-century Prairie Métis economies shaped the spatial characteristics of their communities generally and the Qu'Appelle Valley community in particular" (111). The chapter ends with a compelling account of the "Testimony of a Métis Fiddler and the Red River Jig" (113).

Chapter 7, "Defending the Aboriginal Right to Hunt," revolves around the challenges of answering several complex questions within the legal apparatus in order to defend Aboriginal hunting rights in the courts. For example, in addressing the use of primary and secondary sources in terms of their qualities of validity or significance premised on "Issues of Voice and Silence," Ray recounts how he was asked by his legal team "a series of questions about the points [he] had made about the ways in which evolutionary perspectives had coloured the writing of Métis history" (123). Ray relates this point to the fact that "most of the records pertaining to the Métis were written by 'outsiders'" (123).

In the concluding chapter, "To Educate the Court," Ray brings all of his experiences together in assessing his "twenty-five-year journey" as an expert witness and how he has come to understand that "[t]he courtroom is unlike any university classroom and poses unique teaching challenges. There is only one 'student'—the judge, who sits at the head of the room, flanked on one side by a 'witness-stand' that faces the 'jury-box' on the other" (145).

This is a clear and frank account of one scientist's odyssey through an adversarial and deeply colonial apparatus. *Telling It to the Judge* implicitly asks us to reflect on and question not only our society's legal authority in terms of what is just for the nations, whose lands we (Canadians) live on, but to question as scientists what kinds of stories we are telling and to what ends they are being used?

Joshua Smith, University of Western Ontario

CONTRIBUTORS

Michael Asch, Departments of Anthropology and Political Science, University of Victoria. e-mail: masch@uvic.ca.

Ian Campbell, Department of Political Science, University of Canterbury. e-mail: ian.campbell@canterbury.ac.nz.

Regna Darnell, Department of Anthropology, University of Western Ontario. e-mail: rdarnell@uwo.ca.

Lindy-Lou Flynn, Independent Scholar/Ethnographer. e-mail: lindy-lou.flynn@shaw.ca.

Frederic W. Gleach, Department of Anthropology, Cornell University. e-mail: f.gleach@cornell.edu.

Geoffrey Gray, School of History, Philosophy, Religion, and Classics, University of Queensland. e-mail: g.gray1@uq.edu.au.

Laurel Kendall, Division of Anthropology, American Museum of Natural History. e-mail: lkendall@amnh.org.

Mark Lamont, Department of Anthropology, Goldsmiths, University of London. e-mail: m.lamont@gold.ac.uk.

Charles D. Laughlin, (emeritus) Department of Sociology & Anthropology, Carleton University. e-mail: cdlaughlin@gmail.com.

Doug Munro. School of History, Philosophy, Religion, and Classics, University of Queensland. e-mail: d.munro2@uq.edu.au.

Lars Rodseth, Department of Anthropology, Syracuse University. e-mail: rodseth@maxwell.syr.edu.

Abraham Rosman, (emeritus) Department of Anthropology, Columbia University.

Paula Rubel, (emerita) Department of Anthropology, Columbia University. e-mail: pgr4@columbia.edu.

Joshua Smith, Department of Anthropology, University of Western Ontario. e-mail: actionanth@gmail.com.